FROM COAL SACK
TO WOOLSACK

GEOFF LOFTHOUSE

Pontefract Press

1999

GEOFF LOFTHOUSE

Publisher: **Pontefract Press**

17 Linden Terrace

Pontefract, WF8 4AE

01977 793121

e mail: pontefractpress.demon.co.uk

Distributor: **Yorkshire Art Circus**

School Lane

Glasshoughton

Castleford

WF10 4QH

01977 550401

www.openingline.co.uk

© Text: Geoff Lofthouse

© Cover Photos: Pontefract & Castleford Express
Universal Pictorial Press (London)

Editors: Brian Lewis and Reini Schühle

Cover Design: Jacob Schühle-Lewis, Clockwork Sheep

Production Team: Reini Schühle, Alice Walton, Jane Robinson, Margaret Morton

Printer: FM Repro, Roberttown, Liversedge
Tel: 01924 411011   Fax: 01924 411196

ISBN: 1 900325 17 9

CONTENTS

FOREWORD

THE RIGHT HONOURABLE BETTY BOOTHROYD MP, SPEAKER OF THE HOUSE OF COMMONS

It was Oscar Wilde who said, "Nothing succeeds like *excess*." When he penned that aphorism I doubt if he had modesty in mind. Modesty is certainly a rare quality among politicians, but there are some, like my old friend Geoffrey Lofthouse, who possess it in abundance. This was reflected in the title of his first book, *A Very Miner MP*.

It is an inspiring story about a practical man who overcame social and educational deprivation to become a leader in his coalfield community and eventually Member of Parliament for Pontefract and Castleford.

Geoffrey has now produced a second book, *From Coal Sack to Woolsack*, which is just as compelling and inspirational as the first. Soon after his arrival at Westminster it became clear that Geoffrey possessed all the qualities which are best summed up by that unofficial but widely admired accolade, "a House of Commons man".

It was no surprise when he became Deputy Speaker, and now he has achieved a unique double by becoming a Deputy Speaker, and frequent occupant of the Woolsack, in the House of Lords.

The Speaker must be, and be seen to be, above the party political battle which so often rages on the floor of the House. For that reason the Speaker's chair is a lonely seat.

My task has been made easier by all who have served as Deputy Speaker, but none showed greater willingness than Geoffrey in being ready to undertake an additional stint in the Chair when he recognised the pressures imposed by duties I had to undertake outside the Chamber were at their most intense.

The appearance of Geoffrey's smiling face on those occasions, well ahead of the appointed time, was like a tonic. I had hoped he would continue as Deputy Speaker for a much longer period, and when I learnt of his decision to retire from the Commons he was left in no doubt about my disappointment.

Over the years Geoffrey and I have worked as a team, business-like, mutually supportive, and close personal friends. He is dependable and resolute. Those admirable qualities shine through the pages of the second volume of his autobiography.

Denis Boothroyd
Speaker.

INTRODUCTION
Geoff Lofthouse

Although I am a Peer of the Realm, a Knight Bachelor, have been the Deputy Speaker of the House of Commons and therefore, in the minds of many, a man of privilege, I believe that my honours derive from elsewhere. My privileges come to me because of my birth and early occupation.

I was born into an extended family of mutually supportive adults and children in the small mining town of Featherstone and all my life have lived within a three mile radius of my birthplace in Blacksmith Yard. My workplaces have been a little further off. I have worked in Allerton Bywater, Fryston and Methley Junction, and although this brought me into a slightly bigger area I have never set a pit prop or made decisions at a desk which was more than a twenty minute bike ride away from my home. Before I entered through St Stephen's Entrance as an elected member for Pontefract and Castleford my perspectives were fashioned in a five mile square of Yorkshire. As husband, father, grandfather, miner, trade unionist, councillor, rugby player, politician, mayor, chairman of committees, magistrate and student I have not wandered far. Yet I consider myself as experienced as any man.

The focus of my early history was the subject of my first book, *A Very Miner MP*. Discovery of a wider world is the subject of this one. A closer look will, I hope, show that the division is artificial, and that a miner sat in the Speaker's Chair and for an interval of history directed the greatest debating chamber in this land. My job derived from Featherstone privileges.

I have a number of people to thank. Following the death of Sarah I leant heavily on the companionship of three Labour Party stalwarts, Roy Hill, Eric Tonks and Jack Kershaw. They were constantly at my side in difficult times. Notwithstanding the great debt of friendship I owe them, the love of my dutiful and caring daughter Lynne and her family has been paramount. Their influence on my life has meant to me much more than any of the honours I have received.

I am also indebted to people directly associated with this book. In the first place I would place my secretary Jane Robinson, a loyal patient friend, who has been in the boiler house throughout my parliamentary career, and has always been reliable and trustworthy. Without her skill and assistance I would not have been able to start this text, let alone finish it. Brian Munka, my former House of Commons assistant, did some of the early invaluable research and I thank him for that. Brian Lewis and Reini Schühle edited the book, and their son Jacob was responsible for picture editing and design. I am grateful to Councillor Roy Hirst, Chief Whip Wakefield MDC, for his unselfish assistance. From the first Alice Walton has been more than my devoted friend. From its inception she has been in a very real sense part of this book. She listens intently and never gives bad advice; in every way a real lady.

COAL SACK TO WOOLSACK

In the wake of the humiliating defeat inflicted on the miners by Margaret Thatcher in the Great Strike of 1984/85 there was profound depression and bitterness in Pontefract and Castleford, as there was in every mining community. Families had suffered a loss of savings and of homes, and some had been rent asunder by vicious ideological strife which set father against son and brother against brother. Despite all this, most had retained their dignity and this was due in no small part to the support and deportment of the women of the coalfields.

As MP for Pontefract and Castleford I went through all this trauma with my constituents, fiercely resenting the fact that evidence seemed to indicate this was a naked, political strike manipulated by the Conservative Government with Ian MacGregor as hatchet man and the miners as victims. I was aware of this when I repeatedly questioned Margaret Thatcher in the House of Commons about MacGregor's appointment. That lady never gave me a satisfactory answer, it was as though she knew his job brief.

Although the general public appeared to support the miners in their struggle, I knew that the Government's policy was to minimise the power of the NUM, for it disdained and feared the union leadership's motives. Many people said to me at the time that if Arthur Scargill won, the NUM could unite with the Power Workers Union and so create an industrial monolith with the ability to switch off the country's energy supplies, all this at Scargill's whim. The public feared that this weapon would give him enormous power, which, if he chose to use it for political reasons, would create a state in which no democratically elected government would be able to stand firm. There were many of my constituents who felt it was for this man's pride and ambition that the miners had to suffer. They thought that although the miners had a just cause, and Scargill was probably right in his forecast of the Government's intention to run down the coal industry and move toward privatisation, he was a dangerous leader.

I was at a very low ebb at this time. In my personal life I had suffered from the loss of my dear wife Sarah. I could not find the slightest solace in work, for the continued threat to the existence of the coal industry in general and to the collieries in my constituency in particular drove me to despair. I was also disturbed by the complete absence of Government action and assistance to encourage alternative employment in my constituency. If there was to be a rapid run-down of the coal industry Pontefract and Castleford were going to be faced with an unprecedented unemployment problem. At that time this misery would be compounded by the lack of opportunity for school leavers and youths, many of whom would have previously entered automatically into craft apprenticeships and mining training schemes. There was a traditional path followed straight from school by young men in mining communities, and this was about to be destroyed.

I had taken that path myself. I left school on a Friday in 1939 and commenced work at the Featherstone Pit on the following Monday at 6 am in the pit bottom. There I was, joined by about 70% of boys that had been in the same class at Featherstone School - Doc Richardson, Derek Hufton, Bas Ledbetter and others. Years passed; by 1964 I had become the Manpower Officer for the Castleford area; responsible for recruitment to all pits in the area. Twenty years on, the number of boys coming into the pits was probably down by 20%. My task in the early years was to recruit sufficient numbers for the industry's needs. It wasn't easy although on the surface life in the pit was still attractive, with apprentice craft schemes offering first class training in electrical and mechanical engineering, transferable skills and also specialised apprenticeships for mining. Management schemes were controlled by the Staff Department. Then my biggest problem was persuading boys to accept these jobs. I spent much time in secondary schools showing films and encouraging the boys to come into mining. In all innocence I was mistakenly assuring them of a secure future.

The Pontefract, Castleford and Featherstone area had changed in that 30 years. We had the benefit of nationalisation, but had also seen the growth of a diverse economy. There were some service industries but it was the building of the power station at Ferrybridge which had created alternative jobs for men. I saw that National Coal Board apprentices who completed their apprenticeship were regularly poached to the power stations.

9

Today the situation has radically changed. On the rapid-run down of the mining industry, the apprenticeship scheme ceased and the progression from school to craft apprenticeships disappeared. By 1999 the percentage of school leavers entering the coal industry has dropped off the bottom of the scale. Richard Budge, the owner of the majority of the privatised coal industry, informed me once when he was up at the Prince of Wales Colliery that while they did their level best to maintain employment for some apprenticeships, at that time only one had been recruited to our local colliery.

Now while in recent times the number of women employed across the area has been on the increase, many of the young men I recruited straight from school in the 1960s, and who became redundant in the mid to late 80s, have never found new jobs.

As an MP I knew that I must work in a determined mood to protect Pontefract and Castleford, and by association all other mining communities, from savage attack. At that time I was fortunate to be a member of the Select Committee on Energy and I was able to make good use of this platform in my attempt to provide protection. In the Commons I repeatedly challenged Margaret Thatcher and other relevant Ministers and asked for assurances that the coal industry would not be reduced until other industries had been encouraged to move into this area. I did not get them; rather there were many denials that it was the Government's intention to rapidly run down the coal industry. I was never convinced. From 1985 onwards it was plain that the Government intended to rid the coal industry of all men over 50 by offering them what were - by the standards at the time - very lucrative redundancy settlements. Some were as high as £40,000. These levels of payoff made it easier for the NCB to bring about a run-down without too much trouble.

The end of the Great Strike in 1985 did not totally ease things. During my constituency surgeries I noticed with regret the resentment and hostility that existed between some miners and their families, and the rest of the community. Our area is one in which the extended family still exists. Men who returned to work in such communities could be ostracised as scabs by their mothers, fathers, aunts and uncles. In some cases this was unjustified, for I knew unfortunate men who were subjected to the most intense financial difficulties and who, feeling that the strike was a lost cause as it approached its bitter end, were driven back to work by desperation. They had broken ranks and were branded. Some Featherstone lads I knew went through hell. They had supported the union like tigers throughout the early months but by February 1985 they now wanted a return to some type of normality. Most believed that a compromise should have been sought before Christmas. It wasn't.

I did not experience the 1926 Strike - I was one year old - but I well recall that in my early days in the pits and long after, the word "black" preceded some men's Christian or surname. This was a short form of "black leg" and indeed such men were not allowed into the local working men's clubs; some men carried that nickname to their graves. It is interesting to note that fourteen years after the 1984 strike, although the healing is not absolute, these days I never hear anyone called "black". On occasions you will hear the comment, "He went back, him," but in that observation I do not detect any real malice.

That was not the case in 1985. The good-natured quality of the community response was undergoing change. There was much bitterness against the police who had at times, in my carefully considered opinion, used excessive physical force. I myself had witnessed a demonstration of this whilst acting as an observer at Kellingley Colliery. I was known to be a community leader and an MP but I was roughly pushed aside and struck. These acts of violence did not appear to be committed by members of the West Yorkshire Police under the command of the much respected Chief Constable Sir Colin Sampson, but by outsiders. I know where the men came from who hit me, they weren't from our area. Sir Colin recognised that his force would have to police the area after the strike had ended, and that task would be much easier if the police maintained the goodwill. As an elected representative I was grateful for this common sense approach.

Perhaps the greatest and most understandable rancour existed among the honest hard-working and always law-abiding men who nevertheless found themselves in jail because they had sought to defend our community and its principled way of life. I shall never forget the Saturday morning I visited Armley Prison in Leeds to talk to some of these men and to recognise their utter dejection. I know, even to this day some have not fully recovered from experiences of that period and I know how truly devastated their families were. Armley Prison is a soul destroying place. Going there affected me very deeply and I spared no effort to find the men as much legal protection as was possible. Not every miner is, or was, a saint, and there were undoubtedly some individuals who did deserve punishment for unnecessary violence or foolhardy actions, but the strike did terrible things to a huge number of perfectly decent people and created a dreadful emotional aftermath. It fell to people like me to attempt to soothe, as opposed to heal, their wounds.

Yet it is too easy to emphasise the bad and neglect the good. Whilst the result of the strike was nothing short of disastrous for the mining communities, we should not forget the women who took their place in the front line. Through those dark days women, who had been "seen but not heard" for most of their lives, discovered that they had a voice and could use it to create a better future for themselves and others. The seeds of important change were sown on the picket lines and in the soup kitchens where, standing shoulder to shoulder with their men, the women realised their ability to get things done. The end of the strike did not bring an end to the problems for coalfield women and their families but it did allow a group of local women in my constituency, who had come together in 1984, to recognise their power and it made them determined to improve their lot.

Eighteen months after the strike had ended, with a small grant for premises and a giant will to win, Castleford Women's Centre in Wesley Street was born. I well recall a survey which was conducted just before the opening and which asked people what they would want from such a centre, coming up with an unpredictable answer. They didn't want bingo. 95% of respondents said that they wanted to improve their education but were intimidated by the thought of going to college. Affectionately dubbed The University of Life, originally in Wesley Street, now in the new centre by the railway bridge on York Street, it got in step with Labour's commitment to Life Long Learning well before spin doctors had thought up the phrase. I was delighted, as was the whole district, when the centre formed a partnership with

Leeds Metropolitan University in 1994. The first students have already achieved their certificates in Higher Education. Many are now working towards a BA in Arts and Social Studies. Starting from small beginnings, this unique institution has given Yorkshire women a distinctive voice in Europe by acting as first headquarters for an UK branch of the European Network of Women.

For all its enormous success in the academic field, the Women's Centre is not just an education establishment; the original aim was to ensure that women did not feel alone when coping with the misery of poverty and debt, the biggest hardship experienced in the aftermath of the strike. As Margaret Handforth, one of the founders, said to me, "The centre kept people sane because they knew there was somewhere to go with their troubles. We couldn't solve their problems but they did not have to cope alone."

Whenever I visited the centre it was obvious to me that women gained great confidence when they recognised that all had the same problems. This gave them the faith to carry on. I am sure the centre just held people up long enough to assure them that they could survive. Eventually they did not need assistance but until then the centre was always there for them.

Nowadays all manner of social and personal problems are tackled in the same spirit of support, caring and common sense, that I recognised during the strike. By making educational opportunities accessible to everyone, it provides a friendly, welcoming atmosphere, that has worked wonders. The practical structure of its activities and facilities is a delight. I feel privileged to have seen the Castleford Women's Centre continue to expand and running courses which the people of the area wanted. Already two more centres in Airedale and Knottingley, beyond the boundaries of central Castleford, have been opened.

Now called the Community Learning Centre, over the years the centre has provided all manner of activities including citizen's advice, housing aid and free child-care facilities. In every possible way the team managing the centre have seen themselves as facilitators who enhance the community worth. They have engendered a tradition of excellence within a modern environment. Today the centre continues to provide accessible education and training to the community in a friendly, welcoming environment. Yet for all the new equipment and furniture, its life and soul still lies with the women who knew how to pull themselves out of a nightmare and, barely believing that they could do it, went ahead and realised a dream.

* * * * *

I had a lot of sympathy with the women of the Castleford Women's' Centre because in many ways the way they became educated mirrored my own education. My mother's father, Johnny Fellows, my Grandad, was the first great influence. He had arrived in Featherstone as a young man from Staffordshire as a shaft sinker and had married my grandmother, Annie Bolton, a daughter of a well known North Featherstone family. He was to be the main influence on my life following my father's death. From being four years old I looked to him for protection and it was always there. Whatever Grandad said to me, I was confident it was the right advice. Several phrases come to mind. Whilst he gave me assurance as a small child he obviously realised that when I reached my early teens he had to prepare my mind for my future in the coal industry so he conditioned my mind to the fact that the workers always had to protect themselves: "Never trust the bosses lad, always look after your own. If your own can't help you, those buggers won't." When I started work at Ackton Colliery, those words were in my mind and were influential. Self education was beginning.

I started work at fourteen. At the completion of the very first week when I returned home my grandfather enquired whether I had paid my union fees. I was not aware what I had to do. That evening Grandad took me to Featherstone Miners Welfare. Evan Evans, another Staffordshire man and Miner's Union Secretary, took three pence from me; payment I found difficult because I was working a week in hand. Mister Evans - there was no informality then, since he was an adult and held a prominent position in the community he had to be addressed in a formal way - took my money, made me a brand-new membership card recording that I had paid the weekly rate. I was told by Grandad I must go to the union box every Friday when I left the pit to pay that three pence until I became an adult, and then it would be six pence. Grandad, although I am sure he trusted me, would occasionally check my union card to see that I had paid. When Mr Evans signed me up I became a member of the Yorkshire Miners' Association. My education as a trade unionist and as a politician had begun.

For the first fourteen years of my life down the pit I was no more than a card carrying union member. Trade unionism lay dormant. I attended branch meetings as a young trade unionist but I did not take a major role in the branch, I voted but rarely spoke. I had married at twenty, Lynne was born six years later and I had entered another large extended family. Family life, my work as a face worker, taking home reasonably good money for those times, and of course rugby, dominated my life.

Some politicians map out their lives from their teens up to the point where they become a key statesman. It is said that Michael Heseltine wrote his future career on the back of a wage packet. He would make a lot of money, join the Conservative Party, enter Parliament, become a Cabinet Minister and end up Prime Minister. The start of my political career wasn't mapped on the back of an envelope but was conditioned by the existence of 150 yards of Silkstone coal somewhere 600 yards down below Featherstone.

Luck plays a major part in how we receive our education and how our ambitions develop. It was that way with me. Though in my case it was an act of ill-luck affecting another miner which kick-started my career. One day, while working on the afternoon shift on 45's Face in Ackton Hall, a very good friend of mine, Fred Scranage, the Checker on our face, found himself with a broken conveyor belt. Fred got injured extracting the belt from around the rollers. He had a responsible job, he had been appointed by his workmates to represent their interests. He filled coal like everyone else, but he also had the responsibility to deal with allowances, negotiate with the Deputy of the shift. He checked the amount of coal which was filled each day on behalf of the men and saw that this weight tallied with the record weighed on the surface where a more senior branch official called the checkweighman overlooked the weighing of the coal. In my day the

Ackton Hall checkweighmen were either Percy Woodcock or Jack Parker.

The position of a checkweighman in the history of British trade unions is one of great importance. In one of the mid-nineteenth century Mining Acts a Liberal Government saw the fairness of allowing the owners' records on coal production to be overlooked by a workman. It was agreed in legislation that the workmen should have an elected representative who would have a degree of power as the miners' elected representative in the colliery yard. I suspect, had the Government realised what this meant, they would not have passed the legislation, for not only did it ensure fairness for the working men, something they agreed was appropriate, but - and this is very important - it legitimised the presence of trade unionists at every colliery in the land. From that point on, men like Percy and Jack, following in the footsteps of four generations who had gone before, had the right to negotiate with managers. Two weighmen sat side-by-side in the Checkweigh Box, one on behalf of management and one representing the men. As each tub went over the weighing machine its weight was recorded. Arbitrating about how much coal and how much muck was in a tub of coal was the beginning of the rights of union men to have control over their wages and conditions.

Checkers, and another official called a "clotcher", had similar rights. To be one of these union officials - checkweighman, clotcher or checker - gave you influence amongst the men. That is the company I joined on the day Fred Scranage got injured. Somebody had switched on the power farther up the main gate and Fred found his arm drawn into the machinery. Fred never again worked on the coal face, although he worked at the pit on much lower wages as a day labourer. This meant that our coalface lacked a checker.

I was aged 28, and because I had a reasonable reputation as a good worker and was a known rugby player, the men decided that I should take over Fred's job. My education as a trade unionist was just about to begin. More luck, rather than ill-luck, played a dominant part in what happened next.

The geology of a pit is often decisive when it comes to making money. On one shift sometime earlier the coal completely disappeared. Technically this is called "hitting a fault" and means that the miners have to drift down to locate the coal some way below. As you search for the coal there is minimum pay because there is no coal output and in those days wages were based on weight. At the point when Fred had the accident we had just relocated the seam on 45's. It lay in virgin ground. Since it was the first coal face in the relocated seam, no other coal had been worked around it; no fracturing of the strata had occurred, as there were no close workings the coal had not compacted; it was like cutting butter. The old colliers would say, "It's given itself up Geoff," meaning that the coal was easy to mine and they were right. We filled tub after tub quickly and efficiently and as a consequence the management had to fill our wage packets accordingly. Our money was far in excess of other faces working at the pit.

The geology on 45's made me. I didn't deserve it, but the good pay was believed to be in some way associated with my appointment. My popularity grew.

At that time there would be 2000 men working at the Ackton Hall pit. Of course in the pubs and clubs of Featherstone, especially on a Thursday evening when the checkers on the various faces received their advanced note of the wages for the previous week, this would be discussed. Each Thursday when the 45's note was distributed, there was general discussion and envy from miners working on other faces. They wanted a bit of the action. Men on other faces were not concerned about the reasons why high wages had been achieved, for they knew the reason - it was the ability of the new checker. I never thought to discourage this belief. My confidence grew. Success was educating me and I was learning a number of political truths. Success breeds success, you advance by small increments, but underpinning it all there must be a philosophy. That philosophy had come from my grandad. He had said, "Never trust the bosses."

Sometime in 1954 we had a particularly good week. On the afternoon shift we had filled more coal than ever before and consequently our wages were the highest ever. On the Thursday I received a note from the then Under Manager, Mr Sidney Criddle, asking me to call and see him. Criddle was distrusted by most men at the pit and I was on my guard when I called. When I was in his office he drew my attention to the wages we had earned and said, "Do you want it all this week Geoff?" Having a distrust of Criddle I nearly fell off the chair. My answer was, "Of course we want it, we have earned it." He responded, "You are a young man gathering somewhat of a reputation at this pit, take some advice from an old man: if this is the maximum, every other week when you earn less the men will consider their wages to be down." He said, "Let me put so much in each week, and keep the top rate stable."

I did not take that advice through lack of trust and knowing full well that men know when they have had an exceptional week. It seems to me important that as a leader you never fudge an issue but tell the people who have elected you exactly where they stand and in detail; and never protect those who you mistrust. Do not spin your story. You must have faith in the intelligence of the people you represent. I take the view that if conditions developed where the men could not earn as much as they had done previously, although probably working harder, they should be adequately recompensed for the conditions they were working in and it was up to the checker to argue and negotiate on their behalf.

All this time I was learning new skills. I was learning to be watchful. My mathematical skills were also improving. I was learning that miners, like all human beings, are not perfect but basically decent and intelligent and that I had to try to manage a constantly changing situation. Down the pit there can be few long term plans, for you are subject to the vagaries of geology and personalities. This was good training.

My success on 45's made my reputation in the colliery so that when elections to the branch committee came up I was urged to stand, and did stand.

I knew early on that I was going to win, for George "Ginger" Jones, a close personal friend of mine and a man who had been a checker for many years on other faces, said to me, "You'll walk this election Geoff, Green Lane Club's backing you." This was one of the main clubs where the bulk of Ackton miners gathered and its clientele represented all faces and not just my colleagues on 45's. In the event

I won the election easily. Of the 2,000 men employed at the colliery 1,200 cast their votes; 1,000 for me and 200 for my opponents. Of the 800 missing men many were sick miners and pensioners - in those days pensioners had a right of vote - but since the ballot was at the pit head they did not generally do so. To be elected with such a landslide was a great honour.

In the next two years I took part in two other elections, and by 1956 I had risen from branch member to president and to workmen's inspector. It was at this point I realised I needed more formal education. Fortunately the union provided it. In the Yorkshire coalfield two university courses had been set up, one at Sheffield and one at Leeds. A number of prominent union officials who were later to become well known in trade union, local government and parliamentary arenas - men like Alec Woodall, Arthur Scargill and Jim McFarlane - went to Sheffield but it is the ones who went to Leeds who I knew best.

On the first course twenty miners were accepted for Leeds, having undergone a test at Barnsley officiated over by Professor Albert Johnson, Head of.the Extra Mural Department. Two in particular deserve mention. Jack Smart, a Glasshoughton pit man who was to become the NUM area agent, Freeman of Castleford, Leader of the Wakefield Metropolitan District Council, Chairman of the Association of Metropolitan District Councils (AMA) and knighted for his services to that body, was there. The other was Bill O'Brien, another Glasshoughton miner. He became Councillor for Knottingley, Leader of Knottingley District Council, Deputy Leader of Wakefield Metropolitan District Council and eventually, Member of Parliament for Normanton.

I was apprehensive on the day I walked into the classroom in the University's Brotherton Building. I hadn't sat behind a school desk since I was fourteen. I was particularly afraid that I would be undermined by the nature of the course which I was about to undertake. I felt myself generally ignorant and inferior. That sense of inferiority made me apprehensive though I was comforted by the presence of colleagues feeling the same. When the lecturer arrived I met a man who was to be influential in my future political career. Dr

Patrick Duffy, later to be Minister for the Navy in Callaghan's Government, was at that time a young economics lecturer. He had fought in the war as a pilot in the Fleet Air Arm and had been severely injured. A graduate of Leeds, he was the son of a Rossington miner. That was an asset but he also had a practical knowledge of politics, a grasp of what we needed to know and had the common sense to deal with people, who like me were practical men thirsting for education.

This was not our first encounter. I met him when he ran the Workers' Education Association classes at the Blackamoor Hotel, Pontefract. He was a friendly face and my confidence grew.

In his time Patrick Duffy has taught me many things and has made me appreciate the value of education. From the first he understood our problems. He never talked above our heads, but gradually drew us up to his level. He had the knack of knowing when he got to the stage where we were not following and then came back to explain. When he marked our work he would diplomatically comment what he thought we should have said without ever making us feel inferior. He always treated you as an equal. This created a friendship and admiration which has continued throughout 45 years. I was not to know then that I would one day join him in Parliament, but when I did he was a mentor who always met me as an equal. On many occasions, despite his own academic expertise, he would ask my advice on many practical things. I sometimes wondered whether this was a deliberate gesture to give me confidence though I think he came to appreciate my understanding of the practice of politics. Along with Roy Mason he has been my parliamentary mentor. Always, he has been my friend.

When I decided to write the present volume, he gave me some advice: "Don't let the second volume be just a catalogue of humorous events that you have witnessed in Parliament, too many others have done that; let it be a learned book so that in the future students of politics have a useful, practical reference book."

* * * * *

Gradually-learnt principle and a pragmatic approach to life prepared me for the various jobs I took on in Parliament. In 1984 I had been appointed a Member of the House of Commons Select Committee On Energy. This gave me a visible and influential platform from which to investigate the Conservative Government's plans on privatisation, plans whose existence was routinely denied by the Tories. In the aftermath of the Miners' Strike I especially welcomed this position of power, for it enabled me to be present to question the likes of Ian MacGregor and his lieutenants in the National Coal Board, Sir Kenneth Couzens, M J Edwards and K Moses, respectively Deputy Chairman, Commercial Director and Technical Director. My first real chance came on 26 February 1986 when these gentlemen appeared before the Committee. On that occasion they put on their top team. Sir Kenneth was formally leading for the Coal Board but MacGregor was there to intervene and make reply as or when he wished. I was anxious to engage him and when I did I was astounded at his bland assertion that industrial relations in the coal industry "had never been better". This was said a mere four months after the end of the most lacerating strike the industry had known since 1926.

His response to my questioning on the social and economic consequences of wrongful dismissal without reinstatement, and on pit closures resulting in wholesale unemployment, were evasive and couched in coldly formal terms. There was no expression of regret or sympathy for what he had done to our communities. I came to the conclusion that MacGregor was a very fine actor but I sensed malice behind the make-up.

Although the industry was being run down and colliery yards and offices smashed to rubble and quickly turned into brown sites, I still had obligations to coal communities and needed to know more of the alternative systems favoured by Mrs Thatcher. But before doing that I needed to see my industry in a broader, and especially a transatlantic, context.

The coal strike finished in the spring of 1985 and as a part of the Committee's extensive investigation of the coal industry a year later I had the opportunity to visit the United States. The purpose of the visit was to compare technological and managerial methods, to determine what might be the reasons for differences in the productivity record in each country. We were to assess the US perspective on the international market for coal, and within that remit, hear views on the potential of the UK market for US exports. We also had to study the role which the federal and state governments played in the development of the US coal industry, and consider the comparable legal constraints. This, we hoped, would help us establish what needed to be done to put the UK coal industry on a sound economic basis and provide us with information to maximise the respective roles of the NCB and the Government in achieving this. My gut feeling was that the Government victory over the miners spelled "privatisation" and that America was the model. Observation of the American industry would give us a foretaste of what was to come. As a former miner, I was naturally very keen indeed to see how my American colleagues were faring.

We had a rigorous schedule to maintain. No sooner had we arrived in Washington DC than we were briefed by the Energy Counsellor and the Visits Officer from the British Embassy. A quick change and then we were off to a working dinner hosted by Carl Bagge, Vice President and Chief Executive of the American National Coal Association, a most powerful man in both voice and physique. If ever I saw a man obsessed with capitalism and power, that man was Mr Carl Bagge.

Some see investigatory parliamentary visits as times to relax, but this was no holiday, we were always on the go. After a welcome night's rest it was up with the birds to be briefed again by the Energy Counsellor before a meeting at the US Department of Energy. We then went for a lunch kindly hosted by HM Ambassador at his magnificent residence in Massachusetts Avenue. When our Washington meetings were over we flew to Pittsburgh and stayed at the Hilton Hotel. It was a gruelling day but the highlight of that night was an unscheduled meeting.

When standing at the bar before dinner I was tapped on the shoulder by a young man who had obviously taken note of the names of our delegation. He said to me, "Good evening Mr Lofthouse." Here I was in Pittsburgh and someone, unknown to me, had identified me as Mr

Lofthouse. After exchanging pleasantries I asked him how he knew me. He said, "Well, you come from Featherstone and so do I." This immediately made me feel at home. His name was Millward and that he had been born in Featherstone Square. His father's name was Bill Millward, the Billy Millward I had worked with at Ackton Hall Colliery in the 1950s. This made my evening; Featherstone is never far away.

The following morning we visited the Consolidated Coal Company Underground Mine, near Morgan Town, West Virginia, and then travelled by coach to Zanesville, Ohio, where we had meetings with Mr Millward's company, the UK Mining Equipment Exporters. Next day saw us visiting the Central Ohio Coal Company Opencast Mine near Zanesville. On completion of that engagement we travelled by coach to Columbus, Ohio and from there we flew down to Birmingham, Alabama via Atlanta, Georgia, to attend a working dinner hosted by Bill Carr, President of Jim Walter Resources Inc. He was a Geordie and had previously been a colliery manager in the Northern coalfields. This of course made it very easy for us to communicate with him. He prepared us for our visit on the following day to their No 5 Deep Mine near Brookwood, Alabama. After this all-day visit we returned to Washington that evening by plane. The morning of the next day, 11 April, saw us in meetings with the United Mineworkers Union and then the Bituminous Coal Operators Association, which is the employers' federation. A farewell buffet reception by the Energy Counsellor ended our official programme and we were then left with three hours for a brief tour of the elegant capital city of the US before flying back to London that night. I list this itinerary simply to disprove any notion that a foreign visit undertaken by the Energy Select Committee could be described as a junket. Some of my colleagues' fact finding journeys might be described that way, this was not. It was a gruelling schedule and we worked hard. Mind, that was how we wanted it.

The American experience quickly made me aware of the great differences between our respective industries. There were, for instance, 3,500 privately owned mines in the US. Forgetting very small units, little more than day-holes, all serious mining in the UK at that time was under the ownership of British Coal. I was personally interested in deep shaft mining, the type most common in the UK, and was particularly keen to see mines with similar geological conditions to those operating in the area I knew best, Yorkshire. I had experience and the confidence to challenge where I knew my ground. One of my Conservative colleagues on the Committee, Peter Rost, expressed the view that in the US, under private enterprise management, productivity was two to three times as much per man shift as in the UK and that this was not due to hard work or superior machinery - incidentally most of this British made - but to efficient management and operation. My view, based on experience, was more sophisticated. I saw that it took less time to transport miners to the coal face because more efficient transportation systems were employed, that wider roadways meant that heavier, more productive equipment could be more easily moved about. He considered that because miners were better paid than in the UK, and because there were better industrial relations, there was better motivation. Above all, he thought that the management was better than in the UK, with fewer people above ground servicing those at the coal face, with less bureaucracy and red tape than was found at the London HQ of the National Coal Board. He felt that efficiency and productivity were given a big boost by the American coal companies for they were smaller and regional. My feeling was that his opinions were dominated by ideology and not knowledge. I heard a pretty powerful pitch for privatisation. This simply gave added credence to my cynical view of the Government's plans to privatise.

He had no practical experience of the coal industry; on the other hand I had begun work as a miner at the age of fourteen in 1939, eight years before nationalisation. I knew the industry intimately and had worked in conditions that today would be the cause of justified public outrage. Twice, as a small fourteen year old driving a pony underground, I had the traumatic experience of coming across a dead man crushed because of the collapse of a roof. All we had in those days were wooden pit props which could be snapped like matchsticks even under moderate pressure. Shareholders and dividends dictated working conditions. I felt it a privilege after 1947 to work in a nationalised industry which took pride in safeguarding the lives of its men and which was not motivated purely by profit. The advances I had seen made in colliery safety compared with the pre-nationalised days were staggering. They were not reflected in the US pits we saw.

I found the two deep mines which we visited in the United States, the Consolidated Coal Company Underground Mine near Morgans Town, West Virginia and the Jim Walter Resources No 5 Deep Mine near Brookwood, Alabama, to be very strange places. I came out of them convinced that they were unsafe work places. For instance, I found thousands of metres of roadway without any support at all. I have always been of the view that roof bolts as a permanent support were not as safe as arched girder roads; a view confirmed by the Chief Inspector of Mines when I questioned him in the Select Committee. Here girder routes were virtually unknown.

In one of the American mines I found that men were being taken to work by something like a trolley bus system using only an overhead electric wire to support motive power. This system created sparking as the vehicle travelled to the coal face. I also saw workmen using welding gear that threw off showers of sparks in areas which could easily attract explosions in pockets of gas. All this, I am very glad to say, was quite foreign to me. In the UK the threat of explosions through its ignition was treated with deadly seriousness, but not here. One of my Committee colleagues was my friend Bill O'Brien, the Member of Parliament for the neighbouring constituency of Normanton, who has a similar coalmining background to me, with many years' experience of the coal industry. In one of the deep mines he remarked to me that nothing had made him happier than when we reached the top of the shaft. He said that he had never felt more unsafe in a coal mine. It was a view which I fully shared. Of course, it is possible that the very powerful ventilation system that we found in these mines minimised the build-up of gases, but my own experience has taught me first hand that in coalmining you can never be too careful.

I was very interested in talking to the miners and other employees and I took every opportunity to do so. As we were making our way along one of the roadways we came across a young fellow taking a breather and I approached him and wished him good morning. I could scarcely believe the evidence of my own ears when he proved to be a

25

she! I asked the young woman what she did and her courteous reply was, "I am a stone duster sir." Her job was to dress the roadways with stone dust in a bid to prevent spontaneous combustion of coal dust. This safety practice pleased me. My surprise on meeting her was as nothing compared to what awaited me at the coal face itself. There, heavy-duty chocks were being used to support the roof and as I crawled down the coal face I found a young miner slogging her guts out to move forward one of the chocks which had become embedded in the floor and would not operate properly. This young woman weighed no more than eight stone. This shook me rigid. In England we had abolished the employment of women as underground coal miners in the 1840s.

My fears for the safety of the American miners seemed to be justified when we studied the accident records, which were available. They were much higher than for the UK mines. Accident statistics were only kept at the 40% of American mines which were unionised and whilst this made it nearly impossible to make a comparison, I suspect that accidents were more common in non-unionised collieries.

The US workers had a lot in common with the people who I had worked beside in my teens and twenties, they worked hard in rotten conditions. By contrast, the employers we met struck me as archetypal hard-nosed American businessmen, only capable of measuring success by the sole criterion of who could make the most money. One of these men declared, during one of our working dinners, that he would commit murder to secure an order for one million tonne of coal. I remembered what my grandad said, "Never trust a boss." I am still not sure if the business man was joking.

* * * * *

The first boss I ever saw, I saw in 1931. His name was Archer. Later in life I would sit on the Magistrates' Bench with his son, but that was a long way off. As a boy of tender years I knew him by his notoriety: He was a very hated man in Featherstone, blamed for the closure of the Featherstone Main Colliery in 1935. But though I knew of him, I never saw him. Then one winter's day just before noon - I would be about eight years old - I took my sledge to the steep incline at the back of the Sun Inn at North Featherstone and with mates prepared to slide down to the pit yard.

The timing was important, for like everyone in a pit village I was aware of the times the men surfaced from the pit. Sometimes it was at the normal shift time, that is about 1.30 pm, but if we heard the buzzer blow earlier than that time, we knew it meant the men were being flushed. Flushing happened when the miners digging the coal could no longer be supplied with empty tubs, so to save the owners money, the shift ended prematurely. It also meant that they had not eaten their snap so when we heard the early buzzer we immediately dived for our sledges and sledged to the colliery. Our little empty stomachs were keen to sample the jam sandwiches, cheese sandwiches and occasionally a slice of that home baked delicacy, parkin. Since the sledge track led onto colliery premises, Archer, to protect his investment, came storming out of his office and chased us off the premises.

The Managing Director of the company who owned the first pit I worked at was a man called Careera, but since I never saw it written down I might have the spelling wrong. He lived locally on Pontefract Road in a large semi. He was not the owner of a vast coal empire like the American Carl Bagge, he was just the most important immediate boss of the Hemsworth, South Kirkby, Featherstone Coalmining Company, a relatively small amalgamation of collieries which served our area. The name of that company was a rarity; for more often than not family names were what you got when talk was of the mine ownership. Briggs, Pope and Pearson, Charlesworth and Masham, were names known to all, but their owners were remote people who knew little about their workers' lives and seemed to care less. In their houses they had running water in their homes, but they did not provide it at the pit. There were no pit baths at Ackton Hall until 1957; that is ten years after nationalisation. Up to then we used to leave the mine after a day's work underground still in our pit muck, having donned clothes which had been hung in the mine for the whole of our shift; filthy and dusty coats and trousers matched our bodies. With the smell of sweat on our clothes we boarded a B&S or

West Riding - red'uns and green'uns - to make our way back to Pontefract. Today it would be very embarrassing to board public transport in that condition and sit at the side of people in reasonable clothes; however, I never came across any resentment. People around here were used to this and accepted it as a way of life.

Sarah didn't, she had strict views on cleanliness. Sometimes when the bus arrived at the Chequerfield stop about 50 yards from our home, Sarah and Lynne would be waiting at the gate. Sarah kept Lynne as smart as a pin. On seeing me the two-year-old would dash up to me with Sarah running after her shouting, "Don't pick her up, don't pick her up."

The bosses of my youth and early manhood did not seem to care much about their workers. Even at good pits like Briggs standards were low. Snydale and Whitwood pits were called bread and herring pits. Archer, Pope, Pearson, Masham, Briggs, Charlesworth - these were the bosses I knew or had heard of in my youth, and yet here I was almost 50 years later facing similar men in a Committee Room of the House of Commons; the times had changed. Now I had the ability to question them, and if need be, make them sweat.

* * * * *

The present system of departmental Select Committees in the House of Commons dates back to 1979, one year before I entered the Commons, and replaced the rather makeshift system which had been developing in a piece meal manner since the 1960s. Committees are appointed "to examine the expenditure, administration and policy of the principal government departments and associated public bodies, and more particularly to strengthen the accountability of Ministers to the House of Commons for the discharge of their responsibilities." Members of the Select Committee are not in general expected to concern themselves with draft legislation or Bills, but to question Ministers and civil servants who shape coming legislation.

The system is sounder than I had thought it might be when I sat on it for the first time, but if the Select Committees are to continue and thrive they have to change. I would recommend that increased resources be made available for individual committees in terms of staff and office accommodation; that essential resources extending the policy and research divisions of the House of Commons Library are established, which are staffed by people with the specialist knowledge and experience to handle complex subjects swiftly and efficiently; and that each department should employ an information officer with the responsibility of drawing to the attention of Select Committees information that they may think appropriate to the inquiries being made. There should be increased parliamentary time on the floor of the House of Commons for the presentation of Select Committee reports, and a regular slot where Select Committee findings can be presented to the House should be established.

The system works like this: In questioning Ministers, civil servants and any other persons with a useful contribution to make, Departmental Select Committees have the authority to send for people, papers and records. They can also travel away from Westminster, as we did when some of us went to the USA, and can appoint specialist advisers. Though delegated, these are extensive powers. Theoretically, a committee can pick up any topic it likes within its broad frame of reference, appoint a team of specialist advisers to assist it and spend its time travelling around the country demanding evidence from anyone that it chooses and ask for the disclosure of any private documents that it wishes to see. If a witness will not appear, the House has the power to subpoena. There was one famous case when the Committee had to formally invoke their powers of compulsion to make Arthur Scargill attend a hearing. On that occasion they dispatched that formidable lady, Miss Frampton, from the Serjeant at Arms' Office to the NUM Headquarters to issue the order. It did not beat about the bush. Scargill backed off and appeared before the Committee.

When the present Select Committee system was implemented in 1979, Roy Mason and I were very sceptical. We questioned whether Select Committees would be effective in influencing government or whether the reports would be just pigeonholed after much expenditure of time, talent and money. However, we did agree that they would be useful for eliciting information. We also saw great advantages in the press coverage reports like these would engender: Reporting might cause embarrassment to governments and in that way hopefully would influence the government's attitude. My own experience has been that the information provided to committee members has been more than useful and the knowledge it provided has equipped Members with information which has been very valuable in presenting their arguments in both chambers of the Palace of Westminster. There is certainly evidence that governments do not welcome some of the inquiries. Whether this warrants the formidable expense and time is another question. After 20 years the jury is still out on that one. Do the committees' reports influence government in a direct way? I think not.

The Select Committee finally completed its work and produced its draft report on Wednesday 28 January 1987 *(Appendix A)*. The Report on the coal industry was due for final consideration, paragraph by paragraph. Members wishing to propose amendments to the report had to do so in an approved manner. My chief objective was to elicit the precise intent of the Government on the privatisation of the coal industry, so I decided to place on record my reservations. Despite consistent denials I was convinced that the Government's aim was more privatisation. The attitude of my Conservative colleagues on the Committee did nothing to allay my suspicions.

A major opportunity to probe came at one of the last examinations of witnesses, and before the draft report was composed. Peter Walker, Secretary of State for Energy - now Lord Walker of Worcester - was called. Both myself and Peter Rost, a pro-privatisation Tory who argued his case from a diametrically opposed position, questioned him on the sale of the coal mines. Peter Walker denied that privatisation was on the cards, but I remained unconvinced.

The draft report that we convened to consider in January 1987 was a comprehensive document as befitted the extensive research and examination of witnesses that had been undertaken. When one of the conclusions advanced stated that every opportunity must be given to the private sector to invest in the coal industry, for the sake of my principles, my heritage and my own experience working in the privatised coal mines prior to nationalisation, I knew I must act, for I felt impelled to compose my own report. I was able to do this in good time as the draft report had been circulated amongst us before our meeting. My strategy was simple. I moved a motion that 34 paragraphs should be struck from the draft and replaced by my own. *(Appendix B)*

In defence of my amendments I pointed out that the Chairman of British Coal, Sir Robert Haslam - now Lord Haslam - a man with long experience of the private sector, had bluntly told us that the idea that private industry had a magic wand and could come in and do things beyond the capabilities of the nationalised industries was fantasy. Ian MacGregor, Chairman of British Coal, had described speculation over the privatisation of the coal industry as "an unfortunate diversion" and the General Secretary of the British Association of Colliery Management thought it was very destabilising, so I was not alone. The structure of the industry at that time was, in my view, broadly acceptable and public ownership brought real practical and strategic advantages. I took the view no convincing case for alteration had yet been made. In Parliament I had received an unclear reply about privatisation plans from Mrs Thatcher, the Prime Minister. On 24 November 1986 she had said:

"The Government has privatised one fifth of the state sector of industries which they inherited in 1979 and will have transferred a further one fifth to the private sector by the end of this Parliamentary Session. We have also announced our intention to return most of the remainder of the private sector in the next Parliament. However, there are no current plans for the privatisation of British Coal. The priority for the industry's management is to build on the enormous productivity gains that are now being achieved and to restore the industry to financial viability."

I considered this an evasive answer on the future of British Coal and knew her answer to be an example of a classic parliamentary tactic to avoid answering a direct question. "No current plans" means at that moment in time. It did not take into account the fact that the plans could have altered an hour later. I suggested that the Government should state categorically that there would be no privatisation of British Coal, for I had been assured of this by both Peter Walker and also later by Lord Parkinson, in an enquiry into the privatisation of the electricity industry.

Mrs Thatcher had her views, I had mine. My opposition to privatisation was based on my own direct experience of the pre-1947 coal industry. It had been exploitative and health and safety matters which had been so assiduously attended to by the nationalised industry would be neglected by those driven solely by the profit motive. But there was a third factor. I feared that private owners would be equally neglectful of social and environmental factors. I felt that British Coal, as a nationalised industry, would be expected to take a much wider view of its responsibilities than a privatised one.

I also held the belief that important strategic assets should remain in public control so that any temporary disturbances in world energy markets could be overcome and Britain's principal energy asset preserved for her future needs. I did not feel that there should be a possibility that we could be made hostage to the vagaries of the Polish coal economy. I was convinced, and still am, that the case for running down coal was based on short term economic factors that there would be no long term strategic planning, and that a privately owned industry would rapidly strip the best coal assets if its short term aim for profits required it to do so. That a state owned industry would take a long-term view of the future was endorsed by Peter Walker in 1986: "I very much want to see the coal option as a form of energy to remain active and open. We cannot predict the future supplies and cost of supply of energy and if you have such a resource you would be crazy to close off one industry for a long while or forever."

My view reflected Walker's; the public interest was best served by public ownership of an industry that had received substantial amounts of aid because of its crucial strategic importance. Governmental and parliamentary stewardship of energy provision was, and is, just as important as the supervision of the strategic defence needs.

The most commonly envisaged form of privatisation advanced by right wing doctrinaire Conservatives was one where individual pits would have been sold off, or new licences to mine coal offered to all-comers. Richard J Budge (RJB) was such a successful bidder for the majority of pits that he received most of the British Coal stock. There would be a number of medium sized firms theoretically in competition, but operating with scant regard for the national energy needs, or in consideration of British Coal's traditional remit. Private sector firms would have bought the most profitable mines and, recognising that their principal customer was the electricity supply industry, and this was a monopoly, they would sell their coal at a price which undercut the remaining nationalised pits. Peter Walker described this sort of a system as "absurd and lunatic" and his description was perfect. Other Conservatives argued differently. Professor Robinson listed three gains that he felt had been made from what he described as the "liberalisation" of the industry. For this gentleman the primary gain of privatisation was the "reduced monopoly power of labour". He claimed that he was not suggesting that the power of labour in British Mining should be broken but, given the attitude of the Government during the miners' strike, this seemed disingenuous.

When in the event the House divided against itself in the Coal Bill I recalled the words of Abraham Lincoln: "A house divided against itself cannot stand." To this day I believe that no industry, whether coal or cars or baking pork pies, can ever be truly successful unless management and unions work co-operatively together. We knew that industrial relations post-strike were in terrible shape and talk of privatisation further eroded the morale of the miners, but up to 1984 ours had been a relatively calm industry. My view was, and still is, that the British coal industry should have been allowed to get on with its essential business without being distracted by fashionable ideological nostrums of Thatcherism. Although I recognise my minority report did not eclipse the conclusions of the draft report, I was satisfied that my opinions were now a matter of public record, and that I tried to inject sanity into a crazy decision.

When eventually the Amendment was made the Committee divided. I voted Aye with J D Concannon, Ted Leadbitter and William O'Brien. The "noes" were Michael Brown, Dr Michael Clark, Geoffrey Dickens, James Pawsey and Peter Rost.

On completion of the enquiry, the Committee's report made 50 important recommendations and conclusions. Recommendation 12 contained the treatment of coal and nuclear power. The Committee was disturbed by the uneven treatment given to the coal and nuclear sections of the energy economy by the Government. It recognised that the problems of nuclear power were being glossed over because there was an emotional hostility towards the coal industry. The Committee took the view that the existing generators should not be sold at a discount. They considered that this would be discriminatory.

In a report headed *Consequences of Electricity Privatisation* they looked at the situation after privatisation and expressed a strong view that the closure of deep mines was irreversible. They also emphasised the belief that electricity consumers would gain little or nothing from the precipitant run-down of the British coal industry. The Committee recommended that the Government should permit British Coal to purchase coal fired generating stations where it would be in the British coal industry's interest. The Department were to play an active part in ensuring that a secure source of funds were found to support the Coal Research Establishment, also that the Director General should take steps as soon as possible to reduce the dominance of two generator sites when the electricity market had had time to develop further, but not later than 1995. The report said that the Minister should decide at that time whether the two main generators should be referred to the Monopolies and Mergers Committee and explain fully the reasons for his decision.

Yet despite these powerfully argued recommendations, following both the reports on the coal industry and electricity supply industry, and overwhelming evidence, the Government was not influenced. In the short run it was apparent that the Government was indifferent to the Energy Select Committee's reports.

* * * * *

It is now obvious that the Government completely ignored the warnings in the Energy Select Committee Report on the coal industry in 1986/7 when the committee warned the Government of the possible consequences of running down the coal industry and the effects this could have on our future energy needs. There was also the strong suspicion that pressure was being brought to bear on the Conservative Members not to investigate the Government's proposals to privatise the electricity supply industry prior to the Bill. However, they did not have their way and it was investigated. I was influential in causing the investigation to take place. This is how the change came about.

On the day the Energy Committee sat to decide the future of its investigations I became aware of the Government's intention to produce a Bill to privatise the electricity industry. I believed that its plans should be examined by our Committee. I was determined that we should look beyond coal and look at that aspect of energy policy. At that point I did not know how to advance the case, indeed I believed that the Conservatives on the Committee had been pressurised by the Secretary of State, Cecil Parkinson, not to agree to investigate. However, one morning when we were close to the end of our sessions and when I counted the heads I realised that we were in the majority and that a little push could send their best laid plans into turmoil.

For once not all the Conservatives had turned up. We had four and they had three and not five Members. Judged in terms of appropriate quality our side was better than theirs. Three out of the four Labour people present were ex-miners, the other, Ted Ledbetter, an ex-North Country teacher, was not from our background but was especially experienced in industrial relations and particularly coalmining communities in the North. The opposition had much less experience of our industry. They had a scientist, a journalist, two businessmen and a gentleman of the shires. They were a less cohesive group than ours, therefore dedication to coming to these particular meetings was not so strong.

This particular morning only a minority made the full distance, two had not turned up. Quick as a flash I recognised that against the odds Labour had the majority. Political experience gained in the smoke rooms, trade union lodges and tap rooms of Pontefract told me that if I moved quickly we were in power in this Committee. I suggested that we enquire into the proposed privatisation of the electricity industry

35

and put my proposition to a vote. The Tories immediately recognised their predicament and made some attempt at a delay. No doubt the Government Members hoped that a window of opportunity would open and in would climb the lost majority. It didn't. Seeing they had a problem, one member rose and left the meeting. I knew where he was going, he was off to the Whips' Office. Within minutes he returned accompanied by the Whip. I knew I had to move sharpish and consolidate the position because somewhere across the Palace the Government Whips would be running around to find the missing Members. I formally moved that the Committee carry out "an investigation into the Government's proposals to private the electricity industry." Bill O'Brien, a close political colleague from Knottingley, saw what I was doing and seconded my motion. We were on a roll. We were creating a precedent. This, as far as I am aware, had never been done before: forcing an enquiry by a Select Committee prior to a Bill being produced.

Generation of electricity could potentially come from five sources, coal, gas, nuclear, energy, oil; and alternative sources such as wind, sun and tide power.

I held views on electricity generation using gas but my views were by no means clear cut. I had formed the opinion that whilst we were fortunate that gas had been discovered in the North Sea, it was an unwise policy to use it for industrial purposes. That was because the supply was finite. I considered that it would have been much wiser to reserve the underground reserves for domestic use. I took this view for several reasons. The introduction of North Sea gas had brought about a domestic revolution. Anyone who, like me, had grown up in Featherstone where almost every home burned concessionary coal saw the disadvantages to the environment of solid fuel pollution. Every November time, periods of heavy pollution closed around us and created such enveloping fogs that we couldn't see our hands before us. In my early local government days I had been involved in attempts to produce clean air zones so I was no Luddite as far as restricted coal use was concerned. The bringing in of gas for domestic use was a blessing for the environment, the lack of the fogs since 1960 has proved this point. I took a wide view and saw that air pollution was no help to coal miners who were disabled by the industrial disease emphysema. Since this was the subject of my best work in Parliament I would have been inconsistent to have thought otherwise. I must admit that I liked gas but because we did not know the size of the resource I thought gas should only be used for direct domestic use and not for generation of electricity.

As an ex-miner, clearly recognising the way mining was intimately concerned with employment and community strategy, I was keen that coal powered generators should be encouraged to generate electricity and that the coal fuelled stations should not be abandoned. I was particularly concerned that too little research and development money had not been used to investigate clean coal technology equipment.

If I walked out of my house to the end of Churchbalk Lane, Pontefract, and climbed onto the high land called the Rookeries I could look across towards Hull and see three major power stations: Ferrybridge; Eggborough and Drax. Each of these power stations had a complicated history which was intimately concerned with the de-sulphurisation programme. Ferrybridge was a coal fired station commissioned before the war but expanded in the 1960s. Its future was under threat, for I knew that because of the lack of investment in clean coal technology it would not be able to meet the European targets controlling emissions when they were enforced. Closure of Ferrybridge would have a major effect on unemployment in my constituency, for it not only had its own labour force but it was fed by the two remaining collieries left in this area.

When I became Manpower Officer in 1964, twenty-one collieries were either in my constituency or within five miles of it. Now there were just the Prince of Wales and Kellingley; between them employing less than a thousand men. This number contrasted dramatically with the 21,000 who had worked in the industry twenty-five years earlier. Yet though it was but a small percentage, in towns which had already been hit by pit closures and the collapse of associated industries, it was significant. The power station was also an important employer giving work to something in the region of 600 men. With ancillary workers in supplying industries you could probably double this figure. These raw statistics show that it was essential to maintain this station as a coal fired station and to introduce clean coal technology, and not to countenance closure. Eggborough's situation was similar to Ferrybridge's but because it was four miles beyond the eastern boundary of my constituency the workforce was split between my town and Selby, North Yorkshire. Drax which was farther off by contrast did have some clean coal technology. That was because its commissioning was relatively late. When he was Minister of Fuel and Power, Roy Mason, an ex-coal miner from Barnsley, had made this one of his major gifts to an industry in retreat by insisting that it was coal fired.

The caution displayed by some witnesses occasionally breaks down under questioning in a Select Committee. Senior people become more and more open and you get to see more than was intended. On 27 May 1991 the Select Committee on Energy was busy taking evidence from the then Secretary of State for Energy, John Wakeham MP - now Lord Wakeham - on the subject of clean coal technology.

I had a threefold interest in this topic: a former miner, I had "hands-on" knowledge of the muck that a mine produces, my constituency was host to Ferrybridge, a large, coal fired power station which employed a large number of my constituents and I was conscious of environmental constraints and European Community legislation which said that the amount of sulphur produced by the combustion of coal should be reduced in order to alleviate the ravages of acid rain. The last point was especially important. With a coal fired station, a good way to effect this is to fit flue gas de-sulphurisation - FGD - equipment. This "scrubs" the emissions of sulphur and renders the residue much less toxic. However, like many things that have lasting environmental value, it is expensive.

At that time there were strong rumours circulating in the power industry that PowerGen, which on privatisation became responsible for Ferrybridge, would not fit a FGD. As the official minutes show, I questioned Mr Wakeham about this:

Mr Wakeham- "The position is - and, as you know there was some controversy at the time - that I asked the to-be-privatised generators what in their view was the most commercial way in which they could meet their obligations under the European directive. They produced a plan to fit eight gigawatts of capacity to use British coal. I accepted that plan. That plan is enshrined in the basis upon which we privatised the industry and I do not think that it is for me to speculate on anything else."

Mr Lofthouse - "Let me add this just briefly, Secretary of State. You say that it is enshrined in the basis on which you privatised the industry. Are you telling me that PowerGen are not in a position to withdraw from the FGD programme?"

Mr Wakeham - "My understanding is, no."

Mr Lofthouse -"Thank you, Chairman."

From this and subsequent exchanges I understood that the privatised industry was getting specific financial support to cope with cleaning the output of the station. Subsequently, PowerGen was given £1 billion of taxpayers' money to fit FGD to two stations, Ferrybridge and one in Nottinghamshire. Four years later, however, I was shocked to read in the *Daily Telegraph* that £350 million of the sum allocated to Ferrybridge had, in the words of the newspaper commentator, "vanished".

Fortunately I had remedy to follow this matter through. As a Deputy Speaker in the House of Commons, I found that when I issued an invitation to people who I wished to see, either to a Minister of the Crown or to a person of consequence, this was not treated lightly. I never abused this authority, invoking it only when I felt it necessary. In this case of the missing millions I felt it necessary to interview Ed Wallis, the Chief Executive of PowerGen. He kindly and willingly responded to my invitation to meet.

I told him firmly and frankly I was concerned about the money, but much more than that, my anxiety was for the future of the jobs at Ferrybridge and, by association, at the Prince of Wales and Kellingley Collieries.

We met in my rooms in the House of Commons. Mr Wallis said the best way to maintain the viability of Ferrybridge was to encourage the activities of RJB Mining so as to bring about such a reduction in the price of coal that gas would be uneconomic in comparison. He indicated that despite the shrinking market for coal, because of competition from the likes of nuclear power and French electricity imports, PowerGen still expected to derive 60 per cent of the power it generated from coal. He said that Ferrybridge as one of the big five power stations would not close at all or at least for a very long time. The FGD question simply did not arise as long as emissions from the station were balanced by cleaner stations within the company. From this answer it appeared to me that emissions from Ferrybridge were to be ignored. What mattered was general emissions from his company's plants throughout the country.

When I proceeded to the matter of the *Daily Telegraph's* "vanished" £350 million, Mr Wallis categorically declared that none of the money had vanished. He then explained that the Government's bestowal of £1 billion on PowerGen had in fact been intended for new combined cycle power stations and post CEGB environmental maintenance and repair, and that PowerGen had actually spent £1.3 billion in this cause.

When I mentioned Lord Wakeham's 1991 testimony to the Energy Select Committee Ed Wallis remarked that, for all his many sterling qualities, Lord Wakeham had gone "too far" unalterably committing PowerGen to fit FGD at Ferrybridge and he re-affirmed that PowerGen had no plans to fit FGD.

He departed with a promise to send me a letter which would comprehensively detail PowerGen's plans for Ferrybridge, which he very kindly did. Comprehensive though this letter was, it did little to dispel my fears for the future of the workers at the power station and at the Prince of Wales and Kellingley pits. I found Mr Wallis to be very open and always willing to provide the information I requested, and I was indebted to him. However I regret that currently there is no available technology to bolt onto power stations to reduce carbon dioxide emissions. I have always regretted that I have never had the opportunity of calling Mr Wallis back to the Energy Select Committee to allow the Committee to further examine him and give him the opportunity of explaining to the Committee what he had explained to me, which I am sure he would have been glad to do.

Unfortunately, the Committee had been wound up after the 1992 Election. I have always believed the Government took this decision because of the embarrassment the Committee had created for them during their in-depth examinations on the energy industry. Committee reports can run contrary to government policy and for that reason a government's attitude has not allowed their work to be as effective as I think it should have been.

Yet although I had a committee member's keen interest in oil, it was in the development of the nuclear sector of the economy that I had the more decisive influence. I was aware that the Government supported the extension of the nuclear industry and were keen when making their case to compare the prices of nuclear with those of other fuels. These, they indicated, were much cheaper. First I accepted this as fact. The ability to question in this enquiry, however, gave me more power than I expected. I had somewhat naively believed that the Government knew what it was doing and that the figures were essentially accurate. For that reason I always found it difficult to argue against the economic case and had stressed instead the safety aspects and the dangers of the development of nuclear power. Chernobyl occurred in this period, and a few years earlier America had had the experience of the Three Mile Island incident. When I questioned I was always assured that these "accidents" could not happen here. I would have remained convinced of the economic argument but for my ability to question at a high level. At one sitting I found myself able to question the Chairman of the Nuclear Authority.

Some of the best questions are unprepared. They come from out of the blue as you listen to the debate. The key question which I delivered was a very, very simple one. I asked, "How much does it cost to de-commission a nuclear power station?" The answer surprised me. It also surprised the rest of the Committee - it had not been costed.

On hearing this I asked, "How can you give us such a low figure per thermal unit of generated electricity from a nuclear source when you do not know the answer to such a significant question?" He answered something to the effect that since de-commissioning would be many years ahead it was not possible to produce a total cost. I did not back off: "So what you are saying is, we can never know the cost of producing nuclear power?" The cost of breaking up Ferrybridge

Power Station is minimal. You smash it down, bulldoze the rubble and cart it away in lorries to make hard-core for roads. You don't do that with building materials and land that is polluted with radioactivity.

My question that morning had serious implications and, I believe, affected the complete history of energy privatisation. It was obvious that the Government were to find themselves in great difficulty in attracting buyers for the nuclear generation of electricity, and for that reason they were forced to withdraw any part of the nuclear generation out of the sale of the electricity industry. By doing this, of course there were costs to our communities which went unnoticed. To get them off the hook the Government placed a fuel levy on all consumers including my next door neighbours in Carleton Crest, and on every family, every avenue, street, road and ginnel throughout the land. People who never thought about the mismanagement of nuclear fuels were forced to pay a substantial amount on their energy bills to subsidise an industry which was both dangerous and ill thought through.

It would be too grand a claim to say that with that one question I destroyed nuclear energy but like David, with one pebble to Goliath's forehead, I definitely dented the conceit of nuclear mandarins and helped thwart the Tory Party's ambition to sell off nuclear energy. From then on even their friends stopped rubbing their hands in expectation and realised that nuclear energy was not a marketable proposition.

The Committee spent a lot of time on nuclear energy but the forms they never seriously considered were the alternative ones - wind, sun and tide. Once we went up to the Orkneys and saw a small wind farm there, but it was only on a very minor scale. In all my time in Committee I doubt if we spent more than three hours questioning experts on these forms of energy. Yet it is clear that future generations of constituents in Pontefract and Castleford will have to give serious consideration to the research and generation of such sources if they are to survive in a natural environment with renewable energy resources.

Many of us remembered the way in which some of the Middle Eastern Countries had held the West to ransom thirty years before, therefore the uncertainty of oil prices meant that there was a danger in over-reliance on this source. Like coal emissions oil also polluted the atmosphere and carried other dangers. Shipwrecks could pollute the sea and endanger the coastal economy - features not overemphasised in the rush to displace coal. When considering oil as an energy source we should always remember that whilst it was, and continues to be, important in our overall strategy, the North Sea reserves - like gas - are finite. We should also see that increasingly control of this source has been placed in the hands of private companies in a variety of Scandinavian and northern European countries and that their ownership is complicated.

* * * * *

On the eve of the 1984/85 Miners' Strike, there were 170 deep mine collieries in the United Kingdom. In the next few years both of the pits I had worked in for the bulk of my working life - Ackton Hall as a collier and Fryston as a personnel manager - closed. The collieries of my area were being run down. On 13 October 1992, British Coal made their announcement to cease production at 31 of their 50 deep mine collieries because of the reduced demand for coal. At this time they gave statistics to precisely show what we all knew: 120 pits had been closed from the eve of the Miners' Strike 1984 to the day of the announcement. Now more than half of those remaining were to be closed. This announcement provoked a public outcry. On 19 October 1992, in a statement to the House of Commons, the President of the Board of Trade, Michael Heseltine, in a placatory state said that British Coal would only be allowed to proceed with the closure of 10 pits and that none of these closures would take place until the statutory consultation period of 90 days had been completed and that a moratorium would be imposed on the other closures until early 1993, during which time the Government and British Coal would set out the full case for the closures and enter into a widespread consultation with all those concerned. He didn't convince me. I always recognised this to be a stalling exercise to stem the tide of public criticism, and of course my cynicism unfortunately was proved to be right. The Queen's speech on 18 November 1993 carried the formal announcement that legislation would be introduced to privatise British Coal. The Coal Industry Bill received its second reading in the House of Commons on 17 January 1994.

Despite assurances given by the Government through the different Secretaries of State, that Privatisation of the coal industry was not on a hidden agenda, I was always cynical, so when the Government announced the privatisation, it gave me no pleasure whatsoever to say, "I told you so." Of course I was emotionally involved. The coal industry was like a second family to me and had the greatest formative influence on my youth and young manhood.

Local people didn't go under without a fight. There were protests and marches but one of the most imaginative came from an organisation in my area and one I had, in a way, helped nurture. I cannot say that the arts have been a major feature in my life; however in the early 1990s I began to see that under special circumstances they could be very influential.

During the late 1960s I had become friends with a college lecturer who had worked alongside me to bring more democracy to the Pontefract Party and who was later to be a sounding board when I was devising legislation on industrial illness. Brian Lewis was ten years younger than I was, a bit of a visionary but enough of a pragmatist to keep at least one of his feet on the floor.

At least twice during the time covered in this book the Art Circus intervened in a political way and made a difference. When Michael Heseltine closed the pits they mobilised writers across the coalfield, arranged to meet at Grimethorpe Colliery, one of the target collieries. In one day, using new technology and a lot of old skills - such as talking and writing - they generated a 32,000 word book in fourteen hours. That night, using members' cars, they delivered it all over the coalfield and it was with key speakers at the London rally the next morning. Two days later an abridged copy of *Coal is Energy: Energy is Coal* was printed and selling all over the North; school children even delivered copies to Number Ten Downing Street.

They also responded rapidly when the chairmen of the Rugby League sought to merge the Wakefield, Castleford and Featherstone

Clubs. This time it took a week for the book to reach the streets - using fax they linked up with local clubs like Keighley Cougars but also solicited articles from main people in Australia.

Yorkshire Art Circus was founded in Pontefract, but later established in Castleford and Glasshoughton. I hadn't thought of the arts as being an important feature of communities like Featherstone and Pontefract, but increasingly I saw that the arts did a lot for local people. The Art Circus had its ear to the ground and produced very high quality books and plays, devising an alternative history of England emphasising incidents like these. They took the lives of local people and the lives of communities and transformed them through art so that they had new relevance.

One play I remember very well was about an incident which took place in Featherstone when my grandad was a young miner. The Featherstone Disturbance occurred in September 1893, much of his bitterness regarding the employer came from what he experienced when soldiers came into our village and shot two miners.

I have grown up with the knowledge of this incident and recall, a few weeks after my father's death, my grandad taking me to see his grave. Within 15 metres of where he was buried were the gravestones of these men. As I reached adulthood and my experience increased, I readily understood why my grandad had always advised me to "never trust the bosses". My very close friend Tommy Watton, NUM Branch Secretary, well-known for his left-wing views, would visit the grave annually. The NUM Branch in Featherstone were never allowed to forget this incident.

I was keen to learn more about the Featherstone Riots and saw that not only could I learn about them through books, but also through songs and performances. I was not alone in this feeling. On the occasion when they performed a play about the riots in the local community library, it was totally booked out.

One of the qualities of the Art Circus was that it would not shy away from using the best people it could find. Indeed, money was spent on bringing in a top opera producer to polish up on the last three days of rehearsal of the play, but the hard graft was done by Ian Clayton, a local later to be a well known Yorkshire television personality.

45

I once heard Brian Lewis say, "Working in Fryston Colliery at some time between 1950 and its closure in 1985 were Jack Hulme, a photographer who had an exhibition at The National Museum of Film, Photography and Television; the Manager Jim Bullock who was author of several books; Harry Malkin, a fitter who had an exhibition at the Royal Festival Hall and later designed major statues all over South Yorkshire; Bill Fowkes, one of the Manchester United players who survived the Munich air crash; Dave Wilders who represented England in the Paraplegic Games and wrote the best history of Castleford I have ever read; Geoff Lofthouse, Deputy Speaker of the House of Commons and campaigner on industrial diseases; Keith Fieldhouse, producer to the Pontefract and Featherstone Amateur Dramatic Society and "Nocker" Norton, a great international loose forward for Castleford." Brian continued, "With a list like that, you have to make up your mind. Either there is something special about the water in Fryston or, if you put the right money into any village you'd eventually find this sort of talent. It's just that as a society we have not got the emphasis right."

The Jack Hulme and Harry Malkin Art Circus exhibition at the Royal Festival Hall, not a quarter of mile from the House of Commons, was a great occasion and for me especially memorable because of one picture. As I entered I looked up and saw a massive photograph taken by Jack of a man I knew. It was of Hector Tams, playing an accordion. Hector had been a personal friend of mine over many years. He lived just around the corner from me on Chequerfield Estate. He was a real character; father of eleven children, he would sit on the garden wall, entertain them and others on summer evenings by playing his accordion. This photograph was relevant and brought back a lot of memories.

Hector once told me that one night, after his wife had gone out with her friends, he stayed to look after the children. When Mrs Tams came back and enquired if the children were all right Hector said, "Yes, they are bathed and in bed, all settled barring one. I have been up twice already and he now seems to be settled." Mrs Tams went into the house and came down with the child in her arms, saying, "You silly bugger, this one is not ours." I never knew whether Hector was joking or not.

Their children did Hector and his wife proud. A lot became professional people. One was a consultant at the York Hospital, two of them senior mechanical and electrical mining engineers, and all were children to be very proud of. One I remember particularly well. One day in my position as MP I had to enquire about some small matter at a Featherstone bank. I asked for the manager who was not available at the time, but rang me back half an hour later. She gave the information I required and then said, "You don't know who I am do you? Well I am Muriel Tams." It gave me a great thrill to think I had seen this little girl grow up in this united extended family and I thought, "Another one of Hector's who has done very well."

I have always thought that when there is strong community support, and priority is given to education, our housing estates can produce such people.

My first book *A Very Miner MP* was produced by the Art Circus and launched at the CISWO Disabled Miners' Centre, Halfpenny Lane, Pontefract. This is an interesting and much altered building. Originally it was a Victorian house close to the Pontefract to Featherstone railway lines and the home of Bernard Hartley, the Justice of the Peace who had travelled to the Featherstone Riots and read the Riot Act which resulted in the deaths of James Gibbs and James Duggan.

Roy Hattersley was the main speaker. In the following week in his "End Piece" column in *The Guardian* he spoke of the occasion. He compared it with other launches he attended and said it was something quite different from ones which usually took place in London hotels. He particularly focused on the fact that there were sandwiches, Yorkshire beer and then, after the launch a chance to do a spot of ballroom dancing. This, he said, was the Labour ,movement at its best and that if there were more Geoff Lofthouses in Parliament the Party would not be in the mess they were in at that time. I was flattered but took more pleasure from the fact that at my first book launch I was surrounded by 200 family and friends and parliamentary colleagues, particularly the two Roys, Mason and Hattersley. I had been widowed twelve months and so it was particularly gratifying to have my daughter Lynne and her two children there. The Art Circus launch was one of the few joyful occasions I experienced in that sad period.

On this occasion it was a book launch and I was the recipient, but as an MP you often find yourself at presentations and I regularly attend school prize givings, pensioners functions and retirement do's. Most are predictable but one wasn't. The idea that all miners would take a day a week off work is not true. However, there were a few miners who did just this. They were very handy at playing the system.

When I was Personnel Manager at Fryston I realised that there were some characters who were experts on all aspects of absence, but particularly benefits claims. One week I recall receiving two doctor's certificates referring to the same man. One of them said, "Mr So-and-So says - 'says' underlined - he is suffering from arthritis." The other said, "Mr So-and-So is suffering from - don't know." When he eventually retired I checked this man's records. As far as I could ascertain in the period between Vesting Day - the day nationalisation was proclaimed - and the date of his retirement in the mid-60s, a period of twenty years, he had completed just thirteen full weeks at work. At his retirement party I decided I would present him with a dossier of photocopies of his medical notes and his shovel. What was noticeable about the shovel was that whilst it had been in service for 20 years, the label was still on the shaft.

* * * * *

The British coal industry had been in decline since the end of the Second World War. In 1947, at nationalisation, the National Coal Board employed 718,400 people in collieries and produced 200 million tonnes of coal per year. By 1971 colliery employment had declined to 286,000 and the output was down to 145 million tonnes. In 1983, the year before the last major miners' strike, employment was 233,600 and output was 121 million tonnes. By 1993, employment had declined to 31,700 and output was down to 80,800 tonnes. Clearly these figures show, amongst other things, a dramatic increase in productivity. In 1947 the output per man per year was 267 tonnes. In 1982/83 it had risen to 504 tonnes. In 1992/93 it had increased to 1,611 tonnes.

This was of course mainly brought about by the introduction of unprecedented mechanisation and technology. However, you cannot isolate technology from the men who use it. The workforce had adapted too and played the major part of making the introduction of mechanisation a major success. Men of my generation had served an apprenticeship setting pit props and had retired to self-advancing faces.

In the early 1980s, just before Margaret Thatcher's Conservative Government had embarked upon its privatisation programme, all the major energy industries were state owned and they had definite roles in the system. Direct competition was not a feature of the energy economy. Electricity generation was undertaken by the Central Electricity Generating Board in England and Wales which sold electricity to the local electricity boards. Around 70% of electricity generation came from coal fired power stations and about 20% from nuclear power and about 10% from gas and other sources. At that time gas had no role in generating electricity and oil was considered far too expensive after the sharp oil price increases of the 1970s. There were some oil fired stations which were largely retained as emergency suppliers to cope if the supply of coal was interrupted by economic features like a miners' strike.

The National Coal Board (NCB) sold its coal to the CEGB at an agreed price, over which the Secretary of State for Energy had considerable influence. This was not a free market. The system had evolved to allow coal prices to reflect world prices in order to prevent the CEGB from being disadvantaged by paying higher prices than would have been paid for imports if they had been allowed. There was a three tier pricing system which aimed at charging world prices for a small amount of coal, roughly equivalent to the amount that could be feasibly imported in the short term, a higher price for a larger volume that could have been imported if import facilities were increased, and a final tranche of coal which was charged at full cost. The justification for the third tranche was that there was no feasible alternative to the use of this coal for electricity generation.

49

Privatisation changed this picture completely. The privatisation of British Gas in 1986 roughly coincided with a sharp decline in world oil prices. The price hike of the late 1970s had not yet been reversed. Although as immediate consequence oil's attraction appeared harmful for gas producers, it opened the possibility of supplying gas to new markets of which electricity generation seemed the most promising. There was, however, an EC Directive of 1975 preventing gas from being used for this purpose. This wasn't liked by the Government. It argued that the energy supply position had changed dramatically since the mid-70s. Consequently, the Thatcher Government lobbied hard for a repeal of this directive. They finally achieved this in 1991.

I believed this repeal to be a major mistake. I have always considered that North Sea gas should have been used for domestic purposes. It was a fortunate discovery and the off shore resources should not have been squandered. I argued that if we protected the reserves over a far longer period, this constraint would have had more influence in protecting the environment and preserving the quality of the atmosphere. I believed that coal should have been used for the generation of electricity and I always fought for the introduction of a major clean coal technology programme which would, of course, also protect against atmospheric pollution. Burning coal in cleaner generators and maintaining a viable coal industry could have had long-term benefits for the future energy supplies and could have supported generations to come. Instead we allowed the market and short term gains to dominate our thinking.

The underplaying of coal is a relatively new feature of economic thinking. Recently my colleague, Roy Mason - now Lord Mason of Barnsley - drew my attention to speeches made by Winston Churchill and General Smuts to 3,000 representatives of the coalmining industry at the Central Hall Westminster, on Saturday, 31 October 1942. These speeches were kept a secret at the time, but had the 1980s Conservatives learned from the man who is often venerated as their greatest leader then there would have been more respect for coal in Mrs Thatcher's energy policy.

In 1942 almost every pit in the country had its miners' representative at the meeting, and colliery owners and mine managers were present in large numbers. When they returned home they interpreted to others in the industry their personal impressions of the speeches. It was a speech about the importance of coal to the wartime economy. Churchill started off by calling upon everyone in the industry, management and miners alike, hand in hand, to sweep away all remaining obstacles to maximum production:

"In the crisis of 1940, it is no more than the sober truth to say, we saved the freedom of mankind. We gave Russia time to arm and the United States to organise, but now it is a long cold strain we have to bear, harder perhaps for the British to bear than the shocks which they know so well how to take. We must not cast away our great deliverance, we must carry our work to its final conclusion. We shall not fail and then some day when children ask what did you do to win this inheritance for us and to make our names so respected among men, one will say I was a fighter pilot, another will say, I was in the submarine service, another I marched with the Eighth Army, a fourth will say none of you could have lived without the convoys and the merchant seamen and you in turn will say with equal pride and with equal right, we cut the coal."

Churchill showed how with our massive reserves we were self-sufficient, but by 1992 the heroes who cut the coal in wartime Britain - and Roy and I were two of them - were forgotten. New coal powered stations require ministerial consent, and expansion was therefore at a standstill, but there has been no attempt to restrict the growth of gas fired stations. Once there was a demand for gas for electricity generation, British Gas was happy to supply it. Yet for all the Tory protestations this was not a free market. If the company had had a free hand, prices would have been raised in order to reflect the increasing cost of obtaining the extra supplies. British Gas tried to do so but this attempt fell foul of its regulator. Sir James McKinnon insisted that the company should treat all its customers equally using a published schedule of prices and not changing the terms from one buyer to another. He ruled that British Gas should satisfy the extra demand at listed prices. He was looking for something like a level playing field; the Government, for all it protestations about the market, was not. It was biasing the economy away from coal.

The privatisation of electricity in 1990 had enormous consequences for British Coal, as the National Coal Board became. The CEGB had been virtually the monopoly buyer for British Coal and had relied upon UK supplies for most of its electricity generation. There was some nuclear contribution but not much. We were faced with a major dilemma. Even if British Coal had offered the cheapest supplies, the concentration of supply upon one source would have been unsatisfactory to their two private sector company customers. On the other hand both National Power and PowerGen inherited a stock of coal fired power stations, so needed solid fuel, this meant that the room for manoeuvre was limited. At the time of electricity privatisation it was generally assumed that they would greatly increase their imports of foreign coal, in order to provide competition for British Coal. The result was expected to be a sharp fall in demand for British coal. Things did not turn out as predicted. Even though privatisation operated and strengthened the desire of the electricity industry to seek other fuel supplies, British coal was still needed.

The regional electricity companies (RECs) are the successors of the local electricity boards but they too want more variety of sources of supply than were offered by the two main generating companies, National Power and PowerGen. Gas fired power stations fitted the bill because they could be built cheaply and quickly to expand capacity. Therefore the RECs themselves joined consortia to build gas fired power stations based on combined cycle gas turbines (CCGTs) and agreed to take the electricity thus generated. It is likely that the strategy which made commercial sense for the RECs involved gas generation in order to improve their bargaining position, and will dominate the market in the future. Even when some of the electricity so generated might actually be more expensive than that generated by coal they will stick with gas.

When I came to Parliament in 1978 environmental pollution was not an issue. I had worked in the coal industry since leaving school and had barely heard the concept mentioned. In the 1980s, thank goodness, the problem was forced into our consciousness by a range of environmental emergencies especially the threat to the ozone layer. From that time onwards British Coal faced problems triggered by the environmental concern. The first major worry came with the recognition that acid rain produces sulphur dioxide emissions. All acknowledged that damage is widespread, although there is some disagreement as to the details. Acid rain is one of the causes of extensive damage to trees and also increases acidity in some lakes, thus killing the fish. It is also causing serious weathering damage to historic stone buildings, making them very expensive to repair. Unfortunately British coal is very high in sulphur in these emissions, but there are palliatives. It is possible to remove excessive sulphur dioxide emissions by fitting power stations with flue gas de-sulphurisation. This was my ambition for Ferrybridge Power Station; unfortunately it is an extremely expensive process. Large quantities of limestone are needed to react with the sulphur dioxide to form gypsum, and in the short run limestone quarrying can leave ugly scars on the landscape. Clean air, however, benefits all. In time quarries can be filled and landscaped. We should not too easily dismiss de-sulphurisation.

When international concern about acid rain increases, it becomes relatively more expensive to use British coal and relatively cheaper to use either imported low sulphur coal or other fuels, notably gas. Since the effects of acid rain have an international dimension, the problem is not one that a British government of whatever political hue can ignore even if it wants to. Scandinavian countries in particular blame Britain for their environmental problems and have been highly vocal in their criticism.

There are other problems concerning airborne pollution. Global warming was not expected but is serious and has had tremendous influence on energy policy. To minimise environmental pollution, technological methods for emission reduction require constant development and refinement. It is clear that the burning of coal to provide energy will continue worldwide, especially in China and India where solid fuel will be heavily used. Clean coal technology (CCT) is the term used to describe the wide range of technologies designed to enhance both the efficiency and the environmental acceptability of coal extraction, preparation and use, but they are in their infancy. These technologies increase the energy gained per unit-weight of coal and reduce emissions and waste. Most are in the field of power generation and already there is an array of technologies that are commercially viable, with others set to join them soon. Coal use does not go away because Europe says it ought, but is part of the global economy. That is why Europe should take the lead and investigate ways of making coal a clean fuel.

In the past, it looked as if nuclear power would be the main rival for coal as a source of power for electricity generation. In the event, however, gas is the main competitor and nuclear power has retained much the same role as it has had for the past 20 years, providing about 20% of electricity generated. Neither environmental concerns over airborne pollution nor the desire to diversify sources of supply really assisted nuclear power; on the contrary, privatisation has presented more problems. Originally it was intended to privatise nuclear power with the rest of the nuclear industry, and National Power was made large enough to carry the nuclear power stations. Concerns over possible liabilities resulting from the de-commissioning of the ageing Magnox stations made nuclear power unattractive for the Stock Market so at a late stage the nuclear power stations were withdrawn from privatisation, and transferred instead to Nuclear Electric and Scottish Nuclear but resting within the public sector. To prevent nuclear power becoming uncompetitive, a levy on electricity generated by fossil fuels was introduced with the revenue going mainly to nuclear power. However, such subsidies do not fit in with EC rules and the policy could only be cleared with the EC on condition that it ended in 1998, which was the case. Nuclear power now has to compete on equal terms with other sources of electricity generation. It is not a cheap or attractive alternative.

About 5% of UK electricity is satisfied by imports from France via the cross channel link or inter-connector. Much of base-load French electricity is nuclear generated, but electricity supply through the inter-connector neither paid a levy nor received benefit from it. The electricity was therefore made available to the UK RECs at low prices but the British consumer had to pay more via a higher levy on UK generated electricity to satisfy the statutory obligations. These were disqualified by the Fossil Fuel Levy Act 1998, which removed the advantages that nuclear generated electricity and imported electricity from France enjoyed to ensure that coal and other fuels would enjoy a level playing field.

54

Energy industries have increasingly moved out of the public sector but are by no means entirely in the unregulated private sector. For one thing the Secretary of State retains considerable powers. For example, his approval is required before the building of a new power station can begin. An example of this is close at hand, in the Drax Power Station near Selby in North Yorkshire, constructed in the late 1960s. The then Secretary of State for Energy, Roy Mason MP, ordered that it should be coal fired; no other type of fuel would be entertained by him. Obviously Roy Mason was protecting the coal industry.

Considerable further power in deciding how the industry will develop is left with the regulators - the Director General of Gas Supply and the Director General of Electricity Regulation. These regulators have a powerful role in deciding what prices can be charged and can rule on many points related to the licence which lays down the terms under which the industry operates. Each regional electricity company has a licence which states various conditions including any social obligations and the way in which business is to be conducted, which must be adhered to. It has proved difficult to define the exact role of each regulator since the result has depended to some extent upon the individual personality. In some cases, notably gas, the regulator has recommended that the Government introduce radical changes into the structure of the industry as it stood after privatisation. This is no free Thatcherite market place.

The scale of British Coal's closure programme announced in October 1992 was a colossal shock and led to a wave of protest across the political spectrum. The promised review by the Tories of this policy was followed by the publication of the Government's Coal Review Paper on 25 March 1993. British Coal announced that of the 21 pits reviewed, twelve would continue in production pending the outcome of market testing; six would cease production and would be put in care and maintenance; two with limited economic reserves would close; and one would cease production, go on to development only, and then be brought back into production. Following the Coal Industry Act 1994, the privatisation of British Coal began at the end of that year. British Coal's five regional coal companies and seven care and maintenance deep mines were sold. Sixteen deep mines were bought by RJB Mining. Mining (Scotland) Ltd bought the Scottish mines. In South Wales, Celtic Energy bought the business there. Coal Investments PLC bought six mines but went out of business in 1996. Two of these remained open and were sold to Midlands Mining Limited. The industry has undergone draconian restructuring during the 1990s; concentration exclusively on profitable deposits has resulted in production costs almost as low as those charged anywhere in the world market. This has been a very difficult period, but I am pleased to say we have retained two mines, The Prince of Wales Pontefract, and Kellingley, in our local area.

1 May 1997 saw Labour's triumphant return to office after eighteen years in opposition. The new Government's energy policy is to ensure that there are secure, sustainable, and diverse supplies of energy, including coal, in this country. Unhappily its powers are limited by the Tory privatisation of the energy industries which makes it in large part impossible to intervene in what are now privately owned businesses. However, with regard to the coal industry, the Labour Government has set out the policies that it is pursuing to ensure a successful future for the remaining pits. The Government is taking action to block existing subsidies to German and Spanish coal producers which currently create barriers to sales of UK steam coal, anthracite and the manufactured smokeless fuels in the European Coal and Steel Community. It has also recently set up a review of the Electricity Pool - the buying mechanism through which electricity is sold - to ensure a level playing field; and is encouraging generators to offer unwanted coal power stations to RJB Mining. Further more it is encouraging the electricity regulator to prevent generators from passing on excessive costs under the early take-or-pay gas contracts to ensure that there is no uneven playing field. Last year it passed the Fossil Fuel Levy Act (1998) to remove the advantages that nuclear generated electricity in Britain and imported nuclear generated electricity from France enjoyed. Also it is conducting a review of clean coal technology with the aim of finding ways to support its growth. The environmental challenges presented by coal can be met by technological solutions which will ensure its long-term future, I am sure of that. Finally, the Government is also conducting a review of the planning policy guidance governing opencast mining with a view to tightening it in pursuit of good environmental regulation.

The present Government has taken this action following what I believe to be major mistakes by the Conservative Government when it ran down the coal industry. Their action was based on political dogma and political hysterics. The Country may well come to regret those strategies in the years to come.

* * * * *

My constituents were important to me. I always saw myself as a spokesperson for a local community, someone who spent a lot of his time sorting out problems for local people, before I was a debater in the House of Commons or a Chair of a major committee. Every MP worth their salt is a constituency MP before they are anything else. Although I recognise that ministerial responsibility or, in my case, efficient management of the business of the Commons, rightly took up a lot of my time, I would have felt myself neglectful if I had not paid attention to the rights of people - Labour, Conservative and nonvoters - in the Pontefract area who required my help. Every Saturday, Jane Robinson, my secretary, and I would sit and organise the weekly postbag. Letters would be sent to Ministers, responses would be sent back to householders. Generally our postbag bordered on a hundred letters a week. Some of our responses were automatic. We referred people on to ward councillors, the appropriate officers in Wakefield or onto Ministers of the Crown. I cannot say the responses constituents got were always the response they wanted, what I would say was that I pursued questions through relevant bureaucracies until I got an answer. I always needed to be satisfied that my constituents had been fairly treated, for above all else for that is why I had been elected.

As part of my duties, like the majority of constituency MPs I would take groups of constituents around the Palace of Westminster. This was a privilege because it enabled me to experience, in the company of my peers, constitutional democracy. Trade unionists, party members from all parties, sixth formers, church members, in fact, people from all walks of life, accompanied me on those tours. *(Appendix T)*

The route was always the same. We entered the House at the point the Queen would enter. From the Norman Porch entrance we would proceed through the Robing Room, the Royal Gallery, the Princes Chamber and a corridor hung with pictures of the English Civil War before emerging into the Central Lobby.

The Central Lobby is the hub of parliamentary democracy, for every British citizen has a democratic right to attend there and summon their Member of Parliament. They do this by obtaining a green card from the attendant, and having filled it in, get its message to their Member. On a busy day Central Lobby, the central crossroads of Parliament, is like Briggate in Leeds on a Saturday.

The democratic principle applied by the use of the term "lobby" generally works, though of course it also brings problems. Just as Jane and I receive letters from professional letter writers - people who send us letters every Saturday - so there are professional lobbyists who haunt that area. Organised lobbies, when great numbers converge on this central area, on sensitive issues such as unemployment, fox hunting and abortion, just bring more people than most Members can cope with. When that happens some MPs get neglectful of their obligation. Where unemployment was concerned, especially in the late 1980s, some Government MPs might choose not to be found when people who were out of work appeared. I never applied this sanction. I do not claim to be perfect or have a particular virtue on this matter, for during the eighteen year period of Thatcher it was easy to meet my constituents as I shared their feelings. However, I went to meet people because I felt not to do so would be counterproductive and the processes found in the Central Lobby, with their emphasis on service, are fundamental to the feel of British politics.

After we had looked at the statues and mosaics at that crossroads, I would lead groups from the Central Lobby into the Members' Lobby to explain to them what happened in this area of the Commons. In a local council this room would be called Members' Services or such like. Any message to the MP, either by telephone or letter, passes through this area before it is conveyed on to the Member. We can easily recognise if there is a communication for a light appears under our name.

This is also the place where press men hang out to get official, and more particularly, unofficial briefings. The language which is used in Members' Lobby is particular to the journalist's profession, some conversation is "on" and some "off the record". If a politician says, "This is off the record" he will not expect his name to be quoted in an article. In this way information seeps into the media. On many occasions I have seen a Member chatting to a member of the press, and then recognised the source in a the newspaper the next day.

The Members' Lobby contains statues of politicians who were the Prime Ministers I knew when I was a boy at South Featherstone Modern School: Lloyd George, Winston Churchill and Clement Attlee are there. The last has always had a special place in my affections because in my opinion he was the most effective postwar Prime Minister right up to today's Tony Blair. He was only in office for six years, yet his Government created the Health Service, gave India its independence and nationalised the coal industry; all this in a period directly after the war when soldiers were returning needing employment, the country was on rationing and there was a massive housing shortage.

According to tradition he was a man of very few words. None of his speeches lasted longer than nine minutes. Roy Mason confirms this direct, no nonsense manner. When he first entered Parliament as a man aged 29 years, Attlee sent for him. Roy arrived in a state of nerves and knocked at his door. On the command, "Come in," he entered. All he could see at the end of the room was a bald head lowered studying a green Sports Final. Mr Attlee looked up. "Good morning young man, welcome to the Palace of Westminster, specialise and keep out of the bars, good morning." He was dismissed. Even today this is very sound advice.

Walking from the Members' Gallery in the days when I was a Member of the Commons, I would lead every party of constituents through what is the best known door in England. This is the door where Black Rod knocks three times on his way to summon the Commons to the Lords' Chamber where Her Majesty awaits them on State Opening of Parliament day. He knocks because as an officer of State and not an elected Member, Black Rod does not have automatic access to the House but only enters on the approval of Members. This tradition has a long history. In the mid-seventeenth century the monarch, Charles I, considered that parliamentary democracy represented by the Commons was becoming too powerful, a threat to both the Lords and also the monarchy itself. Having heard that words of treason had been spoken in the Lower House, he turned up to arrest five Members of Parliament. Warned of his arrival in the Palace of Westminster they fled the Chamber. Finding them gone he said, "I see the birds have flown," and asked Speaker Lentham where they were. The answer set a precedent. Lentham replied, "I have no tongue to speak, no eyes to see, no ears to hear without the permission of this House." That is the present position. It governed Betty Boothroyd's conduct and, when I was Deputy Speaker, it also governed me.

The monarch then ordered his people to drag the Speaker from his chair. This story leads directly to the Civil War, the deposition and beheading of Charles I and the establishment of Europe's first modern republic. In the long term it recognised a bigger principle: monarchs only reside with the permission of elected representatives. It is interesting to realise that Charles was tried in Westminster Hall, the very place where I later saw Mandela stand and address both Houses following the establishment of a new South African multiracial republic.

Having got through the door, I turn constituents sharp right into a long narrow room known as the "No Lobby". This room is where Members opposing a motion gather to cast their vote. They do this by passing Clerks, who are sitting at tables and who are equipped with a full list of Members and get their names recorded. They then go through an exit door, past Whips representing the Government, the Opposition and other minor parties. As they pass they nod their head to allow the Whip to take a head count. Having done this, four Whips, two from each Lobby, enter the Chamber and stand in front of the mace facing the Speaker. At this point the Speaker rises, "Order, Order." Then a Whip from the party who has been successful in the count announces the results by stepping forward. "Madam Speaker (or in my case Mr Deputy Speaker) the Ayes to the right 220, the Noes to the left 120." The Clerk then takes the piece of paper from the Whip and brings it to the Speaker for her or him to read. This done the Speaker says, "The Ayes to the right 220, the Noes to the left 120, the Ayes have it. Unlock."

Members have eight minutes to pass through the Lobby before the Lobby doors are closed. Most are happy with this, but not every one. I have found on numerous occasions that Members complain and give various excuses for not getting there on time. Some excuse lateness by saying that they have experienced traffic difficulties in Whitehall, or there are such strong lobbies that access could not be easily gained, crowds outside the Palace of Westminster made access difficult. Occasionally MPs, mindful of the disciplinary action which might be taken by the Whips for missing the vote, complain to the Speaker that eight minutes was not long enough to reach the lobbies, or advance special reasons why the Speaker should have extended a particular Division. They underestimate our system. Commons attendants are all-knowing and give warning of things like traffic difficulties. If I thought they did exist I would extend the time period by a minute or two.

In my time I have heard some outlandish excuses. One lady Member once informed me that she had been dashing off the Circle Line at Westminster to catch the 10 o'clock vote when a baby sitting on its mother's knee next to her on the tube was sick all over her. I saw no visible signs of this on her clothes so I was unsympathetic. Some miss votes because they are "tired and emotional".

The Chamber of the House is done up in green leather, the benches of the Lords are red. Having seen both chambers people often comment on this fact. When we reached this key room I would always point out to the constituents that over the years my work space had varied several times. When I first came into the House I sat as a back-bencher to the right of the Speaker's Chair, from the General Election of 1979 up to 1992, I had sat on the Opposition benches opposite, but for five years I had occupied a place of very great honour in the House. From April 1992 to April 1997 I had sat in the oaken Speaker's Chair.

Compared with many items in the House, this chair is relatively new; it was a gift from the Canadian government, a daughter Parliament, part of our Commonwealth family, and was presented by that government to replace the chair destroyed when Nazi bombs fell on Westminster. Faced on that night with masses of incendiary bombs and knowing that he could not save everything, Churchill made the decision to keep the holy of holies, Westminster Hall, and to let the Commons Chamber burn. As a historian he saw that he could move MPs to the Lords' Chamber, but if it burnt there was no way he could retain the ancient medieval splendour, and especially the roof, of Westminster Hall. It is a sacrifice of which I fully approve, for the stone which made that hall was quarried not half a mile from where my daughter Lynne lived and my grandchildren were born, in Kirk Smeaton, near Pontefract, Yorkshire.

* * * * *

After the 1992 Election a new Speaker was elected following the retirement of Bernard Weatherill - now Lord Weatherill. For many months prior to the election there had been speculation who would succeed him. From the Labour side the names of Harold Walker, Chairman of Ways and Means - now Lord Harold Walker - and Betty Boothroyd, Second Deputy Speaker, seemed to be the favourites. From the Tory side, Peter Brook, Member for the City of Westminster, Giles Shaw, Member for Pudsey and others were mentioned as likely candidates. In the British Parliament the Speaker is invariably an MP of considerable experience. Since 1940 Speakers had always been members of the ruling party when first elected to the Chair of the House and are usually elected without contest. Central to the tradition of the Speakership is the notion of impartiality; everyone accepts that a new Speaker will be above party and will act and behave in a completely independent manner. Even if the government complexion changes, the Speaker will be re-elected to the Chair. Speakers who were former members of the Labour Party were in office 1970, 1979 and 1997, although there was a Conservative administration; and former Conservatives were in post 1964 and 1974, although the country was ruled by Labour administrators.

The Speaker is chosen by election, each Member having one vote. Though at times the Prime Minister and Cabinet will be known to support a particular candidate, back-bench support is vital. When selecting the Speaker, the House is presided over by the Father of the House - the longest sitting Member - who calls upon two Members in turn to move and second the motion to support a candidate. Generally a vote is avoided and a Speaker is elected by his or her fellow MPs without opposition. However on 27 April 1992 for the first time in decades there was a contest between the former Conservative Cabinet Minister, Peter Brook, and the former Second Deputy Speaker of the House, Miss Betty Boothroyd. This caused great interest for several reasons. This was the first time a woman had been nominated for the Speakership, her nomination proposed by a senior Tory, John Biffen - now Lord Biffen. A large section of Tory Members supported Peter Brook, but not all. In the event Miss Boothroyd defeated Mr Brook by 372 votes to 238.

Tradition ordains that the newly elected Speaker should feign a show of reluctance and be dragged to the Chair. Betty didn't display too much resistance, who would? She was making history, the first woman Speaker since the office was established in 1377. It was a great achievement and should be placed in perspective. She was the first Speaker in the twentieth century to be selected from the opposition and she was only the third Speaker ever to have been chosen from the Labour Party.

I was personally thrilled at her appointment. I had known her many years, both as a political colleague and friend. Along with the vast majority of the House, I was certainly pleased that we were going to be governed by a first lady Speaker, who was able to be as formidable, charming and tough as her new role demanded.

I think, though she may not agree with me, being a woman has been helpful to her. Male Members seemed more willing to accept the direction of a woman. She never needed assistance. Through media interest and the televising of the House of Commons, she rapidly became a national and international figure, admired by all and loved by many. She has certainly left her mark on the office and I am sure history will record that her tenure was memorable. She has set a precedent for the new millennium and will be a hard act for a mere male to follow.

Over the years my affection for her has grown. She is naturally kind. One occasion I particularly remember. I had arrived at the House at 9 am to take the Chair at 9.30 for the morning's sitting. On arrival I mentioned to my Assistant, Brian Munka, that I had not been feeling too well in the night and rather wished I didn't have to take the Chair. The procedure was that the Speaker would take the Chair at 9.30 am and I would immediately relieve her following prayers. I had only been in the Chair ten minutes when she sent the Second Deputy Speaker to relieve me. I was surprised at this, but was told to go to Betty's office. It appeared that Brian had informed one of the Clerks in the Ways and Means Office and the information had been rapidly relayed to the Speaker. As I arrived at the Speaker's Office arrangements had already been made for me to be taken to the Westminster Clinic where I was thoroughly tested and advised to rest for a day or two. That done, Betty insisted that I return to Pontefract for a few days' rest. I went. You do not argue with Betty! This was the first sign of the disorder which led to my eventual heart attack in September 1997, the major reason for me taking the decision to leave the House of Commons.

I was appointed to assist the Speaker on 28 April 1992. The appointment came as a surprise. I did not know that I was going to be appointed until Tony Newton, Leader of the House, moved from the Despatch Box that, "Michael Morris, Member for Northampton North, Dame Janet Fookes, Member for Plymouth Drake and Geoffrey Lofthouse, Member for Pontefract and Castleford, should be the Deputy Speakers for the period of the duration of that Parliament." Of course, I had been aware of the rumour and speculation, mainly through the Tea Room chatterers. Furthermore Derek Foster, the Chief Whip, had also indicated to me that I was to be considered, but nothing more. The fact that I was the senior Labour Member on the Chairman's Panel clearly was helpful. This is a key panel of senior Members who chair the Standing Committees and so take legislation through the parliamentary procedures. To this day I am not aware who makes the final decision about deputies but I understand that it is the House of Commons Commission, a body which consists of the Speaker, Leaders of the main parties and Chief Whips.

The new job meant a new suit and I had to move pretty quickly to equip myself with the garments appropriate to the dignity of my new office. A tailor in Tothill Street was recommended. He was a tailor of the old school and had a long connection with the House. He took my measurements, cut a morning suit overnight, by noon the next day had hand stitched it together on an antiquated sewing machine. The bill was a shock, it cost £500, but I must say it was very well made and elegant.

At 4.30 pm I took my place suitably attired in the Chair of the House of Commons, very conscious of the fact that I was wearing a garment that was totally alien to my relaxed style. I felt like Betty's bridegroom. All I needed was the carnation in my buttonhole. As I sat in there and looked at the sea of faces in the Chamber I noticed many new ones who had been elected for the first time and I knew that although in time I would come to know them, I didn't know them now. Things got worse. I could not recollect the names of those who had been my colleagues for many years. The occupant of the Chair must at all times refer to their name when he calls them to speak, and I found this a very unnerving prospect. For a time the problem persisted. In amongst the crowd I saw my very great friend Ray Powell standing and I immediately called him. Sir Raymond, as he is now, repeatedly reminds me that I never called him again, which of course is not true.

This very first stint in the Chair in the House of Commons was the longest two hours of my life. My task was not made easier when I glanced up to the gallery and who should be sat there directly over the clock but my very dear friend Viscount Tonypandy - George Thomas - Speaker when I first came to the House and a man who I very much admired. We were close, he had very kindly written a foreword to the first volume of my autobiography *A Very Miner MP*. I thought, "I am under study here from a real master," and that did not do much for my nerves. However, relief came when, about half way through my first two hour stint, a messenger brought me a note which read, "Congratulations, come over to the Lords and have a cup of tea."

I had had many cups of tea with George when he was the Speaker. Tea was part of the friendship. He would occasionally beckon me to the Chair, mostly on a Monday and say, "Come round for a cup of tea when I leave the Chair, I have got some Welsh Cakes," then lovingly declared, "They are made by my mother." Those were delightful occasions but I think the invitation on that particular day was the most welcome I remember.

I was to find that at times during my five years in the Chair I had a seeming blockage of the mind when calling people I had known for many years to speak. After three or four sessions in the Chair, I confided this to Viscount Tonypandy. He said there was nothing unusual. I recall George's reply with great affection. "Geoffrey," he said, "don't worry - don't call them. They will soon let you know their names." Of course, as ever, George was right. Time and confidence eliminated this problem and all was well.

Having got the job it became important to familiarise myself with the powers and the procedures and dignity of the Deputy Speaker. In this task I was ably assisted by my Research Assistant, Brian Munka. An experienced colleague, he came to me following his uncle, Sir Patrick Duffy's, retirement. To occupy the Speaker's Chair takes you close to a mighty and technically complex heritage. Valuable and essential assistance is rendered by the three Deputies of the Speaker and they must be on top of the job. To chair the House of Commons is a formidable task and one I knew for five years.

I well recall the first day in the Chair when I arrived to take over from Betty. As always she looked resplendent in the Speaker's attire, yet she broke with tradition in one small way. She did not wear the customary wig, she had no need to, because her natural hair was well-blessed. No wig maker could compete. I was dressed in my new morning suit and, never having worn such attire in my life, very conscious of the fact that it was not me. I did not know which was the most comfortable way to sit. Should I sit on the tails or lift them up before I sat down? I must have decided on the latter because my colleague, David Hinchliffe, wisecracked later, "You looked as if you were sitting on the toilet!" Embarrassed I decided I was having no more of this and purchased myself a short black coat. For the following two days I wore it in the Chair until the Clerk to the House diplomatically drew my attention to the change in precedent and indicated that this short coat was unbecoming to the dignity of the Chair.

The kindness of another Member helped me through this awkward stage. Ann Taylor came to the Chair and said, displaying her usual kindness, "You look as though you have been sat there for years, you look the perfect part."

I had known Ann since 1978, she was then the MP for Bolton. She had been seconded to be my minder in the 1978 By-election and I knew from that time on she was a rising star. She later became Shadow Minister of Education, Shadow Leader of the House, and when Labour took office in 1997, Leader of the House and Lord Privy Seal. More recently she has been Government Chief Whip. We have been friends over these years, I always campaigned for her in the Shadow Cabinet elections and she was always successful, much to my pleasure. Clever, but never one of the stupid women's libbers, she strongly believed in the advancement of women in politics, believed women should have equal rights, but not anything more. She did not support 'All Women Shortlists', rather believed all women should be judged on their merits. Her judgement was sound. The Party policy, having flirted with All Women Shortlists with disastrous consequences, came to take a less radical approach. I treasure my friendship with Ann and I shall always recall that she was one of the first visitors during my spell in hospital in 1997. She brought me some interesting reading material and a very kind letter from Tony Blair wishing me well and saying, "Get back down here soon, we need you."

* * * * *

During the early period in the Chair and, indeed, throughout the period I occupied it, I was always grateful to the Clerks. The Clerk of the House and his staff are not civil servants, for they do not serve the government of the day but the House of Commons. Clerks are the be-wigged figures seated in front of the Speaker at the Table of the House. I always found them to be most kind, helpful people who reacted quickly if they sensed the occupant of the Chair was in difficulty. It instilled confidence and I will always be grateful to Sir Clifford Boulton, Sir Donald Limon, Bill MacKay, George Newby and all the 240 members of their staff. During the five years in the Chair, my life was enriched by their friendship. The same applies to the Serjeant at Arms' staff, the Speaker's Secretary, Nicholas Bevan, and all the staff, not least the Train Bearers, Peter Warwick, Don Lord and Nick Wright. Without these people, the House of Commons could not have functioned. Nor could I.

In his Public Information Office factsheet, W R MacKay, the present Clerk to the House, outlines their origins and functions. "Elizabethan Clerks were country gentlemen who, together with the Speaker and a few prominent politicians, huddled round the Chair and represented the government machinery for getting the work of the House done, often to the mystification of those just out of earshot or not alert enough to react to what was being proposed." Today these meetings are conducted slightly differently. At noon each day that the Commons is in session, the Speaker, the three Deputies, the Clerk, his two assistants, the Sergeants at Arms and the Speaker's Secretary discuss the day's business. That is when Betty Boothroyd is at her best. Always a very assured and confident woman, she will listen to any advice offered, but she always makes up her mind very quickly, she never dodges difficult decisions, but is always keen to discuss the previous day in the Chamber, and if there has been any controversy, she gives full support to the occupants of the Chair. She was rock-solid with her support of the Deputies, though always remaining outside the political arena as the position of Speaker demands. Having known her for more than 30 years as a political colleague and friend, we have an inbuilt affection for each other which I will always treasure. For my part I was always keen to help her when the pressures on her were greatest. She never took advantage of my desire to reduce her very great load, supporting me more than ever I was able to support her.

During the morning prior to our meetings, the Speaker would have received many requests, including requests for an emergency debate, private notice questions and requests to question a Minister about any matter which was so urgent that the usual notice could not be given.

The Speaker would inform the meeting of her decision, this was invariably based on a well tried formula. The Clerks advised the Speaker on any business they felt likely to cause procedural problems during the course of that day. That done the Speaker would give her views to her Deputies on what she believed would ensure the smooth running of the House. She regulated those aspects of the daily timetable. The deputies regulated other areas.

During the morning prior to the midday meetings, each Deputy Speaker would receive a list of letters from Members requesting to speak in that day's debate. I would deal with the requests from Labour Members and my two colleagues, Michael Morris and Dame Janet Fookes, would deal with the requests of Conservative Members. We would base our decisions on the times a Member had spoken previously, whether they had a constituency interest in the debate or whether the Member had any special expertise in the subject of debate. The Speaker would discuss our recommendations and either agree or disagree.

I was aware that past occupants of the Chair had never encouraged Members to come to the Chair and enquire whether their names were on the list. I had myself been frustrated by this procedure on many occasions when I was a back-bencher. Waiting all day in the Chamber to speak not knowing when I would be called seemed a waste of time. I well remember one occasion I remained in the Chamber from 2.30 pm to 10 pm and was not called. When appointed I decided that if I thought there was no chance of a Member being called I would inform him or her. Of course if Members were in with a chance, I would also inform them but tell them I expected them to remain in the Chamber to listen to the debate. I thought this was the fairest policy and I continued with this practice during my five years in the Chair. Although I am the first to admit that it has its downside I find it preferable to the other procedure. Members soon became aware that I would inform them of their chances and I found it embarrassing that the moment I took over, Members would leave their seats and form a queue at each side of the Chair requesting to find out if their names were on the list. Sometimes Members would enquire why they were low down and in that way create a new problem. Having produced the list, I was always able to tell them of its reasoning. I found most of them accepted the explanation. I was, however, always annoyed when Members, having been informed of their position, would leave the Chamber and not return until they had seen the television monitor indicating the name who was directly before them. Sometimes they would return looking tired and emotional. If I thought there was a genuine reason for delayed attendance, if they had Standing or Select Committee work, I would not take any action, but if I was not aware of a reason, I would drop them down the order. Sometimes this meant they would not be called in that debate at all. I took discourtesy to the House and their behaviour into consideration in formulating future Speaker lists.

The way the House works is fascinating and one detailed case can perhaps illustrate its complexity. Tom Clark has always been a champion of the disabled and had organised a massive national petition on their behalf. He had made elaborate arrangements to present the petition to the House after the 10 pm vote on the main motion of the day. The Chamber was filled with Members who had come to vote and also support Tom with his petition. At 10 pm I put the question on the main motion and declared the Division in the usual way. If that had been the last Division I would have then called Tom to present his petition. However, the Whips on duty earlier that evening had informed Tom there would be a second Division. On receiving this piece of information he calculated that he could relax, and imagining that the pace was leisurely, he decided to go the toilet. Feeling very relaxed, having time to spare he settled in but, unknown to him, it had been decided not to have a second Division. As the Tellers returned I rose from the Chair to announce the result of the vote. The House was overflowing with Members but I could not see Tom in the seat he had been sat in prior to the Division. Having been aware of the importance of this petition to the disabled people and the efforts Tom had put in, I was concerned and could not understand where he was. The normal procedure would have been that after I had announced the result of the main motion, I would immediately call on Tom to present his petition. I was aware that the petition had received ample press and media coverage and the people of the country, and not least the disabled, would feel Tom had let them down if it was not presented. I recognise it was not the business of the Chair to get involved in such matters, the Chair's job is to see the business of the day was carried out in accordance with the procedures outlined in the Standing Orders of the House. However I have always formed the view that whatever rules, regulations or standing orders you may have, these cannot always cover unforeseen circumstances. On these occasions I have always believed the Chair should use common sense and tolerance. Tom's need for the lavatory, in my book, was an unforeseen circumstance. By this time the Chamber was very noisy. Members on the Government side were cheering in the usual way after the announcement of the vote. Still no Tom. I called the House to order and at length I chastised the Members for their misbehaviour which I knew to be no more than normal. In normal circumstances I would not have done anything. That day I lectured them and gained half a minute or so. Then I went on the chastise Members who stood behind the bar of the House and those others who were roaming about. I told Members taking part in conversations to leave the Chamber quietly. I instructed all other Members to take their seats. I picked out some Members, who did not immediately obey my instruction, for a reprimand. I fumbled with my papers. I developed a coughing attack - and then at last I saw Tom dash through the door to his seat. Whilst Tom was getting his breath back, I calmly called, "Petition, Mr Tom Clark." Tom then proceeded to make his speech and presented his petition to the great cheer of the House. He was a hero.

I was never aware if the Chamber had recognised the tricks I had pulled off on behalf of Tom, but Tom had. He wrote an article for the *Airdrie and Coatbridge Advertiser* the following week headed "The World of Westminster" thanking me. *(Appendix J)*

Traditionally Privy Councillors have priority to speak. This is a custom I do not favour, but take the view that however senior a Member is, all have entered the House in the same way and should have with others an equal right to represent their constituents, this without privilege. On one particular occasion early in my career I fell victim to this preferential procedure. During a debate on the mining industry I waited from 3.30 pm for my turn to speak. About 8.45 pm, when I was thinking it must be nearing my turn to speak, the Privy Councillor Tony Benn arrived. With minutes to spare he had the brass neck to sit at the side of me and in accordance with the Customs of the House, rose when I did. The Speaker called him instead of me. Having the right to speak he used it. He spoke for about 20 minutes, by which time it was time for the wind-up speeches by the Ministers on the Front Bench. On that occasion I was denied the opportunity of speaking in the debate on the mining industry, a subject which of course affected my constituency and on which I had experience. Later in the Tea Room I told him of my feelings. He said, "Yes Geoff, I agree with you. I think I shall resign from being a Privy Councillor." He never did. During my period in the Chair, whilst being expected to abide by the customary procedures, I always avoided calling Privy Councillors if it was possible.

There are many customs and practices in the House which are complicated and through which new Members navigate with difficulty. During debate Members refer to each other only by the name of their constituencies and not their names, the constituency prefixed by The Honourable or The Right Honourable Member for the place they represent. "The Right Honourable" is a Member who is a Privy Councillor, a Member who is a Senior Barrister is the "Right Honourable and Learned Gentleman/Lady the Member for such-and-such".

In the House a Member addresses the Chair. The Speaker alone is "You". There were times when I had to pull up Members time after time. I would just say, "Order, Order. The Honourable Gentleman must not refer to me, I am not responsible for any of his accusations. He must learn to address another Member in the appropriate form using the name of a parliamentary constituency."

New Members naturally found some difficulty in familiarising themselves with the customs. I was always reluctant to pull them up, especially in their early days in the House. I recognised that an intervention from the Chair might knock them off their stride so I tried my best not to unsettle them, especially regarding their maiden speech, for I too well remember my own.

I had written to the Speaker informing him I was desirous of making my maiden speech on 14 December 1978. I was not aware, when I made the request, that this would be the day the then Leader of the

Opposition, Mrs Thatcher, would put down a motion of no confidence in Her Majesty's Government. When I found this was the case, I was tempted to withdraw my name and make my speech another day, but I decided that I would leave my name on the list for the Speaker to consider. Of course I knew that maiden speeches were given precedence.

When the debate commenced at 3.30 pm, the Chamber was full to capacity and bulging at the seams. Mrs Thatcher moved her motion and she had plenty of ammunition. The country was experiencing the first wave of the Winter of Discontent; politically the country was not too happy. Although under pressure, the Prime Minister, James Callaghan, replied skilfully defending his Government. As the Prime Minister sat down at the end of his speech, all Members who had applied to speak rose from their seats in the usual way. I, of course, did likewise thinking I would probably be called midway through the debate. It was then that I heard the Welsh tones of Mr Speaker Thomas call, "Mr Geoffrey Lofthouse." I thought, "You are in it now Geoff, it's muck or nettles." I had prepared my speech with care from notes on what my constituents had been telling me during my election campaign. About half way through the first page, whether through nerves or sheer clumsiness I don't know, I dropped all my papers. I thought, "Don't bother trying to pick them up, just keep going." I was fortunate, I had made many speeches during the election campaign and I drew on my memory to make what I would call an 'off the cuff response'. I think it was probably a better speech than it would have been if I had not dropped my papers; it read well in *Hansard*. *(Appendix Q)*

The next day I was passing the Speaker's Chair. Mr Speaker Thomas leaned over, tapped my shoulder and said, "Excellent yesterday Geoffrey."

I replied, "Thank you Mr Speaker, but you dropped me in it by calling me first after the PM and the Leader of the Opposition."

"Oh no," George replied, in his usual charming voice, "If I had left you waiting in such an important and high-powered debate, you would have been a bag of nerves." I never forgot that and I always tried to practice the same thoughtful kindness on other maiden speech makers in my five year period in the Chair as George Thomas did to me.

* * * * *

During my period as Deputy Speaker from 1992 to 1997, I had a chance to see the workings of the Opposition Whips' Office from an independent perspective. During that period and, indeed prior to it, Derek Foster, Member for Bishop Auckland, was the Opposition Chief Whip. Derek is a man who I have always liked for I have found him to be invariably kind and understanding. He is a man who believes in diplomacy and quiet persuasion; some people view this as a weakness, not me.

On one occasion when a Government Whip failed to make himself heard to anyone but myself, when calling to oppose a motion, Derek rose from his seat and questioned me whether or not the Whip had called to oppose the motion. I replied that I had "heard him." Derek did not make a fuss about it, in his usual understanding way, but I often wondered if he believed me? Of course he accepted the Deputy Speaker's word.

He was the Supreme Commander of the Opposition Whips' office, but had the sense to leave the front line work to his generals Don Dixon and Ray Powell. These generals dealt with the rough and tough side of the job. He was fortunate, for plain speaking Don Dixon - now Lord Dixon - the Member for Jarrow, is one of the straightest men I have ever met. He has no time for diplomacy if it means covering up the truth. Woe betide anyone who crossed Don, especially if it was by deceit. I know many Members who have suffered at his hands when found neglectful of their duties. For my part as a back-bencher I was careful myself to tell him the exact truth if ever he requested information from me. Nevertheless he is a kind man and if anyone has genuine problems Don is always first on hand to assist. I have never met anyone who does not respect and admire him.

In this office, in the 1990s, he was ably assisted by the jolly but shrewd Welshman, Ray Powell - now Sir Raymond Powell - the

Pairing Whip. The Pairing Whip is responsible for maintaining sufficient Members for any vote. Any Member who wished to be absent and made a request to pair with a Member of the Government Party had to get Ray's permission. Pairing means two Members of opposing parties agreeing not to cast their vote on a particular Division, thus cancelling each other's votes. Ray always immediately identified the genuine requests from the not too genuine. If Ray found a Member had deceived him by giving him a false reason for wishing to pair, bang would go that Member's chances of pairing in the future. Like me, Sir Ray was a committed Christian and a major advocate of Keep Sunday Special campaign, something I myself supported though in a private capacity because of my position. Like Ray I felt passionately that the Sunday Trading Bill should be opposed. Unfortunately, our opposition was not successful, but this was not due in any way to lack of effort from Ray. Having vast experience, Don and Ray were experts on parliamentary tactics.

Ten o'clock, two hours before midnight, is the usual time for the main vote of the day. On a normal night, if all was going well, the House may be able rise for about 10.45 pm. If not, 10.00 was when I would see these two men come through the main doors to the Chamber; Don giving a stern look and Ray with a mischievous smile. They would invariably be followed by their storm troopers - Dennis Skinner, Andrew McKinley and Bob Cryer. At that point I would immediately think, "What's happening now?" It would not be long before I found out. On some of these occasions it could mean sitting well into the night.

The British Rail Bill was passing to and fro between the Lords and the Commons. It was towards the end of a parliamentary session and it was 7pm. The House of Lords were waiting for the Bill to return from the House of Commons. Ted Graham - now Lord Graham of Edmonton the Opposition Chief Whip in the Lords - approached Don, his counterpart in the Commons, and informed him that the Lords had suspended their sitting until 9 pm to wait for the return of the Bill. Ted suggested it would be helpful to the Lords if the Commons could hold it up until after 9 pm when the Lords would resume debate. Both Don and Ray recognised they might have difficulty in achieving this. However, they immediately put a plan of action into operation. They decided they would force a Division on every amendment. Considering that each Division took 15 minutes, I recognised that even using that strategy there would not be sufficient time to delay the return of the Bill to the House of Lords until after 9 pm. What could they do? They knew how to play the game to a fine art. They arranged for Members to hang about in the Lobby as long as possible and extend the Divisions to about 20 minutes. I soon spotted these tactics and because the Chair must be above party and impartial at all times, I instructed the Serjeant at Arms to investigate the delays in the Lobbies, the usual instruction on such occasions. If that action was not sufficient, the occupant of the Chair had always the power to announce the vote that had been collected at the time of his instructions so they knew that if they got too clever they might have these powers to contend with.

They continued their delaying tactics on each Division taking about five minutes more than usual each time. With very great skill both Don and Ray just kept inside my patience. However, when the last vote approached they realised that despite their efforts they would not reach their targeted delay. As the minutes ticked by I instructed the Sergeant to investigate the delay and clear the Lobby. Don informed the Sergeant that there were people in the Lobby toilet. The Sergeant then requested him to go and move them out. Don said, "You go, they are lady Members." Alice Mahon, Member for Halifax and Dawn Primarolo, Member for a Bristol seat, had answered a call of nature. I never found out how the Sergeant persuaded the ladies out of the toilet. Even these tactics were not sufficient to reach their target. What did they do next?

Masters of the procedure of the House, they knew that after the occupant of the Chair announces a Division, he will put the motion or amendment and announce two Tellers from each side. These Tellers must then be the same Tellers who count and deliver the vote to the House, otherwise the Division is cancelled and re-run. They did just that and the Bill was delayed until next day.

On another occasion I was in the Chair one Friday morning. A Conservative Member by the name of Brandon Bravo, a Member who represented one of the Nottingham seats, had a Private Member's

Bill to present. Don and Ray had discussed the Bill with him and promised him if he would be brief and allow in the next Bill - a Labour Member's Bill - they would support him by not voting against his Bill. From what I understand Mr Bravo agreed to this rapid processing, but according to received information, in this instance he did not stick to his promise. In Ray's and Don's opinion he had done a deal with the Government Whips to talk at length and stop the next Bill proceeding. They were not so easily thwarted. When Mr Bravo sat down they called a Division and kept Labour Members out of the Lobby. This meant there were not sufficient Members present to form a quorum so the Division was not valid. Bravo lost his Bill. Experience teaches that you don't mess about with two caring, experienced generals.

During one period of non co-operation between the two parties, delaying tactics were common and our Whips were always using the quorum tactic to delay the House. A quorum consists of 40 Members including the occupant of the Chair and four Tellers. This meant that 35 Members must go through the Lobbies. If Don and Ray were aware that there were very few Government Members present they would call a Division. One of them would cry, "I spy strangers!" This is a delaying device often used to force a Division. If this call for a Division was successful, and I have never in my time known it not to be, it would mean that people in the public gallery would have to withdraw. Having called the Division, they kept Labour Members out of the Lobby and ensured that only 31 votes were cast. The cry "I spy strangers!" collapsed the day's business.

Dixon's anger was not always directed at the Tories, sometimes it could be directed at his own side. Late one night Eddie Lloydon, a Liverpool Member, had obtained an Adjournment Debate, a debate at the end of the day's business. It is a device to give back-benchers a chance to advance a case. A Member applies to the Speaker to be considered for such a debate. These requests are decided by lottery.

Eddie's debate was on unemployment in Liverpool. When the Minister was replying to the debate, Ron Brown, Member for Edinburgh Leith, famous for his "Lady in the Bath incident", entered the Chamber; he appeared tired and emotional. He requested the

Minister to give way to allow him to make a point. This the Minister refused to do. This was not uncommon, Ministers often refuse because these debates only last half an hour and time was always limited. Ron was very annoyed that the Minister would not give way and let his anger explode at the end of the debate to such an extent that when the Serjeant at Arms rose to take the Mace from the Chamber, the usual practice at the end of the day's proceedings, Ron grabbed it and it fell to the floor, damaged.

Next day Don discussed this with the Speaker and the Clerks and they agreed: provided Ron gave an apology on the floor of the House, this would be acceptable. Following the reasonable approach an agreed statement was prepared. Don put it to Ron who agreed to make the statement at the beginning of business that day. But when the time came, he refused to make it in the agreed form and made one of his own. Up jumped Don, a big man, walked to the seat where Ron Brown was sitting, took him by the scruff of the neck and marched him out of the Chamber! Brown was suspended from the House without pay for a period, and had to pay for the repairs of the Mace, a substantial figure. Don never tolerated discourtesy to the House.

* * * * *

Most people fix upon one particular achievement after a lifetime of public service, which gives them more satisfaction than the rest combined. Mine was winning my battle for compensation for mineworkers suffering from bronchitis and emphysema. I have spent a lifetime representing and defending the British coal miner. Therefore I know that of the many hardships which the miners have had to endure it is not only the dramatic ones like explosions and roof falls that injure and kill my fellow miners but chronic chest diseases caused by their exposure to coal and stone dust. Getting them their rights has been my greatest achievement.

Prior to nationalisation, when coal owners were bent on exploiting miners as much as possible with little regard for their health and safety, and indeed after nationalisation when mechanisation was introduced, the powerful machines which were brought in created working conditions dominated by a colossal amount of dust. Dust suppression measures, water sprays in particular which drenched the machines, were an attempt to control this dust, but they were never adequate. As a result I had seen many colleagues stricken and suffer great agony from dust related illnesses. In my time I have seen men who I had known to have been big strong hard-working miners reduced to physical wrecks. I had seen them fighting for breath, not able to walk a yard, needing to be carried about, not able to lift a cup of tea to their lips - and yet they were continually being denied any form of compensation, for people with lung illnesses were virtually ignored. The excuses given usually denied both justice and common sense.

For many years it had been denied that the dust was the main cause of their condition. Although there had been inquiries by the Industrial Injuries Advisory Council, for all its work it had never been able to recommend that bronchitis and emphysema should be a prescribed disease deserving industrial injuries benefit. Invariably their excuse was cosmetic. They made great play of the fact that a major contributor to the acquisition of the disease was cigarette smoking. I knew this was not the case. Having seen friends and colleagues, such as George Harland, Bertram Lee and many others die after years of agony, I knew that I had to do something about it. When I entered the House of Commons I was convinced of the great injustice which had been done to these men and was determined to address the issue because of its personal significance. I was determined to secure compensation for these coal miners whose health had been destroyed by the ravages of bronchitis and emphysema, not least those who had confided to me that death would be a welcome release from their wretched existence. With these bitter memories in mind, I made it the cardinal goal of my parliamentary career to do something to improve their lives and to get them the recompense they deserved.

Between 20 October 1982 and 25 October 1989 I made five attempts to launch a Private Members Bill seeking compensation for those afflicted with bronchitis/emphysema. On each occasion I used a parliamentary procedure known as a Ten-Minute Rule Bill. This way of obtaining a ten minute slot in the parliamentary timetable is somewhat antiquated. These slots are mainly used by Members to highlight a constituency problem through the publicity that they obtain. If a Member is interested in obtaining one of these slots, they have to be outside the office issuing these bills at 10 am on the appropriate day. There is always great demand for these slots so they are issued on a first-come-first-served basis. To get a chance often necessitates a Member sitting outside the office hours before the bills are issued. I took no chances. To make sure I obtained my private bill, I sat outside the office from 9 pm the previous evening, all through the night until 10 am next morning. This was the only way I could be sure that I obtained a slot to present the miners' case.

From the first I was aware that the bills themselves would not get anywhere in the House of Commons. My ambitions lay elsewhere. My goal was to highlight the problem and attempt to get House of Commons backing for my campaign. On all the five occasions there was no opposition to my bill. The evidence I presented to the House was based on learned research, which I hoped would influence the thinking of the Industrial Injuries Advisory Council (IIAC). On every occasion I invited them to take note of the evidence presented. I later gave both verbal and written evidence to the IIAC to press my case. I was determined that bronchitis/emphysema should be recognised as an industrial disease for the purpose of the Industrial Injuries Act.

In my crusade I was helped by people of distinction like Dr Ann Cockroft, a young woman who had many papers published on the subject in the pre-eminent medical journal *The Lancet*. Her in-depth research paper on nonsmoking mineworkers indicated that a mineworker was ten times more likely to develop bronchitis/ emphysema than a member of the general public. I also had great assistance from Dr Michael Peake, Consultant in Chest Diseases at the Pontefract General Infirmary, a man whose work and commitment was a major factor in conclusively proving that bronchitis/ emphysema was an industrial disease. They and their fellow researchers, with lengthy and thorough investigation, had given academic credence and respectability to what I knew from observation: coalmining - not cigarettes - produces bronchitis/ emphysema sufferers.

The campaign was complicated. As a layman, after studying the work of Doctors Cockroft, Peake and others I knew that merely X-raying the lungs is not enough to make a conclusive diagnosis. Lung function testing and exercise tolerance needed to be taken into account when making a diagnosis. By 1989 I also knew that medical research could do no more. The case had been proven beyond doubt. All that was now needed was political will.

I will always regret that despite this unimpeachable body of evidence the political will of both Parliament and the IIAC took a long time to summon. In 1963, my predecessor Joe Harper had been told that although emphysema had been kept under constant review by the Pneumoconiosis Research Unit of the Medical Research Council, those concerned had up to date found no causal relationship between dust and coalmining and the disease. What utter nonsense! When I inherited both Joe's seat and his cause that attitude had not changed. In fact I was told at the beginning of March 1983 that cases that might be due to such employment couldn't be clinically distinguished from others. I was convinced that it was not true. In my speech in the House of Commons of 22 March 1983, I said, "if the word "lies" was not un-parliamentary, I would say, as a former coal miner, that it was a lie." I had been told in a parliamentary question in 1978 that the matter was subject to close study, was under review. I informed the House, that was not enough because "for some, study can be a lifetime's occupation." The sick miner had not that sort of time allocation. Experience of industrial disease research was turning me into a cynic.

A report issued by the Industrial Injuries Advisory Board in May 1988, which persisted in ignoring the learned evidence I had provided, left me unimpressed. I was particularly concerned at the IIAC's custom of only investigating the prevalence of bronchitis/emphysema every 10 years. I had been campaigning since 1978 and by 1989 it appeared all my work during that decade failed to persuade them. I was despondent, always asking, "How many ill and deteriorating miners will be left by 1998 at the next review?" This prompted my last bill in 1989. This again failed to find parliamentary time, although it received parliamentary support. However, in 1992, my prospects of success were drastically transformed. The IIAC decided to investigate the inclusion of bronchitis/emphysema as a prescribed disease earlier than was usual, not to wait ten years. I don't know if it was my persistence which achieved this result, but I like to think I had some part to play in the making of this decision.

Another breakthrough occurred that year. In May 1992 I became a Deputy Speaker in the House of Commons, a position that brought with it the status of a Minister of the Crown. This meant that I would no longer I have to take my chances with hundreds of other back-benchers in the competition for parliamentary time. From that date onwards I found I could speak directly to relevant Ministers about making bronchitis/emphysema a prescribed disease under the terms of the Industrial Injuries Act without sitting up all night. Although it was difficult dealing with the Conservative administration, it was not always difficult dealing with some individual Ministers of that party. However, my concern about the passing of valuable time and the delay in the implementation of legislation did nothing to allay my mounting sense of frustration. A bolt from the blue brought matters to a head.

An anonymous fax proved to be the catalyst. Obviously my championship of the miners' case was known beyond the confines of the Palace of Westminster and therefore I was the prime recipient of any document about industrial illness. Yet although that was the case, up to then I had never been the recipient of a leaked document. I do not agree with such practices on grounds of responsibility and accountability, but in this case I was glad to make an exception.

This document plainly stated that the appropriate government departments intended to delay the implementation of legislation to compensate miners with bronchitis/emphysema for as long as possible so that by the time legislation was in place, a great many miners would have died and saved the Exchequer a great deal of money. This was cold-blooded, callous and cynical, monstrous to an almost unprecedented degree. The leaked memo alerted me to the fact that the IIAC had in fact taken a decision to recommend to the Government that bronchitis/emphysema should be a prescribed disease and the IIAC report was to be published as a command paper on 25 November 1992. Sure in this knowledge I immediately corresponded with Professor J Harrington, Chairman of the IIAC, who confirmed that the Council had in fact recommended this to the Government. I was incensed. The leak told me a government department, presumably the Department of Social Security - the one trusted with the well-being of the citizens of this country - was making a request to another department, the Department of Trade and Industry, to delay the implementation of the recommendation despite a request to act coming from a learned body. For no better reason than the desire to save money arising out of miners' deaths they were happy to delay action.

I saw this as a call to arms and the time to seriously consider my position. I was privileged to be a Deputy Speaker, but this office placed constraints on my activities in the House. I was unable to speak upon partisan topics as the Chair had a policy of complete impartiality. On the other hand I had ministerial status, so that I could press constituency issues outside the channels available to regular back-benchers. My situation was complicated. This document was so infamous that I had to decide whether it might not be better for me to resign the Chair and return to the back-benches where I could speak openly and seek the maximum publicity and bring shame on a Government that contemplated such callous tactics, or remain where I was and fight in other ways. Thousands of coal miners had died without receiving compensation, this was not a light decision. I was amazed that any government would stoop so low as this and therefore believed that such actions should be exposed to public scrutiny in as direct a way as possible.

Quietly, I decided on my course of action. I would use my ministerial privilege to approach the Prime Minister and I would seek from him an assurance that the recommendation of the IIAC would be implemented quickly and in full. If he felt unable to give me any such assurance, I would ask the advice of the then Clerk of the House, Sir Clifford Bolton, a kind and learned gentleman, on the procedures for the resignation as Deputy Speaker. In the event I modified the order for action. On consideration I decided to see Sir Clifford first. At my request he called into my office and I told him what I intended to do, and although he did not make any comment on the document, I could tell that he was very disturbed, for my proposed action was unprecedented. As he left I told him that I intended seeing the Prime Minister and I would take things from there. He thought that was the appropriate action at that stage and said that he would gladly see me again if I thought it necessary.

An appointment with John Major was quickly arranged. In his personal office I told him how very strongly I felt. He withheld comment on the document but I knew him well enough to see he was concerned. He suddenly made a dramatic decision. He gave me a firm promise that Peter Lilley, then Secretary of State for Social Services, would make an announcement the very next day stating the Government would be implementing the IIAC's recommendations in full. To say that I was pleased is an understatement.

The next step was to meet with Nicholas Scott, the then Parliamentary Under-Secretary of State at the Department of Social Security, who would have direct responsibility for the implementation. He too, very kindly, called on me. When people call on you at Westminster, that is when you begin to appreciate that your status has changed. He sought my advice, which in this case I was only too ready to give. I told him it was a great step forward, but reminded him that it had come only after years of injustice and that many miners had died without any of the help that they deserved. I then went on to express my reservations about some of the conditions within the recommendations that I felt were flawed. There was, for instance, a 20 year rule, which meant that to qualify for compensation, a miner would have to have worked underground for at least 20 years. You can breathe in a lot of coal dust in less than 20 years' underground, believe me, and the problems are not only located underground, there is plenty of coal dust floating around above ground at a colliery, too. In addition, I was concerned over the proposed X-ray and breathing test which I felt were too stringent, especially for the more debilitated miners. I took care to inform the Chairman of the IIAC, Professor Harrington, of my concerns.

I regret to say that later on my fears were confirmed. Many miners were refused benefits because of these tests, but continued pressure did bring about some modifications. Both the X-ray and breathing tests were abolished. Unfortunately the 20 year rule still stands.

Nicholas Scott said that he was in full agreement that the most severely afflicted should be compensated first. All this took place in February 1993. Even with the best intentions, the wheels of administration grind slowly, but on 13 September 1993 emphysema and bronchitis were awarded the status of prescribed diseases under the terms of the Industrial Injuries Act. The process of reparation had begun. The passing of the Act was only the first step. In my experience miners are owed much, but ask for little, so it will always be a matter of concern for me to see that they get what they deserve.

The many telephone calls I received after the act was passed will always live in my memory. Many miners, some who I have never met, others who I have known and worked with, contacted me to say that they had been awarded compensation and to express their grateful thanks. One case in particular sticks in my mind.

One Sunday, a little time after the disease had been prescribed an industrial disease, I sat in my usual pew at All Saints Church, Pontefract and heard the Vicar announce the deaths and the funerals that had taken place the previous week. At that time I heard that a very dear friend of mine, a pal through our school days and our working life, Johnny Malpass, had passed away. Soon after the passing of the Act he had rung me. Listening on the telephone I could hear he could hardly breathe, yet there he was, expressing his grateful thanks to me because he had just received his award of compensation. His wife had died only a few weeks previously and John was at a very low ebb. However, this award had helped to lift his spirits. Now, a month later, our Vicar, the Reverend Kevin Partington, announced his funeral. Johnny, like many others, had suffered many years without compensation, some had never received any; Johnny had received his for a few weeks, but had no time to enjoy it. What an injustice!

Following my success with my campaign to obtain industrial injuries benefits for coal miners suffering from bronchitis/emphysema, I was delighted that the National Association of Colliery Overmen, Deputies and Shotfirers (NACODS), through their excellent General Secretary, Peter McNestry, also made a claim for compensation for their members who were suffering from bronchitis/emphysema. The claim was made against the Government after the liability to defend and manage such claims was transferred to the Government from British Coal.

I always considered Peter to be a leader in the Joe Gormley mould - tough and very realistic in a quiet and modest way. I take pride in Peter's success when he became Leader of NACODS. I had first met him in my position as Manpower Officer for the Wakefield/Castleford Area of the National Coal Board. I was recruiting men in the northern coalfields to staff Kellingley Colliery and I persuaded him to come to Kellingley. At that time I little realised that this move would result in Peter becoming a great asset to the coalmining industry. Thirty years later the name of Peter McNestry and his union were associated with my efforts for justice for coal miners and mining deputies. The early hearings of the claim were in Cardiff, but the most significant hearing took place before Mr Justice Turner sitting in the Royal Courts of Justice in London on 21 January 1998. To my great delight he ruled in the deputies' favour. In his summary His Lordship was extremely critical of the British Coal Corporation, both in respect of health and safety and indeed, its defence of the litigation. This was a major breakthrough, but there was a problem on how to produce a formula to deal with individual cases. I was concerned that if all the claimants had to go through a medical assessment, the delay this would cause would mean many of the miners would have died before their cases were settled. Mr Justice Turner's ruling removed that.

I had been pressing the Government for three years before the Lord Justice Turner decision, through correspondence with the Lord Chancellor and Tim Eggar, then Minister of State at the DTI. I requested that instead of preparing for years of litigation, I would consider it equitable and consensual for the defendants to give earnest consideration to setting up a bronchitis/emphysema compensation scheme. I informed them I believed this would avoid massive litigation costs and the subsequent enormous expenditure on legal aid costs over the years. I very much regret my request fell on deaf ears. I believe the Conservative Government thought they would be successful in defending a compensation claim.

When I was elevated to the House of Lords in 1997 I had new resources, so decided to highlight my fear about the possible delays in settling the claims by applying for a debate. In that Place there is a system called "un-starred questions". It means that an hour and a half of debate can be held on any subject of the Members' choice. This is similar to an Adjournment Debate in the House of Commons. I was fortunate in obtaining a debate which took place on 16 November 1998, and I was delighted but less than pleased that the debate did not commence until 11 pm and ended at 12.25 am. This displeasure was not any less when I considered that the House had spent from 3.08 pm to 5.14 pm a little earlier discussing whether the Lord Chancellor should be allowed to wear his trousers rather than breeches, buckles and tights. Their Lordships do seem to do crazy things sometimes. In the mining community, our work attire was either banickers - specialised knee length trousers made out of flannelette to absorb the sweat - or football shorts. I could not understand their elevated concerns. On many occasions, in hot conditions and when these garments got saturated with sweat, I have managed to work without anything on at all. Now I am not suggesting the Lord Chancellor should do likewise, but it is of no great concern to me if he wears trousers or breeches, buckles and tights. What is more important is the nonsense of having time spent on a rarefied debate rather than social justice. I know what was of the greater importance to me.

The Lords' debate brought two stalwarts from mining history into the argument, Derek Ezra and Roy Mason. I knew Lord Ezra very well when he was Chairman of the National Coal Board between 1971 and 1982. A very nice man, he sent me a letter of congratulations following my maiden speech. Technically he was a boss, but I recognised that he cared very much for the coal industry and particularly the welfare of its employees. I always thought that the working relationship he had with Joe Gormley, the President of the NUM from 1971-1982, was of great benefit to the industry. It was interesting they both received a peerage; Joe in 1982 and Lord Ezra in 1983. Unfortunately Joe suffered a stroke and died in the year Derek Ezra came to the Lords. I thought it a great pity they could not continue their partnership.

In his speech Lord Ezra paid me the tribute of being a strong advocate for the miners, and I thought of a conversation I had with

Joe. It was during a journey from Kings Cross Station. I was returning to Wakefield and he was travelling to the northern coalfields to attend a miners' gathering. During our conversation Joe said, "Geoff, never stop your fight for the Industrial Injuries Benefits for the miners suffering from bronchitis/emphysema. Do not get disillusioned, keep battling because the case is irrefutable." I certainly felt Joe's presence with me as I made my speech that night. *(Appendix D)*

I was also grateful for the support of Lord Mason of Barnsley - a powerful voice if ever there was one. Roy like myself had started work down a coal mine when he was fourteen. I first heard of him when he was adopted as the Labour candidate for Bridlington in 1951. Two years later he was elected Member of Parliament for Barnsley and remained in the House of Commons as Member of Parliament for the Barnsley Constituency until 1987.

Roy's talents were first brought to my notice when I attended an NUM summer school at Bingley College in the mid 1950s. These annual schools, organised for NUM members, brought different national figures from politics and the trade unions to lecture young trade unionists. One of the lecturers was Harold Wilson. He encouraged the NUM members to join the Labour Party and said, "What I want the NUM to do is send us some more Roy Masons." I consider that Roy one of the most outstanding Members of Parliament to have come from the coal industry. He has, I believe, been a Minister of State and Secretary of State of seven departments. His record is more than equal to any other mining sponsored MP and this includes the great Nye Bevan and Tom Williams, a South Yorkshire Miner who was Minister of Agriculture in the 1945 Attlee Government.

I recall strong rumours that, following the retirement of Lord Ezra from the National Coal Board, Roy Mason had been offered the Chairmanship, but the then Prime Minister, Margaret Thatcher, had intervened and stopped the appointment. No doubt she was aware there would be no chance of Roy Mason becoming a government puppet and doing her a hatchet job. That was left to Ian McGregor. We would still have a significant coal industry if Roy Mason had been appointed.

In the Lords' debate I was also supported by my very close friend and colleague, Lord Dixon of Jarrow. Following a meeting with John Battle, the then Minister of State at the DTI - and therefore responsible for the payments the miners would receive - I recognised that we had turned a corner. I found our meeting very refreshing indeed, unlike my meetings with former Conservative Ministers, some of whom had no doubt been responsible for the policy detected in the leaked document. John was enthusiastic to help the miners. He was also in a unique position for he had money available, something like £2 billion, to meet the claims. With that sort of cash he would not find it necessary to go cap in hand to the Treasury. From early on he pressurised the lawyers on both sides to produce a formula for the assessment of these awards as soon as possible. This should have been of no surprise to me, knowing the work John had put in when he was a back-bench MP for people suffering from asbestosis arising out of their employment and living in the vicinity of a factory in his Leeds constituency.

On 21 December 1998, John Battle announced that an agreement had been reached that day on the level of general damages which would henceforth compensate an ex-miner for pain and suffering. It was anticipated that 100,000 claims would be made and an award would be based on individual disability and would range from £4,000 to £50,000.

* * * * *

In 1987 the political backdrop was dominated by the shock of Labour's defeat at the hands of the Tories for the third time. Looking back I see that this was a period of change which produced the stimulus for the transformation of the Labour Party. Change was demanded, for there were no obvious excuses for defeat in that election as there had been in 1979 and 1983. In 1979, defeat could be explained by the unpopularity of some Labour Government policies and by trade unionists' militancy in the winter of 1978/79; in 1983 by factional divisions, the unfavourable public perception of Michael Foot as Labour Leader, and the successful rescue of the Falkland Islands from Argentinian invasion under the leadership of Margaret Thatcher. In 1987 it was difficult to pinpoint anything definite, although it was apparent to most Labour MPs and union leaders that voters did not like the Party's policies. The immediate dilemma facing us appeared to be that if we abandoned many of our traditional policies - support for trade union demarcation, nationalisation of the means of production and distribution, the purist 1948 welfare state packages - they would provoke internecine Party warfare as the grassroots activists stoutly defended traditional points of view. It was not recognised that a majority of our grassroots were also desperately keen to win the next general election and therefore would either willingly acquiesce in the changes that occurred or else remain loyally silent. At all levels within the Party most were heartily sick of opposition politics, they wanted government. Neil Kinnock understood this and initiated a programme driven by determination, to move us away from this unsuccessful past. He initiated reforms that went beyond what most envisaged. By 1991 Labour had been moulded very much to his image. He laid a foundation for the further programmes of reform executed by his two successors, John Smith and Tony Blair. Neil Kinnock made the Party electable and he began this process in 1985 when he made a most powerful speech at the Labour Party conference attacking militants. When he attacked the Liverpool Mafia, and the delivery of redundancy notices by taxi, he spoke the language the country wanted to hear.

Labour's 1987 Election Manifesto had already begun to shift away from some of the unpopular commitments of 1983. Public ownership was now reserved only for the specific public utilities of gas, water, and telecommunications. Workers' individual rights were now emphasised rather more than collective trade union legal immunities, and there were no proposals to repeal the trade union reforms initiated by the Conservative Government. The Party replaced its anti-Economic Community stance with a commitment to work constructively with the EC countries, though promising to stand up for British interests. What was not modified was its non-nuclear commitment. Policy shifts had occurred by 1987, but after the following election defeat, Labour embarked upon a fundamental reappraisal of its entire political strategy.

After the 1987 General Election, various interpretations of the Party defeat were presented to the National Executive Committee (NEC), and eventually from these emerged a commitment to a wide ranging policy review. This was the most comprehensive attempt to reconsider the nature of the Party's political commitments since the writing of the Party's original constitution in 1918. After two years' work by seven review groups under the ultimate guidance of Neil Kinnock, *Meet the Challenge - Make the Change*, was published in 1989. Two major themes emerged from the booklet: firstly, Labour Party notions of public and private ownership were outdated; and secondly, the quality of public services could be improved if we put the needs of the user before those of the producer.

In the public/private ownership debate, the report came down in favour of private ownership and affirmed that a Labour Government's task would be to stimulate a successful market economy and that it would intervene only where the stimulation was not coming from market forces. Throughout the report there was a stress on the essential role of the market. This emphasis was new. In the past, the Party had never wanted to eliminate private enterprise, but rather stress its unpleasant characteristics. Now it took a more positive stance.

Party rhetoric had traditionally equated private enterprise with profit, and public enterprise with service and made clear its preference for the latter. Labour now adopted the "responsible social market model" in which government would only intervene when provision was necessary. Only if the market was not providing - such as in the areas of labour training and environmental protection - or in order to establish agencies to control exploitation of market power, would it intervene. Labour wanted an active "developmental" state, centring on generating growth and efficiency; not featherbedding but challenging to secure needs.

Meet the Challenge made clear that public ownership was not a fundamental priority. Some forms of common ownership were appropriate for the public utilities, particularly British Telecom and

Water, but what would be returned to public ownership would depend on the situation when the Party was returned to office. It was not a fundamental obligation. What was stressed was the need for the major utilities to be more sensitive to consumer needs. It was considered that this was where market forces were flawed. From this it followed that the utilities should be answerable to regulatory commissions which would oversee pricing, investment and service standards.

Regarding the second theme, the quality of public services, the emphasis was now on the need to improve public services from the consumers', not the producers', point of view. This was an attempt to shift the Party away from its close identification with the public sector trade unions and to flag up its awareness of the public criticism of a welfare state which benefited the producer rather than the user. For example, the blue print suggested that local authorities would be required to agree service agreements with their customers, and that, if the agreed service levels were not achieved or met, then financial sanctions would result.

The commitment to market forces and service-friendly public sector utilities were the two most important themes running through *Meet the Challenge - Make the Change*, while the two most significant specific changes it contained were the redefinition of the Party's non-nuclear, and industrial relations, policies. The report declared that Britain's defence was an essential component of foreign policy and the prime responsibility of any government was that British forces would be efficiently and effectively trained and equipped. Britain's contribution to NATO - including the nuclear deterrent - would be maintained. However, in an attempt to part meet the Party's recent objections to nuclear weaponry there was a commitment to cancel the fourth Trident submarine, then on order, to adopt a policy of no-first-use of nuclear weapons, to seek to place Britain's nuclear weaponry into international disarmament negotiations, and to end the testing of all British nuclear devices. The report however contained no proposals to end Britain's nuclear capability or to remove American nuclear bases.

It also made clear that trade unions had a central role to play in a successful economy, but placed no emphasis on the commitment to restore and maintain collective rights for trade unions. Instead, it shifted towards guaranteeing basic legal rights for individual workers including their negotiation of decent wages and working conditions. Their protection from discrimination for union activities and from unfair dismissal, their ability to take time off work for family care, and their entitlement to union representation were also stressed. The report made no commitment to repeal the recent Tory laws on the closed shop or on picketing. The only proposed repeals of Conservative legislation were those allowing workers to be sacked after a strike ballot decision, those enabling employers to split companies in such a way as to legally avoid primary dispute action, and finally, those enabling employers to use judicial injunctions to curb industrial action. It said that Conservative legislation requiring ballots of union members prior to strike action and for the election of union executives would also be retained.

This section of the policy review introduced a shift of major proportion in the Party's commitments. Labour's non-nuclear stance between 1983 and 1987 had been a temporary aberration from its previous orthodox defence record; therefore the proposal to retain Britain's nuclear forces was no more than a return to the political mainstream. In contrast, its previous industrial relations commitments had always concentrated on the maintenance of the unions' legal immunities; the shift in policy from protecting collective union immunities to asserting individual rights at work was a major break with past definitions of one of the central ideals of the Party/trades unions relationship; trade union freedom.

What the policy review managed to do most effectively was to loosen the Party's commitment to specific, electorally unattractive policies, such as nationalisation, unilateral nuclear disarmament, and the trade unions' legal immunities. It had expunged these unpopular policies, restricted the number of commitments that might cause electoral embarrassment and made some specific proposals to move the Party in new directions.

There were only three topics - public ownership, trade union rights, and defence - on which any significant opposition was expressed by delegates at the 1989 Party Conference. Critics of the social market idea argued that capitalism would not act in a socially responsible manner and therefore demanded that the Party maintain its commitment to public ownership. But the case for public ownership mustered less than half a million votes in a total ballot of 6 million and was therefore overwhelmingly rejected. Opponents of the trade unions' proposals demanded the repeal of all the Conservative Government's trade union legislation, but they too were defeated, albeit by a smaller majority than in the case of public ownership. The sharpest debate and the closest vote came over the Party's defence policies. Critics of the policy review demanded a continuing commitment to unilateral nuclear disarmament and a sharp reduction in Britain's defence expenditures. The unilateralist position was defeated, but the Party voted, against the leadership's wishes, to reduce defence expenditures to the average of other European countries. *Meet The Challenge* and the conference which followed at its heels were the beginning of the Labour Party's return to power in 1997.

The fact that Neil Kinnock had succeeded in convincing the Party's main deliberative body to affirm enormous changes in policy on nationalisation, trade union laws, and unilateralism was extraordinary. Most people in the Labour Party faced up to the dilemma of reconciling deeply-held beliefs and the need to win power by opting for the latter. I believe Neil Kinnock deserves considerable credit for creating a climate of opinion which accepted change, however painful it might be, in the interest of the future of the whole Labour Party. Surrounded by a small group of personal supporters in his private political office, the Party Headquarters, the Shadow Cabinet and the NEC, he displayed a clear and consistent drive towards elected office. He capitalised on the mood within the Party to reverse its decline and to become again a governing party. There were institutional, structural, cultural and personal obstacles to his renewal project. He had constantly to mobilise majorities in the Party outside Parliament to calculate the trade union response to his reforms, face opposition from many Party activists; and he was criticised by those who claimed that he jettisoned his socialist principles. I always believed the bulk of this opposition to be nonsense. The Labour Party has never been an easy one to lead, but the problems and difficulties that

Neil Kinnock experienced when he was first elected were considerable. However by 1991 he had developed into the most powerful leader of the Party since Clement Attlee. His goal was office, and the bulk of the Party proved willing to follow in his tracks to achieve that goal.

Despite all this he could not get the blessings of the country. Labour had to endure an unprecedented fourth defeat in the 1992 General Election. This campaign was conducted in the midst of a severe economic recession - some might call it depression - which had undermined the Conservatives' reputation for economic competence, yet the Conservatives won the election almost solely on claims about Labour's economic incompetence. From late 1991 onwards, Conservative Cabinet Ministers hammered out the claim that Labour would bungle and blunder and that its policies would fuel inflation. Unemployment would rise, there would be increased interest rates which would make mortgages expensive and difficult to get, cause financial chaos, reduce competitiveness and bring back the winter of discontent. Like all good political messages, this one was short, simple and clear: no matter how bad the economy might be, it would be much worse under Labour. It turned out to be the Conservatives' main argument for the rest of the campaign. Almost every Labour criticism of Conservative economic policy brought forth not a defence of the policy, but an attack on Labour's economic competence. Neil Kinnock was condemned as an economic illiterate whose policies would mean permanent recession for the country.

Against the backdrop of bad economic news, the first two months of 1992 were given largely to economic claims and counterclaims between the parties. Labour went on the attack with the concerted criticism of government economic incompetence and complacency and presented its alternative of modest tax increases to fund better services and to invest for growth. The Conservatives defended themselves with a poster campaign attacking Labour's tax policy. They produced a large poster showing a huge black bomb labelled "Labour's Tax Bombshell" and the slogan "You'd pay £1,000 more tax per year with Labour." The mark was later raised to £1,250. Approval of the Conservatives' economic record was low but trust in Labour's ability to handle the economy remained still lower. Many voters believed that Labour would introduce large tax increases; over half believed that income tax would rise by 10p.

The rancorous argument between the two main parties about economic policy and economic competence was fuelled with speculation about the March budget. The Government really needed two budgets; the economy required fiscal stringency and prudent investment for economic recovery; the election needed an interest rate cut and tax cuts. Whichever course was chosen, room for manoeuvre was strictly limited. The Government desperately needed to cut interest rates in order to stimulate the economy and relieve mortgage holders; but for its own reasons it had joined the European Exchange Rate Mechanism (ERM) in October 1990 at what many regarded as too high a rate. The pound had drifted to the bottom of its rate, and an interest rate cut might well have provoked a sterling crisis. Since this would have severely damaged the Tory campaign, attention turned to tax cuts. Here again, options were limited. The recession had reduced the Government's tax revenues and, in spite of the massive privatisation receipts of previous years, the cupboard was now bare. In addition, Labour had limited the Government's options by forcing it to state that it would not increase VAT. Income tax cuts, therefore, would mean government borrowing - something contrary to Thatcherite principles of good management and not recommended in the depths of a severe recession by many economists either. Notwithstanding all this, the Tories were still lagging behind in the opinion polls and had pinned their hopes on budget generosity. Tax cuts would also highlight, they believed, the differences between them and Labour. The polls showed that many voters believed that tax cuts were as good a way as any of kick-starting the economy.

In the event, budget day on 10 March produced something of a surprise. Instead of taking a penny off the standard rate of tax, as had been widely expected, the Chancellor of the Exchequer, Norman Lamont MP - now Lord Lamont - lowered the lowest tax rate band to 20p, thus helping 4 million people on low earnings. Various other measures were designed to appeal to the motor trade, farmers, small businesses, and pensioners. Lamont announced that the package meant that government borrowing would double from £14 million to £28 million.

Labour savaged the whole package, and Neil Kinnock's claim that the budget tried to bribe the voters with borrowed money was true. The Gallup poll of March 1992 reported that 57% thought that the budget had been generous for election purposes and only 31% thought it a serious attempt to handle the economic situation. As many thought it fair (45%) as unfair (44%) but, more importantly, 70% approved of the new 20p tax band.

The Tories obviously thought that they had pulled off a marvellous coup. John Major spent his time during Lamont's speech laughing and gesturing derisively towards the Labour Front Bench, yet the public turned out to be indifferent. In the March Gallup poll 16% said that the Budget had made them favour the Tories more, 38% were less than impressed, and 42% said that it made no difference.

For the first time in British political history the Opposition did not rest content with its criticism of the budget but produced its own full-dress affair and presented it with a photo-opportunity of John Smith MP, the Shadow Chancellor, and his colleagues standing on the Treasury steps trying to look as much like a real Treasury team as possible. The alternative budget was designed partly to distract attention from the Government's tax cuts and partly to show Labour as prudent and responsible. The Labour "budget" reversed the new 20p lower tax rate but raised the threshold below which no tax or National Insurance contributions were to be paid. At the other end of the income scale, it introduced a 50p rate for those earning £40,000 or more and abolished the National Insurance ceiling of £21,000. An important part of the package, but one often overlooked in the discussion of tax, was that child benefit and pensions were to be increased.

Because it was generally recognised that the economic situation provided little room for manoeuvre, John Smith's budget differed mainly in detail from Norman Lamont's. Nevertheless, there were differences of principle. The Tories opted for tax cuts, even borrowing to achieve them, whereas Labour planned for some redistribution of income, some tax increases to pay for better health and education services, and for investment financed by borrowing. Labour had announced its general plans for a tax increase in January 1992, in order to avoid last minute shocks, and although the proposed tax increases applied only to high earners, the Party was still gambling on the apparent preference of the electorate for higher taxes and better services. Survey evidence over many years showed that the majority of voters were willing to pay higher taxes provided that they were spent on the right things - notably health, education and some social services - and provided that the extra money produced better services. But whatever people tell opinion polls, many still vote for tax cuts in the privacy of a polling booth. In Britain in 1992, announcing even small tax increases gave the Conservatives the opportunity for stories about Labour's irresponsibility and its "real" plans for huge tax increases for everyone. They seized the opportunity with real vigour, and repeated the same message over and over again: Labour, they said, was the party of large tax increases.

This was fertile ground. A Gallup poll at the end of February 1992 showed that 58% of people thought that their taxes would go up a great deal under a Labour Government. The issue in the electorate's mind seemed to be not small tax and spending increases - which they approved of as long as they were spent efficiently and on the right services - but large tax increases which they feared if Labour were elected. Therefore the Conservatives concentrated on their message about the £1,250 tax increase and reinforced it with pictures of bombs. Much of this seems to have struck home with the public. In fact, the tax proposals of the two parties were rather similar. *The Financial Times* of 17 March 1992 said that there was not much to choose between the parties, and the Institute for Fiscal Studies calculated that under Labour's tax plans, four out of five families would gain, while 9% - those earning more than £30,000 - would lose. Under the Conservative budget, the Institute found 74% of families would gain and 4% would lose.

The economic situation was such that economic and tax issues dominated the campaign and drove out virtually every other competence issue. Matters such as defence, Europe, law and order, local government finance, transport and energy, barely made an appearance. The National Health Service, however, did. Health was a vote winner for Labour. Labour had, after all, set up the NHS in 1948 and was still seen as its protector in 1992. There was widespread concern that the Conservatives' NHS reforms would in effect privatise parts of it and create a two-tier service for the rich and the poor. The Tories did their best to persuade the public that they had spent more on health than ever before, that hospital waiting lists had been reduced, and that their hospital trust reforms had worked and did not amount to privatisation. The public, rightly, remained fixedly sceptical. A poll in April 1992 found that 53% believed that the NHS was unsafe in Tory hands, and 57% did not believe the Government's claim that it would not privatise the NHS. Labour maintained a large lead over the Tories on the health issue, and throughout the campaign Labour was judged the best party to handle the NHS by a majority of around two to one.

The problem for Labour was that the 1992 election was exceedingly narrow in its range. The recession dominated everything. Given this, it was in Labour's interest to attack the soft target of the Conservatives' economic performance. The Conservatives thought that they could best defend themselves by attacking Labour's tax plans and reputation for economic incompetence. When Labour tried to raise caring issues such as the NHS, it was in the Tories' interest to deflect the discussion and turn it into an argument about Labour's lies and untrustworthiness. And a prime target was Neil Kinnock.

Notwithstanding the fact that Kinnock picked up support in 1992, as he had in 1987, polling throughout the campaign showed that by far the most frequently cited reason for not voting Labour was the feeling that Neil Kinnock would not make a good Prime Minister. Many were conscious of his change of mind on important political matters, such as nuclear defence, and in interviews he often spoke in long and winding sentences. Fewer than a third believed that he was a good Labour leader, compared with well over a half who thought that Paddy Ashdown was a good leader for the Liberal Democrats and about half who were satisfied with John Major. In March 1992 on most personal qualities except "caring", Kinnock was ranked well below Major by the public and by Gallup. It is also true that as the Labour leader Neil Kinnock was subjected to an unprecedented vituperative attack by the Conservative press, who carped on about his dismal failures as a future Prime Minister, as a Labour leader, as a human being, culminating in the infamous *Sun* front page on 9 April

1992, Election Day, that showed a picture of Neil Kinnock in a light bulb, with the words, "If Kinnock wins today, will the last person to leave Britain please turn out the lights."

The Red Rose Sheffield rally held on 1 April - not the most appropriate of dates - has been widely criticised for its triumphant show-business manner and the "we have already won" style. Following this the Tories attacked on what was perceived to be Labour's weakest point - Neil Kinnock. It seems likely that Kinnock's weak image was in part responsible for the consolidation of Conservative support that seemed to take place at the very end of the campaign. The Tories' campaign, especially John Major's decision to go back to the campaign trail on a soap box in selected market towns, showed him a populist of the old style. The critical factor underpinning the Tory victory, however, was that they persuaded enough people, drawn from all social groups, to vote according to their wallets. Many voters were irritated with the Tories for imposing a lengthy period of high interest rates upon them. They were concerned about the length of the recession and the fact that unemployment was still rising but this cut little ice. In the nine months or so before the election, the beneficial effects of the interest rate reductions initiated in October 1990 were starting to feed through. Economic optimism was rising and even began to accelerate during the final weeks of the campaign. The political triumph of the Tories was to make the satisfaction of these rising expectations conditional on a Tory victory. By the end of the campaign almost half the electorate believed that they would be worse off under Labour's taxation policies and a large proportion of them - most of them falsely avowing to the pollsters that taxation had not been an issue affecting their vote - duly voted Conservative. To these people, there were signs that the Conservatives had just about turned the economic corner and things were better. In this situation, they voted for the devil they knew. They thought it was better to vote Conservative - just to be on the safe side.

* * * * *

On the morning of Friday 10 April 1992 the Conservative Party found themselves unexpectedly returned to office with a comfortable majority of 21 seats. This was devastating for Labour. Many in the country who had genuinely thought Labour would be victorious, had grown over-optimistic. Against the background of a deep recession and after entering the General Election campaign with a sustained poll lead, Labour could still only achieve 34.4% of the vote, barely 3.6% more than in 1987. Neil Kinnock, the man who had done so much to bring Labour back from the electoral abyss, announced immediately after the election that he would stand down from the leadership of the Party as soon as a new leader could be chosen.

The contenders for the leadership were John Smith and Bryan Gould - now Vice Chancellor of the University of Waikato - and for the Deputy leadership, Bryan Gould again, Margaret Beckett and John Prescott. In acknowledgement of Smith's senior position within the Party, virtually all other leadership candidates - Gordon Brown, Tony Blair, Robin Cook, and Jack Cunningham - decided not to stand against him. Robin Cook in fact ran John Smith's campaign. The result announced on Saturday 18 July 1992 was, as expected, a victory for John Smith with Margaret Beckett as his Deputy. Both were elected with substantial majorities.

Most, myself included, thought Bryan Gould had made a tactical mistake by standing for both positions. I sensed resentment coming from a substantial number of Party members. They thought him overambitious in going for both positions and, indeed, for challenging John Smith. I believed at the time, and I do to this day, that if Bryan Gould had just stood for the position of Deputy Leader, he might have been successful. He would then have found himself in a very strong position to succeed John Smith and could now be the Prime Minister. These days Bryan Gould may possibly be aware of this mistaken strategy and the accident of history which took John Smith and left him isolated. I think it may be the origin of the bile which seems to cause him to address New Labour as "Not Labour" and to say that he is glad that he is not part of it. He still holds to the old Labour policies which were persistently rejected by the electorate; yet if he had been Deputy then he might now be Prime Minister, or more probably, Leader of Her Majesty's Loyal Opposition.

John Smith was confirmed as the new Leader of the Party after the House of Commons had gone into Recess for the summer and was given the opportunity to make his parliamentary debut as Leader under dramatic circumstances the following September when the Commons was recalled to debate the circumstances of Britain's humiliating abandonment of the Exchange Rate Mechanism (ERM). It was a performance as dazzling as it was confident, as it was polished. It had a tremendous, uplifting effect on the morale of the Party in Parliament and in the Country. In the face of it the Conservatives slumped into dejection. I myself thought that this speech was the beginning of the end of Norman Lamont as Chancellor of the Exchequer. The Conservatives had no answer to this stunning performance and it was plain to all that this was the real beginning of a Labour revival. In show business terms our "star" had been given the opportunity to shine. Of all the speeches I have heard in the House of Commons, both from the back-bencher and the Speaker's Chair, I don't think I have seen his performance surpassed.

With John Smith's election it seemed clear that Neil Kinnock's commitment to the modernisation of the Party's policies and organisation would be maintained, the process of ideological revision would continue. The only doubts surrounding Smith's inheritance concerned the pace and the manner in which ideological change would be promoted. The reason for such reservations lay in his style of leadership. John was a unifier who took a conciliatory approach towards Labour's internecine strife, and substantial political benefits flowed from this. By seeking to mediate in the debate between modernisers and traditionalists, he underlined the importance of the Party's gained unity. The practical effect was that, without promoting the modernisers' cause as openly as his predecessor had done, he nevertheless managed to extend the process of organisational change by establishing in October 1993 the principle of "One Member, One Vote" for the selection of parliamentary candidates. This curbed the power of the trade unions' block vote within the Party. John Prescott, the present Deputy Leader, and an influential trade unionist, made a major contribution, and together they won the day.

With regard to Labour's ideological stance, John Smith's inclination was to further the Party's gradual transition from traditional state socialism to a variant of European social democracy. This process had been going on since the policy review of the late 1980s. That this ideological revision was entirely in harmony with his own standpoint as a social democrat is key to an understanding of the change in the political climate. As a Labour MP from 1970, and a Minister in the Labour Government of 1974/79, he had been a supporter of a mixed economy and an advocate of social improvement within the framework which it provided. John Smith's social democratic stance stood on a firm Christian Socialist base. As he made clear in his R H Tawney Memorial Lecture given in March 1993, the distinctive features of this ethical socialism for him rested on a belief in community values, the independence of individual freedom and collective action. I found myself in agreement and supportive of John Smith, we embraced the same views.

The moral basis of this Christian Socialism, bequeathed by socialists and theologians like R H Tawney, William Temple and others, consisted of the overriding belief that the individual was best fulfilled in the context of a strong community bound together in friendship. John Smith planned in 1994 to publish a revised version of his lecture to form a personal statement of democratic socialist values. He then intended to offer his beliefs as a supplement to, rather than as a replacement for, Clause Four in the Party's constitution. This, he believed, would help lower any tensions over Clause Four by demonstrating that it had been superseded by his new statement.

This belief system, especially his initiative on Clause Four, was consistent with the gradualist and conciliatory style which was not to the taste of all his colleagues. Jack Straw - now Home Secretary - published a pamphlet called *Policy and Ideology* which called for a complete revision of Clause Four, so that the Party's objectives related directly to the circumstances existing in the Britain of the 1990s, rather than 1918. This pamphlet appeared in March 1993 during Smith's struggle to secure the backing of trade union leaders for One Member, One Vote, and was regarded by him with displeasure, an unhelpful intervention.

Neil Kinnock echoed Straw's views in February 1994, when he too recommended the re-casting of Clause Four. In spite of these two resonant contributions to the case for directly changing Clause Four without much subtlety, John Smith continued to adhere to a more indirect approach to this potentially divisive, explosive issue, making preparations through the drafting of his supplementary statement of values which in due course would be discussed by the Party. He hoped it would be adopted by the 1995 Party Conference. More broadly, he pursued his long-term strategy, shelving further organisational reforms and placing emphasis on Party unity and on the preparation of Party policy.

Although the strategy appeared at times to Labour modernisers such as Jack Straw, Tony Blair and Gordon Brown, to be pedestrian and overcautious, John Smith's leadership of the Labour Party ensured popularity in the country. When he died on 12 May 1994, he left the Labour Party broadly united, and the process of its modernisation was continuing, albeit at a moderate pace. John Smith's death cast a gloom not only over politics, but also over the country as a whole. It was not always possible to recognise this popularity during his lifetime but it was highlighted in his death.

* * * * *

On 12 May 1994 I arrived at the House of Commons at 8 am, as was my practice. At the Members' Entrance the policeman on duty asked me if I had heard about John Smith being taken to hospital. I had not. I was very surprised because I knew John had been making a major speech the previous night and I had been informed he had been on top form, the speech a great success at a glittering affair. I requested more information but he was unable to give me any details. After arriving at my office, I immediately went to the Tea Room, the unofficial nerve centre of the House, and found the place a-buzz with rumour.

Throughout the building, members of staff were gathered in groups. I immediately attempted to ascertain the extent of John's illness but no-one seemed to know. By 9 am the Tea Room had become crowded, all tables were taken and there was an atmosphere of deep concern and high tension. Different rumours continued to seep through but without any foundation. However, soon after it was officially announced that John had died. We were all stunned. No-one knew really what to say. There were tears flowing and there was a great feeling of disbelief, disillusionment and shock from Members of all parties and staff. Truly I have never experienced anything like it in Parliament, nobody really knew exactly what to say. Labour Party Members who had so much faith in him and had pinned their hopes on him to bring Labour back from the wilderness and return the Party to government were shocked, but so were Conservatives. The House sat at the usual time of 2.30 pm. At that time the Speaker rose, as is the custom, and informed the House: "I regret to inform the House of the death of John Smith, Right Honourable Member for Monklands East, and the House will join me in expressing our deepest sympathy to the family." The Prime Minister, John Major, and Margaret Beckett, the Deputy Leader of the Labour Party, who had immediately become Acting Leader of the Party until an election to replace John Smith, led the House in paying tribute to his memory. The House then adjourned for the day.

It was a great personal loss and created a void in my parliamentary life. I was always very close to him for I saw in him a caring and passionate person. When I first became Deputy Speaker, I watched with great interest the performance of Members who had been elected to Parliament at the 1992 Elections. I used to while away my time in the Chair assessing the potential for future prominence of these people. And just as a matter of interest, I informed John of these names. I never knew whether John valued my opinion to the extent that he would consider them if he became Prime Minister, but many of the names I have highlighted are now Ministers. He did not suffer fools gladly but always recognised genuine people.

When I was being challenged on re-selection as candidate for the 1992 election I well recall him requesting me to go and see him in his office. John expressed his concern to me and it was obvious he was less than pleased that I was being challenged in my home town. Like myself he recognised that nobody had a God-given right to go unchallenged, but he wanted to know about my opposition's motivation. I recall him saying to me, "You have an excellent parliamentary record and I have never heard a single complaint about your constituency work. To the contrary, I have heard nothing but high praise, not least for your work for the miners in the coal industry. I can assure you Geoff, your work as Deputy Speaker has been outstanding." He enquired if the man who was challenging me was one of the candidates who had been interviewed for the Hemsworth by-election when Derek Enright was the candidate. I told him that was the case.

My affectionate memories of John Smith have never dimmed. He was a special man and so I could not rest until I had visited his grave on Iona. I did this in September 1998. There, on this remote but holy Scottish Island, under a plain slab of local stone, lies the body of this great man. The inscription on the stone is devoid of all the styles and titles that one would expect to find on the stone of one so distinguished. It just reads:

John Smith - An honest man's the noblest work of God

I am not aware that this was at the personal request of John, but it distils the essential directness and humility of his character. As I knelt, reading this inscription, the Iona breeze blowing, my thinning hair upright, I knew John would be saying, "What are you doing here Lofthouse, cut out the mourning, get back and get on with the job."

* * * * *

I clearly remember that in the Tea Room, after the announcement of John's death, there was immediate speculation on who would be the new Leader. I overheard a group of senior Tories speculating and I clearly heard one of them say, "Let us hope, for our party's sake, they don't elect young Blair." This remark was brought vividly to my mind when the events of the subsequent leadership campaign unfolded. Very little consideration had been given to a replacement for John Smith and no one had been groomed. Now Tories were saying how much they feared Tony Blair.

I had always admired this young man from the time he entered Parliament in 1983. It didn't take long to pick him out as something special. From the start he could command the attention of the House, was always articulate and well informed but also had a blend of eloquence and wit. It soon became evident that Members on the Conservative Government side respected him and were very cautious when attempting to take him on. I immediately liked him and became very friendly with him. I found him to be modest and particularly recall one of his first appointments as a Shadow Minister. I had been playing a leading part in the major energy debates and because I was a senior member of the Energy Select Committee there was some anticipation that I might be appointed Shadow Minister in the Energy Department, with the coal industry portfolio. This was not to be and Tony was appointed Shadow Minister for Energy. I never resented his fortune but I do recall Tony coming to sit with me in the Tea Room. "I hope you are not too disappointed, Geoff, that I have got the post and hope I shall always be able to come to you to tap into your own experiences." He never failed to do this. Unlike some academics he never flaunted his intellect and never condescended to people of my generation, who because of the social conditions prevailing before the war, had not been given the opportunity to seek higher education. This I very much appreciated.

Tony Blair's election to the Labour Leadership in July 1994 after securing 57% of the votes of Party members soon led to an acceleration of the pace of modernisation within the Party. Along with Gordon Brown, he had been amongst the most prominent of Labour's modernisers since the late 1980s, had supported the policy changes and organisational reforms, and particularly the late John Smith's 1993 successful stand on "One Member, One Vote".

Under the leadership of Tony Blair, modernisation continued apace in the Labour Party. In April 1995 Clause Four of the Party Constitution was replaced by a statement of values, removing Labour's historic commitment to nationalisation. Tony Blair was determined to make New Labour more receptive to the free market and the middle classes, in this way reflecting economic and demographic changes in the country.

Modernisation, for Tony Blair, was about Labour working in its traditional role as a majority mainstream party and advancing the interests of the broad majority of people. Modern socialism, for him, consisted not in a particular form of economic organisation based on public ownership, but rather in a collection of values found in community enterprise and sharing. This he knew was strengthened by invoking the concept of the public interest supportive of the individual, rather than of the mass. His notion of socialism was person centred rather than based on notions of class or social unity. The primary task of Tony Blair's new agenda was to translate this concept into practical public action aimed at enhancing the individual's freedom and interests. Over time the main features of the ideological revision which Blair was advocating as the governing philosophy of New Labour were becoming clear. They appeared to stress that inclusive community promoted public interest, that there must be rejection of the elevated status previously accorded to public ownership, and that an unqualified regard for the merits of a competitive market economy, once judged by socialists as incompatible with their ideals, was not incompatible with the Welfare State.

In maintaining that socialist values were compatible with a market economy, Tony Blair made himself vulnerable to the charge that there was a basic contradiction between the ideals of community, solidarity, mutual obligation and social responsibility on the one hand, and the acquisitive and materialistic values of the market - as seen through the development of individual wants - on the other. In spite of these problems, it soon became clear that he was not concerned with developing his position only at an abstract level. He would challenge traditional values. At the end of his first conference speech as Party Leader he indicated that the Party would rewrite Clause Four of the Party Constitution.

When, on 4 October 1994, Blair advanced this controversial proposal, it was at the end of his speech. There and then he told his audience that Labour required a modern constitution that would unmistakably state what Labour was about and which the Tories would be unable to misrepresent. He wanted the whole Party to be involved, and reminded his audience that a political party that did not modify its philosophies to suit the circumstances of the times would become a fossil, a useless curiosity. Thus Tony Blair became the first Labour Leader since Hugh Gaitskell in 1959 to openly challenge the status of Clause Four as the formal expression of the Party's socialist purpose. Like Gaitskell, he considered that revising Clause Four was necessary not only in the light of important economic and social changes in Britain, but also in order to avoid misunderstanding or misrepresentation.

Blair's modernising project gained momentum in December 1994 when the Party's National Executive agreed a timetable for a special Party Conference to vote on the proposed constitutional change. This was to take place in April 1995. In January of that year the NEC decided to urge constituency parties to ballot their members on the proposal, and Blair himself began a nationwide tour in order to argue his case for change face-to-face with Party members.

In Tony Blair's judgement, Clause Four needed revision for three reasons. In the first place Clause Four committed Labour to common ownership with no boundaries, and hence to common ownership of industry, retailing and finance, rather than to a mixed economy. Such a commitment made no sense on the grounds of either socialist principle or economic reality. Second, Clause Four's position at the centre of its manifesto as a statement of objectives which no government could or would implement, had helped to divide the Party from its leaders and must go. Since no Labour election manifesto had ever contained a pledge to carry Clause Four into practice, Blair felt that the gap between the philosophy suggested by Clause Four and the policies of Labour governments led to the charge that the leadership was too timid to tread the path of true Socialism. Thirdly, he maintained that public ownership as enshrined in Clause Four was only ever the means to an end, it did not on its own reflect Labour's values or Labour's overall view of the economy. It was a distraction, not a help.

Free of such limitations, he considered that the new Clause Four ought to define Labour's purpose as a political party embodying socialist values. These included social justice, equality, freedom, democracy and solidarity, enduring values which, in Blair's view, ought to underlie and inspire Labour's new statement of purpose.

By the beginning of 1995, the circumstances facing Tony Blair seemed more favourable than those that had confronted Hugh Gaitskell in 1959. Unlike Gaitskell, Blair had carefully prepared the ground in advance. He had consulted with, and gained the support of, prominent colleagues such as John Prescott and Peter Mandelson and had made a point of declaring that an open debate on the issue would take place amongst Labour's mass membership and that a new statement of aims, composed by himself and Prescott, would in due course be submitted to both the Party's National Executive and to a Special Party Conference. Second, Blair's proposal was unlikely to face such fierce opposition from the trade unions as Hugh Gaitskell had faced. Blair was dealing with a trade union movement which, as a result of Labour's organisational reforms since 1987 - especially the reduction in 1993 of the union's block vote to 70% of total conference votes - did not exercise the same decisive political leverage within the Party as in Gaitskell's day. Prior to 1993 this had amounted to the unions controlling the conference decisions. Nevertheless, Blair needed to tread with some care in this area, as many of Labour's affiliated unions still had objectives similar to those of Clause Four written into their own constitutions and rule books.

Against this background and in accordance with the timetable agreed in December 1994, the new text of Clause Four was eventually published in March 1995 and approved by the National Executive on 13 March. The emphasis was on the values of community, social justice and democracy, rather than economic goals. Part One declared the Labour Party to be a democratic socialist party, believing that by the strength of common endeavour people achieve more than they achieve alone, creating for all the means to realise their individual potential and for all a community in which power, wealth and opportunity are in the hands of the many, not the few, where the rights that people enjoy reflect the duties that they owe, and where all live together freely and in a spirit of solidarity, tolerance and respect. Part Two contained the most heretical aspect of Blair's undertaking; it redefined Labour's economic aims and embraced notions of a competitive market economy operating in the public interest and of a fruitful partnership between private and public ownership.

With the new Clause Four, Labour was committed to the goal of a dynamic economy, serving the public interest in which the enterprise of the market and the rigour of competition were to be joined with the forces of partnership and co-operation in order to produce the wealth needed by the nation: opportunity for all to work and prosper, with a thriving public sector and high quality public services, where undertakings essential to the common good were either owned by the public or accountable to them. Part Two also referred to Labour's commitment to strive for a just society and an open democracy in which government would be held to account by the people. It argued that decisions should be taken, as far as was practical, by the communities that they would affect, and where human rights could be guaranteed.

Boosted by widespread press recognition of its ideological significance, Tony Blair's modernising project reached the final stage of the six month campaign when on 29 April 1995, at the Special Party Conference held at the Methodist Central Hall Westminster, it was presented to the Party. The original Clause Four had been adopted in February 1918. Eighty years ago the then Party Leader secured the approval by a 65% vote. Tony Blair's support included 90% of the constituency vote and 54.6% of the union vote. Well before the 1997 election he had overwhelming support for his strategy and stance.

As New Labour moved close to the election campaign, Tony Blair gained support of the Party for his modernisation policies under the *Road to Manifesto*. He toured the country advocating and promoting the aims and policies of New Labour. Party members were balloted on Party policy, leading Tony Blair to proclaim that "for the first time a political party will be entering a general election with its programme for government voted on by its members." This policy review resulted in five key policy pledges, including reducing class sizes, fast track punishment for young offenders, cutting of NHS waiting lists, getting 250,000 unemployed 16-25 year olds off benefit and into work, and a pledge to maintain low inflation.

As well as policies laid out in the *Road to Manifesto* process, Labour had been working hard to shed its "tax and spend" image. As Shadow Chancellor, Gordon Brown pledged that if elected, he would not increase income tax for the life of the next Parliament. New Labour also tried hard to become the party of law and order in the mind of the public. Tony Blair's famous pledge to be "Tough on Crime and Tough on the Causes of Crime" was reinforced by Jack Straw, the then Shadow Home Secretary, who promoted a tough stance on juvenile crime and advocated curfews for 10 year olds.

New Labour entered the General Election, called on 17 March 1997, in good shape. The consistently positive poll ratings and an impressive by-election victory in Wirral South in February augured well. Even so, the spectre of 1992's unexpected defeat prevented even the most optimistic Labour forecasters from daring to predict anything like the landslide or record breaking outcome that they ultimately secured. Labour won 44.4% of the votes cast, which meant 419 seats in total (including the Speaker's seat), up 146 on the 1992/97 Parliament. Labour's majority was a formidable 179 and the landslide represented an unprecedented swing of 10.3% from the Conservatives to Labour. Of the brand-new intake of 260 MPs, 183 were Labour.

Three factors underpinned this extraordinary transformation of the Labour and Conservative fortunes. The first of these was the Conservatives' loss of their previous reputation for competence in economic management. This Conservative weakness on economic competence was reinforced by Shadow Chancellor Gordon Brown's determination to present Labour's tax and spending plans as being no more threatening to "middle Britain" than those of the Tories. In 1992 the Conservatives were seen by 52% of voters as the "best party" if Britain got into economic difficulties, compared with Labour on 31%. By March 1997 the position had been almost exactly reversed with Labour seen as the "best party" by 49%, and the Tories by 35%.

The second factor underpinning Labour's remarkable transformation was undoubtedly Tony Blair's obvious ability as a competent political manager who would preside over a moderate, sensible government. In contrast to John Major's utter failure to quieten the seething discontent over Europe that continually festered within the Tory ranks, Tony Blair was able to present himself as a leader who had not only removed the outdated Clause Four from Labour's constitution, but who had also modernised British social democracy to the point where it now firmly embraced monetary orthodoxy and financial prudence.

Anyone who could lead a modernised and united Labour Party so decisively to the centre ground and centre left of British politics was also qualified to lead the country into the 21st century. Enough voters accepted this for New Labour to achieve victory. Fully 93% of Labour voters considered Tony Blair's leadership strengths to have been either very or fairly important in their decision to vote New Labour, complementing the 67% who thought that John Major's weaknesses played an important part in their decision. The sense that New Labour was a more moderate and more responsible party under Tony Blair was seen as very important by 66% of Labour voters - and by 74% of those who converted directly from voting Conservative to voting Labour between 1992 and 1997. The overwhelming majority of Labour voters - 97% - also cited the Party's promises to improve the NHS and education as important reasons for voting Labour. This was a clear and damning indictment of the Tories' record on health and education over the previous eighteen years.

A third factor, which made a great contribution to the changing positions of the parties, was sleaze. Throughout the 1992/97 Parliament, the Conservatives were hit by a series of sexual and financial scandals. Notwithstanding John Major's decision to establish the Nolan Committee on standards in public life in 1994, Tory Ministers were consistently unable to quell the public disquiet that the various allegations of corruption engendered. I deeply regretted this state of affairs. By the 1990s the reputation of politicians, in the eyes of the public, had sunk to its lowest ebb in living memory. This was a deeply unfair slur on the integrity and reputation of the overwhelming majority of Members on both sides of the House who were - and are - hard-working and dedicated to the interests of their constituents. Nevertheless the dispute over the propriety of some Members persisted to the very end of the election campaign, and the view that the various acts of individual corruption were the consequence of the arrogance of eighteen years of power was widespread amongst the voters. I always regretted that John Major never appeared to use his authority to discipline these individuals, and indeed tended to protect them. Whilst this was the action of a kind and caring man, it was not good political judgement. 80% of Labour voters identified Conservative sleaze and corruption as being a very important factor in their voting decision. Sleaze, moreover, symbolised the tiredness and ineptness of the Conservative Government. It was "time for change".

Undoubtedly, Tony Blair's brilliant charisma and acute political and emotional intelligence played a major role in New Labour's outstanding poll victory. But in managing New Labour, he also has unique advantages as leader which were never available to his predecessors. He was the first Labour Prime Minister to be elected by the whole Party, via an electoral college. This made him virtually immune to any damaging speculation about the Parliamentary Labour Party displacing him in a leadership contest. This was a problem that persistently clouded Harold Wilson's Government after the 1967 devaluation of the pound. Only if he fails badly to get New Labour re-elected as the government will Tony Blair's leadership be in serious question, and today that seems unlikely.

In recent years, because of Party reform, the previously dominant voting influence of the trade unions at the Party Conference and in elections for the National Executive Committee has been greatly reduced in favour of the constituency membership. This in turn has been much increased and has become more representative of voters generally. Under Tony Blair - and before him Neil Kinnock and John Smith - the internal Party structure has been much simplified, with clearer power given to the Leader and the Parliamentary Labour Party Leadership for determining Party policy than ever before. By rewriting Clause Four in the Party Constitution, Tony Blair removed a potent rallying point for the Left from debate, and secured his position by submitting the Party's 1997 election programme to a vote of the Party membership. Since this occurred a whole six months before the 1997 General Election Blair will have no need to be closely bound by the Party Conference when coming up for re-election in 2001 or 2002. He could simply repeat the same exercise, and probably secure similar levels of mass membership support against any dissenters. Tony Blair also ran a very personalised and personally directed New Labour election campaign so that he could rely upon solid support from the raft of new MPs brought into Parliament by the landslide victory. Protected by his youth and by the Electoral College endorsement, he has no serious challengers for the Labour leadership to worry about. As the century closes, I think he can probably be ranked as second only to Winston Churchill as the most remarkable British politician of the 20th Century. It should be remembered that Winston Churchill was a wartime Prime Minister and this tended to magnify his talents and achievements.

* * * * *

On 17 March 1997 John Major stood outside Number 10 Downing Street and announced the beginning of the longest general election campaign of modern time, a six-week marathon with polling dates scheduled for 1 May. On 2 May, much to my delight, Tony Blair, accompanied by his wife and young family, made his way along Downing Street through cheering crowds to No 10 on his return from Buckingham Palace, with the Queen's commission to form a new Government.

The scope and breadth of the Conservative defeat was unprecedented in modern history. One by one, the records fell: the largest Labour majority ever; the lowest Conservative vote this century (by a full 6%); the first time since 1906 that Conservatives would number less than 200 in the House of Commons; the largest anti-Conservative tide since 1945. This was the first time ever the Conservatives would hold no seats in Scotland or Wales; the biggest Liberal success in 70 years; and to top it all off, Tony Blair, at 43, became the youngest Prime Minister in two centuries, since William Pitt the Younger.

This was a defeat I had been waiting for and it had been a long time coming. Electorally, the Tories had held power tenuously for eighteen years. Their share of the vote never topped 43% and for much of the 1980s they were blessed with a badly divided opposition. It is fair to say that for most of their eighteen years in power, the Tories were behind in the opinion polls, only to score lucky wins come election time. Most of their policies were also deeply unpopular. As the eighties wore on, a considerable margin in the opinion polls indicated that people preferred the Welfare State to Margaret Thatcher's capitalist revival. It was obvious to me: after eighteen years of one-party rule, Britain was ready for a change. I also believe that Tony Blair has earned the reputation as man of change in changing times. His promise of a kinder, gentler style of government "for the many, not the few" struck a resounding chord with the electorate. This appeal was tremendously enhanced by the fact that the Tories simply did themselves in, that John Major's Government simply lost all credibility.

It had promised tax cuts and delivered 22 tax increases. Five months after the surprise Tory election victory in April 1992, interest rates were raised to 15% in just one day, the infamous 'Black Wednesday' when the pound was ignominiously forced out of the European Monitoring System at a cost of £22 billion. I always believed John Major to be a man of honourable intentions, but I also took the view that the Parliamentary Conservative Party knew a little too much about self-righteousness and pride and too little about humility.

Labour promised to build a modern and fair country. I am pleased to report at the time of writing, that Tony Blair and the Labour Government have been serving the people and keeping Labour's election pledges. A Bill to cut class sizes for all 5, 6 and 7 year olds is law; the first £22 million is going to cutting class sizes for 100,000 children. An extra £1.3 billion has gone to improving school buildings and equipment, plus an extra £1.25 billion to raise standards in schools. The NHS has been given £2 billion more than under the plans of John Major's Tories. The windfall tax, levied on the enormous profits of the Tory privatisation of utilities, has brought what I believe will be the biggest ever programme to get the young and long-term unemployed back to work, and is working well. Corporation tax has also been cut to the lowest in Europe.

Labour's attack on social issues has been broad based. Childcare has been put within the reach of all families, with £300 million over 5 years going to provide after-school places for nearly a million children. The poorest 20% of families will gain four times as much as the wealthiest 20% from the announcements made in the 1999 budget. All pensioners are to get generous cash payments to cope with winter fuel bills on top of the cut in VAT on heating, which has been reduced to its lowest level to help pensioners. Child benefit has seen a record increase, pensioners will benefit from the abolition of eye test charges introduced by the Tories, and the new 10p tax rate amounts to a tax cut for income tax payers. I am delighted that the Crime and Disorder Bill before the House of Commons will, when it becomes law, deliver twelve manifesto commitments, including Labour's pledge to ensure swift justice for persistent offenders. All handguns have been banned.

It is a delight and great satisfaction to me that after Labour's hard campaigning during the Tory years against exploitation and low pay, two million workers are now benefiting from the minimum wage of £3 a hour for 16 to 21 year olds, and £3.60 an hour for all those older. Of the 2 million workers benefiting, 1.3 million are women and 1.2 million are part-timers. 200,000 are young people; 80,000 are home workers, and 200,000 are single parents, and about 130,000 are ethnic minority workers. The minimum wage is a victory for enterprise and fairness, and whilst I would have liked to have seen it a little higher, it is in stark contrast to the Tories' "market determines wage level". It really shows that Labour is for the many, not the few.

The greatest benefit of Labour's programme is to education, its Number One priority. Between 1999 and 2002 an additional £19 billion is proposed for investment to modernise schools and raise standards. This comes on top of the total of £2.5 billion given to education since May 1997. The money will support projects including extending schools and building new classrooms. The amount being spent on renewing schools has been doubled, and all in all Labour is delivering a 5% real terms increase in education spending to the end of this Parliament in 2002. This compares to just 1.4% during the eighteen years of the Tories.

I believe that Labour is fulfilling its pledge to build a modern and dependable NHS with a fast, high quality service, based on need, not on the ability to pay. Over the first two years of government an extra £2.25 billion has been found for the NHS and moves have been set in train to end the divisive internal market. Waiting lists have been falling steadily from the record level inherited from the Tories and I think it is fair to expect they should keep on falling now the investment programme of £21 billion has been launched on 1 April 1999.

Abroad British military strength has been deployed in support of an ethical foreign policy which will not see Britain, in concert with her allies, ignoring atrocities committed against humanity by foreign tyrants. In Ireland thirty bloody years of terrorist warfare in Northern Ireland hopefully seem to be coming to an end. The outstanding achievements of Tony Blair, Marjorie Mowlam and others have brought about a cease-fire and now both sides are talking to each other. Though there are still great obstacles to overcome, like the de-commissioning of arms, things are improving. I often recall Winston Churchill's words, "Jaw, jaw is better than war, war."

To bring peace to Ireland after 800 years of friction and bloodshed between Britain and Ireland would be a phenomenal achievement. I believe it is a measure of Labour's talent and vision in government that they have brought this within grasp and I hope that by the time this book is published that its efforts will have been rewarded, and peace will have been brought to this troubled island.

* * * * *

When the Football Bill was proceeding through the Standing Committee stage, the Government Whip was not being very co-operative. The late Dennis Howell, former Sports Minister - later Lord Howell - was leading for the Opposition. It was one Thursday evening and the Members of the Committee were keen to end the day's business at 10 pm. So was the occupant of the Chair, but of course I could not express my views.

Thursday evening is always a difficult time because Members are keen to return to their constituencies on that evening. Dennis Howell had requested the Government Whip on duty to indicate what time he intended the Committee to rise. The only answer he could get was, "I will consider it later." That answer did not satisfy Dennis and he sent for Don Dixon, former Deputy Chief Whip, who requested the same information. Don received the same answer but was having none of it.

He immediately informed his Government counterpart, "If you keep these Members here after 10 pm, I will keep all Government Members in the Chamber all night."

He would have little difficulty doing this because on that day the Financial Secretary to the Treasury was presenting estimates for the Armed Forces and Royal Household. This would normally go through "on the nod" but need not. Don gathered the storm troopers - Skinner, Cryer, McKinley and others - and started to organise votes against every motion. This meant that just by keeping a few Labour Members in place he could keep the Government Members up all night. When David Waddington - now Lord Waddington - who was the Government Chief Whip at the time, heard what was happening, he approached Don and requested to be informed of the problems. Suffice it to say, the Football Committee adjourned at 10 pm. The generals and storm troopers had won.

Apart from his duty as Pairing Whip, Sir Raymond Powell also had the responsibility of allocating office accommodation for Members and was the Chairman of the Accommodation and Works Committee. He combined both these duties to great effect. When he took over, the office accommodation for Members was very sparse. When I was first elected I was months without any accommodation of any sort, not even a desk or a telephone. When I was eventually allocated one, it was in a small office accommodating twelve Members. As I said at the time if this had been done outside Parliament, it would have been completely in breach of the Office and Shops Act.

Over the period Ray held these positions there has been a transformation of the accommodation provided for Members. Accommodation has now been made in Parliament Street and Millbank, most of it well equipped and with television where Members can enjoy viewing the channel of their choice or watching the debate in the Chamber from their own office. Some take the view that this has resulted in the lack of attendance of Members in the Chamber. I recognise the argument but I think the advantages have far outweighed the disadvantages. I certainly found it very useful when I was Deputy Speaker. Currently there is new accommodation being built, called Portcullis House, immediately adjacent to the House of

119

Commons. I am sure that future Members of Parliament who will have the benefits of these offices will be grateful to Roy.

One of Ray's triumphs was persuading the Accommodation and Works Committee to undertake an audit of office accommodation. At first the Serjeant at Arms objected, saying that no survey had ever been done before and this one would be unfruitful. However, Ray got his way. When the survey was conducted some offices were found to be empty - they had been allocated to past Members, including Members who had died. They also found accommodation which had been built for a previous Speaker with six children. No one knew it was there; it had last been used by Air Raid Wardens during the War. Above this flat they found 25 unused rooms, some so high you needed a ladder to close the windows. Ray's perseverance resulted in them being converted for Members' use. Today the Members' accommodation is far better than I remember from my early days.

Ray says he had to be very careful that Members who wanted to share offices did so for secretarial purposes. He also tells many humorous stories. One Member thought she had the right to pick her office. Ray brought her down to earth. She was so angry she called him right wing and illegitimate! After this, however hard he tried, he could not find an office for her; eventually, much to Ray's distress, she waited two years. Once I heard Ray tell a new Member that the type of room he got would depend on how much he was prepared to pay to the Whips' Benevolent Fund. He must have been convincing because a Member later asked me if it was correct.

There was always a lot of joviality and kidology between Don Dixon, former Deputy Chief Whip, and Ray Powell. Once Don was speaking from the back-benches about his experiences in the ship yards. He was making reference to what was known as "the market system", this was a system where men would turn up for work on a morning and have to stand about waiting to see if there was any work available. Don said he had stood on many occasions in torrential rain, wet through and water coming through his lace holes. Ray intervened immediately. "On a Point of Order Mr Speaker, did I hear my Honourable Friend correctly? He did say, 'lace holes' or what?!"

* * * * *

Television reached Parliament in 1989. The House of Lords began its broadcasts before the Commons, initially on an experimental basis in 1984. Following rejection in 1966, 1971, 1975 and 1985, public popularity and a desire to see how democracy works, led to the Commons to agree in February 1988 that broadcasting of its own proceedings also should begin on an experimental basis in 1989. The vote on this decision was a free one and was close: 324 for, 266 against. I voted for the motion although I had my reservations. On balance I took the view that the nation had a right to see their parliamentarians in debate. I think time has proved that it has been popular in the eyes of the public, although I think some of the public have not always been pleased with what they have seen. On many occasions I have heard people saying, especially after they have been watching Question Time, that the Members are just a bunch of spoiled children. Televising mostly from the Commons has not given the public the right image. I would have preferred much more emphasis to be placed on televising Select and Standing Committee work, for this is where the major work on the legislation programme takes place. However, television - the media which gives the majority of people their news - had finally arrived after rejection.

On the very first day the cameras rolled Mrs Thatcher arrived in all her glory for Question Time. She intended to be the first politician to speak in the House of Commons as it was being televised. She hadn't reckoned with the parliamentary skill and the opportunism of the late Bob Cryer. Before she had the opportunity to rise Bob was up and calling, "Point of Order." He then turned around and smiled at us all. Using an old and tried debating device a Labour Member from below the Gangway, as they say, was the first televised MP. He said afterwards, "I was determined she wasn't going to get on before me." Typical of Bob!

However, many opponents of the scheme felt that the customs and proceedings of Parliament would be trivialised and that the more charismatic or eccentric Members would be favoured along with the front-benchers, at the expense of the more ordinary MPs, those who worked quietly but effectively in the service of their constituents and who, of course, are the overwhelming majority. Proponents argued that Parliament can only maintain public support and approval if the

121

Chamber and Committees are presented at regular times on television. There was a common fear that viewers might be antagonised by the sight of a large and empty Chamber, not realising that many Members were fully occupied working hard on different committees, in the Committee Rooms. Advocates of the scheme have also pointed out that public interest fostered by the scheme would extend understanding of the true workings of the Commons.

In the *New Yorker* in 1990, the Rt Hon Bernard Weatherill - now Lord Weatherill - then Speaker of the House of Commons, described television from the Commons as the "Best Show on Earth". That was not a unanimous opinion, not everyone liked it. Sir Peter Emery, said, "I think it has altered things and for the worse." The eminent Conservative Leader, Sir Geoffrey Howe, took the opposite view: "If anything, in my judgement, television is diminishing the likelihood of bad behaviour. My impression is that the domestic viewer is asserting rather better standards of expectation of good behaviour than happened previously."

When the cameras started to roll in 1989, there was a noticeable change in the sartorial style of Members. The overwhelming majority had always been smartly dressed in recognition of their public position, but now sleek new suits and fashionable haircuts were sported by the men. This may have had more to do with their wives than the cameras: "I am not going to be the laughing stock of the country, having people see you looking like that." But the general effect was improving. Lady Members had no need to change their ways, for the most part they had always been chic and attractive in their dress and looks. Such exceptions as there were simply carried on.

The increase in lady Members since 1992 has added a welcome note of colour and beauty to what previously was a rather drab Chamber and this in itself has made for good television. The ladies' perfume certainly added a more pleasant aroma. Some changes in style occurred because of technical consideration. We were told that red was a photogenic colour so red ties, hankies, socks and in one or two cases, shirts and jackets, appeared on the men. The ladies appeared in any and every sort of red garment and accessory which could be worn with elegance. What some didn't know was that some shades of red are transmitted far more effectively than others. Some came across as the very model of sartorial splendour, others looked as though they had been doused with a bucket of blood, and a minority glowed like neon signs. It took some time for exhibitionist tendencies to come under control.

Then there was "doughnutting." This, I understand, is an American expression and became most apparent at Prime Minister's Question Times. By reading the Order Paper of the day, those wishing to enhance their image discovered which Member had been successful in the ballot to be called to put their question. They would then arrive in the Chamber and sit beside or behind that Member. This placing more or less guaranteed that they would be seen on television. To some extent I could understand their reasoning, they felt it was necessary to doughnut. When they returned to their constituencies at the weekend, people would say to them, "I never see you in the Chamber." Doughnutting became so blatant that during my period as Deputy Speaker I would look through the Order Paper each morning and identify to my Assistant, Brian Munka, which Members would be today's doughnut. I was never wrong!

One practice which developed following the introduction of television I deplore. It occurs on the day of the State Opening of Parliament. On that occasion, according to custom and tradition Black Rod arrives at the Commons and knocks on its door three times with his wand. Then he is allowed into the Chamber to summons us to the Upper House. The Speaker rises, the Prime Minister and Leader of Opposition, and Secretaries of State follow him to the door. Members then follow on from their seats in the Chamber.

After the cameras arrived however, some Members would deliberately not go into the Chamber but instead they would loiter about in the Members' Lobby and immediately the Speaker's procession entered would sneak into position as near as possible behind the Speaker. On some occasions they even got in front of the Ministers. A position close to the Bar of the House in the House of Lords, listening to the Queen's address, would again guarantee them maximum television coverage. I always thought it needed brass necks to behave in such a rude manner. Unfortunately this practice still continues to this day.

* * * * *

The House of Commons has been my university. I have presided at key national debates including those on Maastricht and I have had many hours of interest in the Chair listening to thousands of speeches over my five years' occupying that very privileged seat. Some of them were serious, well thought out and researched, genuine speeches, many of them spoken from the heart, some entertaining, some effective and I regret to say, some just plain boring! The vast majority were average speeches making points on legislation which was being debated or making constituency speeches in Adjournment Debates but crucial all the same. Parliament is not a theatre, it is a legislating chamber. Our society is changed by adjustments to law not by rhetoric. Many of the best speeches take place when a Member has a special constituency problem and is desirous of bringing it to the notice of the appropriate Minister. I regret that the majority of speeches which I heard did not achieve their objective but perhaps that was bound to be the case. Many of them receive a little local publicity and that is all. They find themselves recorded in *Hansard* and then remain buried in the archives.

On the other hand there are some speeches of high drama which I believe were very effective. One was the resignation speech of Sir Geoffrey Howe. I believe this speech was the beginning of the end of Mrs Thatcher's reign as Prime Minister. Another was the Norman Lamont speech which damaged John Major. *(Appendices G and H)*

Geoffrey Howe's was a devastating speech. Looking up at the Strangers' Gallery, I could see Lady Elspeth Howe, Geoffrey's wife, looking down on her husband with admiration. Later, after the speech was over, I heard some Members unkindly say, "That was Elspeth's speech." He would have been unusual if he had not rehearsed it with her but make no mistake, it was his speech and by any standards it was devastating. When I looked at Mrs Thatcher's face I could see she recognised that this was not a day when she had been savaged by Lord Dennis Healey's dead sheep. I can hear it now:

"People throughout Europe see our Prime Minister's finger wagging and hear her passionate "No, No, No," much clearer than the content of the carefully worded formula texts." ....It is too easy for them to believe that we all share her attitudes, for why else has she been our Prime Minister for so long?"

Norman Lamont's resignation speech 9 June 1993 was also decisive. This speech I believe had a similar effect to Geoffrey Howe's speech, this time marking the beginning of the end of John Major's premiership. Although John was not thrown out by his own party, his Government was overwhelmingly rejected in the 1997 election and some of this rejection can be traced to Lord Lamont's Trustees of the Nation speech.

I believe that when he uttered the words, "We give the impression of being in office but not in power," he put an end to John Major and his Government. The Tories did not replace Major as Leader prior to the 1997 election; the electorate undoubtedly did. Whilst I believe there were many other factors, not least sleaze, Norman Lamont's resignation speech certainly contributed to the Tories' downfall.

These were speeches of high politics and drama but alongside these I would place a speech of great worth, made on a point of principle and delivered for no other reason than that it was right to deliver it. It represents Parliament at its best.

Andrew Mackinlay, Member for Thurrock, is not a household name, but since he entered Parliament in 1992, he has been very active and tireless in causes he really believes in. One of them concerns First World War executions. On 19 October 1993, late in the evening, Andrew made a speech whilst I was in the Chair which certainly impressed me by its content, presentation and sincerity. He moved a Bill to pardon soldiers convicted and executed during the Great War, for offences like cowardice, desertion, sleeping at post, throwing away arms and striking a superior officer.

He explained to the House the nature of a Bill which would facilitate the granting of pardons to 307 soldiers of the British Empire Forces who fought in the 1914-18 war and were executed by firing squad. Andrew told the House many of these soldiers were young men, some teenagers. They were drawn from every corner of the United Kingdom, many were not conscripts, but volunteers, and that some had spent not months but years in the trenches enduring constant shellfire, sniping. They lacked food and sleep and were constantly wet and cold. He said it was hardly surprising that in many cases their spirit broke. Andrew took the view that all 307 soldiers were denied the operation of rules of natural justice. They were not given the opportunity to prepare a defence and in many cases there was no advocacy whatsoever, and when there was it was not conducted by a legally qualified person. Above all, none of the soldiers were given the opportunity to appeal against the sentence of death. Invariably, they were given only 12 - 24 hours' notice before the sentence was carried out. He said that those men had endured grave injustice and it was time the record was put straight.

Andrew emphasised that we knew from the documents that have become available, following the 75 Year Public Records rule, that many of these men were sick, traumatised and suffering from shell-shock. For that reason he said the House should begin to put the records straight to ensure that such men are held in high national esteem. He said he was motivated to bring the Bill before the House because many dependants of these men sought redress, and because there were still among us a few thousand veterans of the Great War, in the evening of their lives, to whom nothing would give greater satisfaction or contentment than knowing - albeit late in the day - that their comrades in arms were fully exonerated. He said it had been suggested that he was seeking to rewrite history. Andrew rejected that, he said he was seeking to ensure that history is written with clarity and precision; that those things that are uncomfortable to the establishment are brought into the open.

He reminded the House that Her Majesty the Queen, the Prime Minister and the Leader of the Opposition would within the next few weeks be at the Cenotaph, and other Right Honourable and Honourable Members would rightly be at their local war memorials. He said we attend such memorials not to remember the veterans of the Crimean War, the Napoleonic Wars or the Cromwellian Wars, but to remember soldiers of the Great War because they are of our time, that almost all of us had grandfathers, fathers and uncles who were in the Great War. That is something which could not be ignored. Those dead soldiers were not merely history. In his opinion the remedy sought was overdue; we should heal the reputations of men broken during the sham trials. He went on to request a blanket pardon for the 307 soldiers, and if that was not appropriate, he suggested the Secretary of State should refer each case to a panel of High Court Judges to test whether or not there had been injustice and whether or not there should be a pardon. He said he could not see what could be wrong with that, other than that some people might not like the truth coming out. He said that the demand for this remedy is like a cry from the grave. "It is time that this House of Commons took hold of the matter, put aside the objections of the establishment and said that these soldiers of the Great War who were executed are deemed worthy to be among those we will remember on Remembrance Sunday."

This struck a direct chord, for Andrew Mckinlay's campaign had particular relevance to me. My father had fought in that war and had been injured in the Battle of the Somme. He was one of the lucky ones. Tens of thousands were killed in the first hours of that campaign and many of his friends never returned. His arm was shattered and this restricted his chances of work. As a boy I remember him telling me that as he lay in his trench he was constantly praying, "Put me on a train to Blighty." He always worked, eventually as a farm labourer at Hough's Farm, North Featherstone, now Day's Farm. I believe that his premature death at 35 was a result of the wounds he received in that senseless battle. For that reason Armistice parades are very important to me.

After the speech Andrew continued his campaign and on 24 July 1998 I was pleased to read in *Hansard* that the Labour Minister for the Armed Forces, Dr John Reid, made a statement on this matter and ended his speech like this:

"Today, there are four things that we can do in this House, which sanctioned and passed the laws under which these men were executed. First, with the knowledge now available to us, we can express our deep sense of regret at the loss of life. There remain only a very few of our fellow countrymen who have a real understanding or memory of life and death in the trenches and on the battlefields of the First World War. This year marks the 80th anniversary of the end of that war, and we are recalling and remembering the conditions of that war, and all those who endured them, both those who died at the hands of the enemy, and those who were executed. We remember too, those who did their awful duty in the firing squads.

Secondly, in our regret, and as we approach a new century, let us remember that pardon implies more than legality and legal formality. Pardon involves understanding, forgiveness, tolerance and wisdom. I trust that Honourable Members will agree that, while the passage of time has distanced us from the evidence and the possibility of distinguishing guilt from innocence, and has rendered the formality of pardon impossible, it has also cast great doubt on the stigma of condemnation.

If some of the men were indeed found wanting, it was not because they all lacked courage, backbone or moral fibre. Among those executed were men who had bravely volunteered to serve their country. Many had given good and loyal service. In a sense, those who were executed were as much victims of the war as the soldiers and airmen who were killed in action, or who died of wounds or disease, like the civilians killed by aerial or naval bombardment, or like those who were lost at sea. As the 20th century draws to a close, they all deserve to have their sacrifice acknowledged afresh. I ask Honourable Members to join me in recognising those who were executed for what they were - the victims, with millions of others, of a cataclysmic and ghastly war.

Thirdly, we hope that others outside the House will recognise all that, and that they will consider allowing the missing names to be added to books of remembrance and war memorials throughout the land.

Finally, there is one other thing that we can do as we look forward to the new millennium. The death penalty is still enshrined in our military law for five offences, including misconduct in action and mutiny. I can tell the House that Defence Ministers will invite

Parliament to abolish the death penalty for military offences in the British Armed Forces in peace and in war."

Regrettably, Andrew had not got the pardon for these men as he had requested, but at least Dr Reid had taken great interest and, in fact, gone some way towards wiping away the stigma from these men. That sort of charity was not present when the then Conservative Minister, Roger Evans gave his response on 19 October 1993.

He said that the speech of the Honourable Member for Thurrock - Mr Mackinlay - was plausible and emotional, but fundamentally misconceived and wrong in principle, he said that history was littered with injustice, and that it was entirely inappropriate at this stage in the century to examine what happened between 1914 and 1918. If ever there was an argument against open government and in favour of keeping the files closed for even longer, it could be made now. He asked, "What are we hoping to achieve by this measure?"

I have emphasised this particular speech by Andrew Mackinlay to highlight the hard and sincere effort many more MPs like him put into their work. I have always thought how unfair it is when the few MPs who get involved with sleaze attract headlines yet men of his worth are not usually mentioned. In and through newspapers our people tend to perceive that all Members of Parliament are lacking in worth or, worse, are corrupt. Indeed I have witnessed a period when the image of MPs is very low in the public's eye. The average MP, who does not seek the headlines but works hard, makes up the majority of Members in the House of Commons.

* * * * *

There have been many occasions when I have found myself having to make spontaneous judgements with no time to refer to the book of parliamentary procedure, *Erskine May*, or to the learned Clerks. As I look back I recognise that the House always responds to good-natured humour and Members are always kind when the Chair finds itself in a difficult position. On such occasions they invariably accept the Chair's ruling. Such occasions are often marked by bi-partisan respect rather than diatribe. In that spirit I recall one time when I was able to save the face of a Conservative Government Whip.

The Whip was on duty to "shout out" on behalf of the Government when the Division was called. The vote was to be at 10 pm. I noticed the Whip enter the Chamber about 9.50 pm, slightly tired and emotional. He sat on the Government Front-Bench and I noticed that his mind was in under-drive. At 10 pm I put the question, "All those in favour of the amendment say, 'Aye'." The Whip on the Opposition Front-Bench shouted loudly, "Aye." - "All those to the contrary say 'No'." Not a pip.

The Government Whip seemed to be dreaming. I put the question again with a similar result. I then gave the call for a Division, "Clear the Lobbies." Derek Foster, the Opposition Chief Whip, rose to the Despatch Box and said, "Mr Deputy Speaker, I did not hear the Government Bench oppose the motion."

I simply said, "I did. Division."

It was not necessary to embarrass the Conservative Whip. As a pragmatist I knew that the Government would have found a way to correct the decision at a later date and in that circumstance I considered that more debate would have been a waste of parliamentary time. I still say I heard the Whip shout 'No', but I know that the House would never have questioned the word of the Deputy Speaker. In that case the Whip in question was saved a real telling off from his Chief Whip.

Another occasion was much nearer to my heart. I had returned to my constituency one Friday evening. It was in April 1995 at the time when the chairmen of the rugby league football clubs, including my own clubs, Featherstone and Castleford, had signed an agreement with News International, the Murdoch Empire. It had been signed quite suddenly without much consultation with club members or shareholders. Along with many other rugby league supporters, I felt that because we were not aware of the contents of the agreement, we could not understand what effect it would have on the future game. I knew that something had to be done and that parliamentary consideration of some sort was called for. I also knew my position as Deputy Speaker prohibited me from initiating action.

When I arrived home there was a message on my answerphone asking me to telephone my colleague David Hinchliffe, MP for Wakefield. David told me he had received a message from the Speaker's Office informing him that he had obtained an Adjournment Debate on the signing of the rugby league agreement.

I said, "Excellent."

David said, "Yes, but I have not put in for one."

"Now David, I am aware how very hard you work and you are always under pressure. You must have forgotten you applied for the debate. I have noticed you have become quite forgetful recently."

An Adjournment Debate of the type David had been successful in obtaining took place on a Wednesday morning. There are two types of debate that can take place, one lasts ninety minutes, the other thirty minutes. David had been successful in obtaining one of the ninety minute debates. His debate, which I chaired, was a great success. It highlighted the fears of the rugby league world and indeed attracted the largest number of MPs I had seen at one of these sort of debates. There were over 40 MPs present. As I opened the debate I made reference to the interest Members had shown. Yet successful or not, to this day David always insists that he did not apply for the debate and I always comment on his lapses of memory.

Sidney Chapman MP, a Conservative Government Whip, held the title of Comptroller of the Queen's Household. One of his duties was presenting messages to the Commons from the Queen. Once Sidney duly presented himself at the Bar of the House dressed in his morning suit and carrying his 'wand', a wooden stick about four foot in length. As he stood to attention at the Bar of the House, wand in his left hand, waiting for the Speaker to call him to deliver the Queen's message, up jumped Dennis Skinner, MP for Bolsover, billiard chalk in his hand and proceeded to treat Sidney's wand in the way cues are treated when their tips are getting tired. I reprimanded Dennis but the House saw the funny side. I said I could not find any guidelines in *Erskine May* on my response to Dennis' action. Poor Sidney!

The House has its characters and so I always enjoyed the antics of Sir Nicholas Fairburn, although I had to be especially alert when he entered the Chamber. Even when tired and emotional he was formidable.

Nicky Fairburn, as he was affectionately known, was a lawyer of high reputation in Scotland. He had been Her Majesty's Solicitor General for Scotland (1979-82) but was a controversial, bordering on the eccentric, character. A very talented man he enjoyed dressing up in Scottish attire and indeed, in other forms of clothing not quite so traditional. Outlandish almost, he described himself in *Who's Who* as "raconteur and wit". He was certainly a man of many talents. Apart from being a QC, he was an author, forester, painter, poet, TV and radio broadcaster, dress designer, landscape gardener and bon viveur. He liked a drink. Called to the Scottish Bar in 1957 he was successful in his practice. I always enjoyed his conversation. He would tell fascinating stories, not least about his work in the Scottish courts. He used to proudly tell me he had never lost a case when defending someone on a murder charge. Eventually he published an autobiography, *A Life Is Too Short*. A prophetic title, for I regret that Nicky may have contributed to his own short life span. He died on 19 February 1995 but I will always remember his friendship and not least the pleasure he got when trying to put one over on me when I was in the Chair. Equally I recall the enjoyment it gave me to be able to use the power of my office to control this brilliant lawyer, though I must confess it was not always easy.

The most embarrassing moment Nicky gave me was during the debate on lowering the age of consent for homosexual activities from 18 to 16 years. It was 21 February 1994, the Chamber was full and overflowing, the public gallery was likewise. There was a great deal of emotion and some members were showing antagonism to the differing points of view. This was not helped by the people who were packed in above us. Many of them appeared to be homosexual and in fact some of them were actually showing open affection for one another. I was tempted to refer the kissing to the Serjeant at Arms, but I thought if I did it might inflame the situation. Whilst I was considering what action I could take, Nicky, attired in his Scottish tartan trousers and fancy coat, entered. He looked worse for wear, but he may not have been. Sometimes he put this image on deliberately.

Tony Blair, then Shadow Home Secretary, was at that moment speaking from the Dispatch Box. He was speaking on the New Clause Three on the Criminal Justice and Public Order Bill, which had been moved by Mrs Edwina Currie, Member for South-East Derbyshire. The clause was attempting to reduce the age of consent for homosexuals from 18 to 16 years.

Nicky rose from his seat. "On a Point of Order, Mr Deputy Speaker."

I called, "Point of Order Sir Nicholas Fairburn," while thinking, "What is he going to test me with now?"

As Tony Blair sat down on Nicky's Point of Order, Sir Nicholas Fairburn went straight to the point. "Mr Deputy Speaker. I hope that the Committee will not be misled by the fact that heterosexual activity is normal and homosexual activity is not." In very graphic language he went on to describe the intimate act of homosexuals. All is recorded in *Hansard* on 21 February 1994. I was immediately on my feet with, "Order, Order." I could not recall anything in *Erskine May* to deal with the situation. Nicky attempted to continue, "Order, Order, we can well do without talk like that. The Honourable Gentleman must take his seat." Nicky gave me his mischievous smile, "I surprised you there."

As he sat Tony Blair rose with, "I do not think that I will answer that intervention."

Nicky had opened the playground. Now Bill Walker, another Scottish MP, followed with a Point of Order, but put more politely than Nicky Fairburn's had been. "On a Point of Order, Mr Lofthouse. For those of us who wish to speak in the debate, may I ask whether it would be in order to describe what it is we are debating. The actual act." Trying to save me some Honourable Members shouted, "We all know." Bill Walker went on. "In order to debate, it must be in order to describe an actual act so that we can be absolutely certain that there is no doubt outside this Chamber about what we are debating."

Now it was my turn. I just replied, "It is a matter of the words and language that are used. And long interventions do not help." I think Bill Walker was aware that I was less than pleased at the type of questioning and he did not pursue the matter.

In the early days of my Deputy Speakership, I did not give much consideration to controlling my liquid input before assuming the chair. I had reached the age when male waterworks are not reliable. I recall that on several occasions in my two hour stints, I only just managed to complete the period without needing the toilet. Gradually I learnt to control my input to perfection and to deny myself liquids for about two hours before I took the Chair. This was successful apart from one occasion. One Friday I took the Chair at 12.15 pm, knowing that the House was to adjourn at 3 pm. I felt the urge about 2 pm. I was getting very desperate about 2.30 pm when fortunately for me a Division was moved. I called the Division and left the Chair unoccupied as I ran for the toilet. I do not think anyone noticed that the Chair was vacant. I got away with it, though if some mischievous MP had spotted the empty Chair and had moved a Point of Order, I would have been in big trouble.

In days past, or so I've heard, there used to be a curtain around the Chair and a bucket under it. If the Speaker found himself in a similar position as I found myself that day he would draw the curtain and relieve himself in the bucket.

* * * * *

There have been many times, especially in the last ten years, which have brought home to me what a privileged person I have become because of the wonderful occasions I have been able to experience. As Deputy Speaker I was entitled to a front seat when visiting heads of state were addressing both Houses of Parliament. I occupied a front seat on 10 November 1992 in the Royal Gallery when President Yeltsin, President of Russia - the first President of Russia the world has known - addressed us. Only briefly meeting President Yeltsin I formed the opinion that he was a very cold and tough character.

The Clintons were just the opposite, witty and able to reach out to people. On 29 November 1995 I took my seat as Deputy Speaker on the front row in the Royal Gallery when William Jefferson Clinton, President of the USA, addressed both Houses of Parliament. He is a very smart, impressive figure, big and good looking, who seems to dwarf all around him. I noticed that the Churchill family - Lady Soames, Churchill's daughter, his grandsons Winston and Nicholas - were seated at the side of the platform. I was later informed that the Clintons had made a special request to meet them. The United States Navy had named a powerful guided missile destroyer after her father, and Lady Soames had been given the honour of presiding at its launching. She is the first American warship to be named after a 'foreigner'. I suspect the meeting had been arranged to ask for permission of the Churchill family for this honour to be conferred upon the late Sir Winston.

In Madam Speaker's address she was once again her impressive self and I quote her speech in full as an example of the sort of oratory expected of the Speaker of the House of Commons on these occasions, at which Betty excelled. *(Appendix L)*

Following the speeches, the President and Mrs Clinton and their entourage went on a conducted tour of the Palace. They shook hands with everyone they passed and had several conversations in the Lordship's Lobby, with peers, senior officers and junior staff. I am informed that both the President and Mrs Clinton displayed a special interest in what is known as the Modesty Curtains which are directly in front of the seats reserved on the balcony for the wives of their Lordships. I understand these curtains were placed in that position to stop amorous peers looking up the ladies' skirts and getting excited, which could become too much for them and possibly create high blood pressure problems. If the Clintons did show such interest, for the life of me I cannot understand why.

I was especially impressed by Mrs Clinton, her elegance and poise and her obvious intelligence. This led me to think of an apocryphal story which I was once told: It seems that the Clintons pulled up at a gas station. Whilst the attendant was filling the tank, Mrs Clinton left the car and approached the attendant with enthusiasm. After she returned to the car, the President said, "You were keen to speak to that man." Mrs Clinton replied, "He was my first boyfriend when we are at high school." The President replied, "I bet you are glad you married me. You are the First Lady of the United States. If you had married him you would have been the wife of a gas jockey." Mrs Clinton replied, "No dear, he would have been the President of the United States!"

I have formed the opinion that Bill Clinton was of strong character and will, high intelligence and charm. This was borne out by the great pressures he must have experienced during the period of his impeachment. I never thought I would live to see the day when an American President would be impeached, but Clinton's inner strength and political success as President stood him in good stead, but I think it impossible to overestimate the pressures to which he must have been subjected. These surely must have been overcome by the character of the man and the support of the formidable First Lady.

On 15 May 1996 I sat on the front row when the President of France, President Chirac, addressed both Houses of Parliament in the Royal Gallery. There had been some rumours that the authorities responsible for making the arrangements were in some difficulty in using the Royal Gallery of the Lords because it was thought that the large paintings of the Battle of Trafalgar and the Battle of Waterloo, two great French defeats at the hands of the British, would cause offence. Rumour had it that President De Gaulle addressed both Houses of Parliament on 7 April 1960 from Westminster Hall for this reason. It is said that prior to President Chirac's visit our Ambassador to France telephoned Black Rod and suggested it may be appropriate to cover up the paintings. Black Rod disagreed. He took the view that if he was to see the Royal Gallery, he must see the paintings. However, I noticed that President Chirac did not leave the Royal Gallery by passing the paintings. He made his exit via the Robing Room, beyond the Royal Gallery.

The Speaker could always set the right tone. Never an elitist, her enthusiasms were always close to the enthusiasms of the people as this speech to President Chirac shows:

"You will have noticed the flags of our two Countries flying side by side in the streets of London in honour of your visit. What you may not know is that throughout last weekend the tricolour was borne in triumph by thousands of people through the streets of Manchester. It was not, I fear, in honour of any of your great statesmen or philosophers or generals, it was a tribute to somebody who many of my fellow countrymen, not altogether light-heartedly, regard as the greatest living Frenchman. I refer to Eric Cantona who scored the winning goal in the Football Cup Final on Saturday and became the hero of a large proportion of the British sporting public. His success drawing attention to the increased interchange of football players between our two countries is only part of the innumerable contacts between France and the United Kingdom and outstandingly, there is now the Channel Tunnel. The Tunnel is not just a matter of making travelling easier between our two countries, though it carried 13 million passengers last year with its numbers growing daily. It brought you to London in speed and comfort this week. The Tunnel is a symbol of the closeness of the United Kingdom and France. It demonstrates the fact that though there may be occasional political differences between our two countries - and let's admit it, there are bound to be differences from time to time between democracies - we are now joined physically as well as being part of the European union. As we stand here in the Royal Gallery of the Palace of Westminster, it seems appropriate to remember how our history and our destiny have been intertwined and to emphasise how many common values are shared by our two different nations."

On 11 July 1996 I was again present in my usual front row seat on the occasion of the visit of Nelson Mandela, President of the Republic of South Africa. I had previously met him when he visited Britain not long after his release from prison. Then he had come to Britain to address a meeting of the Anti-Apartheid movement. My friend, Bob Hughes - at that time Member of Parliament for Aberdeen - now Lord Hughes, had been active for many years in the Anti-Apartheid movement and the 'Free Nelson Mandela' campaign. Bob kindly introduced me to this great man. It was an experience I will never forget. As he shook my hand it was like an electric shock going through me. Here was a man who had spent more than a third of his life in jail because he was determined to end Apartheid yet whose spirit was far stronger than that of his captors. He was very remarkable, for he had emerged with no feeling of personal bitterness to those who had denied his freedom. I was humbled, for here I was meeting a man who held the key to establishing a new and multiracial

South Africa. What a privilege for me. It was certainly the highlight of my political life.

I was not to know that I would once more have the opportunity to meet this great man when he had become the President of the Republic of South Africa, and less was I to know I would be Deputy Speaker of the House of Commons. President Mandela's address was given in Westminster Hall and not in the Royal Gallery. This was only the third time a visiting head of state had addressed both Houses of Parliament from this great hall during the last sixty years; on 23 March 1939 President Le Brun of France, on 7 April 1960 President De Gaulle of France; and then President Mandela.

On this occasion, the Great Hall was full. Although it was the Royal Courts of Justice until 1882, it resonated with history. This is where state trials, including those of Thomas Moore and Charles I, took place, and where in more recent years monarchs and distinguished statesmen had laid in state. As I arrived, dressed in the Deputy Speaker's morning suit, I walked through the middle gangway with hundreds of people sitting on each side and took my seat on the front row in an atmosphere of great excitement. We all felt privileged to have the opportunity to hear and meet a great man. After the platform party had arrived, and after being announced by a fanfare of trumpets, the Speaker, the Lord Chancellor and their staff arrived and also took their seats. The Prime Minister, the Leader of the Opposition and Members of Government and Shadow Ministers all sat in the front rows.

A fanfare of trumpets announced the arrival of the "President of the Republic of South Africa, Mr Nelson Mandela, accompanied by his daughter, Princess Zenani Mandela Dlamini". On this the Speaker and the Lord Chancellor rose from their seats and climbed the steps towards St Stephen's Entrance. As the President and his party arrived at the entrance steps to Westminster Hall accompanied by the Speaker and the Lord Chancellor, it was noticeable the President looked rather unsteady on his feet. Typical of Betty, she immediately took his hand and assisted him down the steps. As I sat and watched her assisting this great man, I thought to myself, "Betty, of the many highlights in your period of Speaker, this one will never be surpassed."

As I listened to the Lord Chancellor's introductory speech I was reminded of the enthusiasm with which the formerly disenfranchised black South Africans had queued for days to have the opportunity of casting their vote. I contrasted this with the complacency and apathy of many British voters who no longer feel obliged to cast theirs. They are privileged to have lived in a country that founded parliamentary democracy and yet the Conservative administration was sustained for nearly 20 years by no more than 43% of the population.

He spoke with great passion of Macmillan's Wind Of Change speech and the need to construct a new universal order in which we are each our brothers' and our sisters' keeper. *(Appendix M)*

Then it was Betty's turn. She noted that the past century had witnessed many horrors but that there had been great triumphs and one of the greatest belonged to the President and the new South Africa. He represented an outstanding victory of the human spirit over evil, for one of the major immoralities of the century was Apartheid. In the end through his generosity of spirit he held the key not only to his own release, but also that to establishing a new and multiracial nation which, although suffering difficult birth pangs, even now was steadily taking form.

More than most of us Betty had a right to speak, for she had belonged to the Black Sash Movement, an organisation of ordinary white women driven by a sense of decency and fair play, who would stand in silent vigil outside South Africa House in Trafalgar Square, draped in black sashes hoping to instil some sense of shame into the people inside. The last thing in her mind in those days, she said, was that as Speaker of the House of Commons she would one day travel to a free South Africa and sit in at local government meetings where members of all races would be represented and speak with each other in an atmosphere of mutual respect. Even less did she expect that she would receive Nelson Mandela in Westminster Hall as President of the South African Republic and see him honoured rapturously by both Houses of Parliament.

What a privilege for me to have been part of it. No occasion I have taken part in through my political career has ever surpassed the emotion of that particular day. At the end of the proceedings, the

President, holding his daughter's hand, left the platform and walked down the middle gangway between the many hundreds of people. As he moved past the rows of seats, the people seated to the end of the rows near the gangways put their hands out to touch him. He acknowledged everyone by shaking their hands. How touched we all were at this man's presence. It was truly unforgettable.

I later discussed the occasion with Black Rod, General Sir Edward Jones, the man who had been involved with making the arrangements for the visit. Like me he had been fascinated by Betty leading Nelson Mandela down the steps but he added a lovely story about Nelson Mandela.

At about 7 am on the morning of the great occasion, a black limousine pulled up at St Stephen's entrance and much to the surprise of the policeman on duty, from it out got Nelson Mandela. The policeman said, "Good morning sir, but you are a little early." The statesman explained. Prior to his imprisonment, he had visited London and had a photograph taken outside St Stephen's entrance and he was keen to do so again, just by himself.

Imagine General Jones' surprise to be told, by the duty policeman, when he arrived much later at St Stephen's entrance on his way to his office to organise the Lords for the great occasion, "Sorry sir, he has been and gone."

I was also privileged to be present in Westminster Hall on 5 May 1995 for the address by Her Majesty the Queen to both Houses of Parliament to commemorate the 50th Anniversary of the end of World War II. I walked to my seat on the front row like many times before, sometimes in the early hours of the morning during the period when I was on the back-benches. At that time I occupied an office in St Stephen's Tower and I always walked through this great hall on my way to and fro for Divisions. I found the vast empty space relaxing. I could always feel its history. However, this particular morning I felt very different. Here I was, dressed up in my Deputy Speaker's gear, going to take my place as Deputy Speaker of the House of Commons, to hear Her Majesty speak on this very special day.

I thought, "Here I am, a lad from the coal mines who had spent most of his working life down a big hole in the ground, crawling in the earth under Featherstone. How have I got here? And what an honour and privilege it was to be part of this as Deputy Speaker of the House of Commons." I was not to know that within a few weeks I would be meeting Her Majesty again at Buckingham Palace when she would bestow on me the great honour of a knighthood. I was also not to know that two years later I was to be honoured by becoming a Peer of the Realm.

The Great Hall is the only remaining part of the Ancient Palace of Westminster. The original hall was completed in 1099 and is 230 feet long, 68 feet wide and 90 feet high. It has suffered the ravage of death watch beetle. Very extensive restorations were concluded in 1992 and it can now be seen at its best. The beautiful roof was severely damaged by incendiary bombs in 1941 and again in 1944, and repairs were not completed until 1950. Perhaps because its history is as chequered as mine I can yet have some ownership. It is close to me in another way. There is some opinion that the original stone came from Kirk Smeaton near Pontefract and was quarried not half a mile from where my two grandchildren were born.

Shortly after taking my seat on the front row, the fanfare by the State trumpeters announced the arrival of Her Majesty accompanied by HRH Prince Philip, Duke of Edinburgh, HRH Prince of Wales and HRH Princess Margaret, Countess of Snowdon. They had been preceded by the Lord Chancellor, Madam Speaker and the Archbishop of Canterbury.

That day's ceremony belongs to a long and well established tradition of communications between the Sovereign and the Houses of Parliament. The first of these addresses to both Houses is recorded in 1540. Until the end of the 19th century, addresses presented to both Houses as a whole were received at one of the Royal residences but in 1897 both Houses presented addresses to Queen Victoria at Buckingham Palace to congratulate Her Majesty on the completion of the sixtieth year of her reign. In the twentieth century it has been the practice for the Sovereign to come to Westminster to receive addresses. On the first occasion, the Armistice of November 1918, the ceremony took place in the Royal Gallery. In 1945 the addresses marking the end of the war in Europe and victory over Japan were also presented in the Royal Gallery. The first event when addresses were presented in Westminster Hall was in 1935 on the occasion of the Silver Jubilee of King George V. This was only the sixth occasion on which addresses had been presented in the Hall. The others had been the opening of the new Commons Chamber in 1950, the 700th anniversary of the Parliament of Simon de Montfort in 1965, the Queen's Silver Jubilee in 1977 and the 300th anniversary of the Glorious Revolution in 1988.

Considering that only three heads of state have addressed both Houses from Westminster Hall since 1939, I have often heard conversations about who makes the decisions on who should be invited and which Hall visitors should speak from. There are different opinions. Some say that the French will not tolerate the pictures of Waterloo and Trafalgar. As I understand it, Westminster Hall is subject to control by three parties: The Queen, The Lord Chancellor and the Speaker, and the use of the Hall is subject to their joint decision. Any request, either internal or external - for instance from the Foreign and Commonwealth Office - is referred to the Speaker, who will state the view of the House to Black Rod, who will obtain the views of the Lord Great Chamberlain, and the Lord Chancellor. Officials of the three parties may consult amongst themselves before producing what is usually a joint view. I understand the basic guidelines for the use of the Hall are that it should be used only for parliamentary purposes, with relevance to one or both Houses, or for historical reasons connected with the Hall and previous events there.

I understand the use of the Royal Gallery is administered by Black Rod through both the Lord Great Chamberlain and the Lord Chancellor. It does appear to me that great consideration is given to the status of the person and the expected attendance. I am sure due consideration will be given by the decision-makers if they feel the attendance may be insufficient to warrant the use of Westminster Hall. However, there is still a little mystery to how the decisions are made.

These authorities will not be bullied. When President Reagan addressed both Houses on 8 June 1992, Mrs Thatcher was keen that he should give his address from Westminster Hall, but in her dictatorial way according to House of Commons rumours, she had not consulted the appropriate authorities. It is said that Michael Foot, then Leader of the Opposition, objected to not being consulted. Whether this is true or not, President Reagan did not get the Hall but made his address from the Royal Gallery.

* * * * *

Derek Enright had been a personal and political friend of mine for over 40 years. A classical Latin scholar and the Deputy Headmaster at St Wilfrid's Roman Catholic High School at Featherstone prior to his parliamentary career, he was elected as a Member of the first European Parliament representing Leeds. He later lost that seat on a re-selection but was nominated as the Party's candidate and eventually elected Member of Parliament for the Hemsworth Constituency following the untimely death of George Buckley. From there he served that constituency with great distinction until his death.

In the 74 years I have lived, I regard him to be one of the finest human beings I was ever privileged to be associated with. He was a scholar who always used his great academic gifts for the benefits of those less intellectually endowed. He was a kind and caring man. I never, on any occasion, heard him speak ill of anyone. During political confrontations he would never take part in political intrigue but would always attempt to defend any person who was under attack. I am afraid I used to say to him sometimes, "You are rather politically naïve Derek." But he would have none of it.

It was a great sadness to me when Derek fell the victim of cancer. He told me early on of the medical findings, which must have been a very severe blow to him, but he never showed it. As the months rolled by he rapidly deteriorated. I will never forget meeting him at the Brighton Labour Party Conference in 1995. By that time he was barely recognisable. He appeared to be so weak and it was incredible that he had managed to be present. As I watched Jane assist him, my personal emotions got the better of me. But when I went to speak to Derek, even though his voice was weak, he immediately put me at my ease. He made no reference to his illness and just talked about the wonderful speech Tony Blair had made. Just a few days after the conference Derek was admitted to St Thomas' Hospital. I recall sitting on the Terrace mostly on evenings with other Members, and Derek would wave from his window from his room in St Thomas' overlooking the Palace of Westminster,.

My lasting memories of him come from my frequent visits to the hospital. I have never experienced anyone so close to death being so brave. He would talk so easily about dying. My previous experience when visiting seriously ill people was that I found it somewhat difficult to discuss death. There was none of this with Derek, he would talk of his coming end quite openly. I well recall my last visit. His words to me were, "Well I shall not be long now Geoff. Hell of a pity I am not going to be here for the election, I would have loved to have been here for when Labour forms the next government."

Derek died in October 1995. This was the same month he attended the Labour Party Conference. I was greatly honoured when Jane, Derek's wife, invited me to give the eulogy at his funeral. I consider it to be a mark both of the esteem in which he was held by the Roman Catholic hierarchy and his popularity with his parliamentary colleagues, that his funeral service was conducted in Westminster Cathedral. This huge and magnificent building, dominated by a tower of 300ft, stands less than a mile from the Palace of Westminster. It is the principal Roman Catholic place of worship in the United Kingdom and it was also one of the few Roman Catholic churches in London or elsewhere big enough to accommodate Derek's mourners, many of whom had travelled down from Pontefract and District. They travelled the 200 miles to recall this modest, dignified man.

Although I had walked past the Cathedral many times, I had never been inside. I was impressed by the vast, shadowy, soaring space inside. The lower walls and pillars are faced with marble in shades of jade, rust and cream. The upper reaches are being sheathed in glittering mosaic as money permits to happen, but there are still large expanses of brick, blackened now by the soot of a century. This darkness adds much to the massive grandeur of the interior, which nonetheless has a feeling of warmth and welcome.

The officiating priest was an old pupil of Derek's and he told how he would have them translating the *Guardian* leaders into Ciceronian Latin before the school-day began. I found the nave was so long that the pulpit from which I was to give my eulogy was half way down. This meant that I had a little walk from where I was seated. The congregation was led by Tony Blair and the Shadow Cabinet and included a great many of Derek's friends who he had made in the course of an active and varied life. I felt humbled to be addressing them all, and in such splendid surroundings.

I knew, through my conversations with Derek during the latter days of his life, he would not want me to be mournful and after expressing my tributes to his life, I highlighted two occasions which I thought he would like. As I stood in the pulpit the roof of Westminster Cathedral seemed to go on forever and I have to admit to being nervous. The setting was awe-inspiring, three priests were either side of me, a young man to lead me in quiet dignity to the microphone. I recognised most of the people present. They were a mixed bag of both political parties, media people and a real mixed bag of Pontefract folk. There were his fellows Catholics, Anglicans like myself, nonconformists, and here and there an agnostic or even an atheist or two, all brought together through their love and affection for a remarkable man. Although I wanted to speak as I found him; honourable, sincere, amusing, brave - a friend, I was not sure if I could carry this one off. I knew how easily my emotions could take over. My personal uncertainty however was held in check by what I saw in front of me. All these most powerful men and women in the land were gathered with local people who didn't have much influence at all. For once I realised politics was a million miles away. What united them was genuine affection for Derek. I told two stories which I know would very much have been appreciated by him. One was the occasion when Sir Nicholas Fairburn, in what we in the House call a tired and emotional state, goaded Derek into singing the famous Beatles classic *Yellow Submarine* in Latin. I also told them the story of Derek's usual kindness when my late wife Sarah was approaching the end of her life. It was a Friday. Sarah was very ill with cancer and I was standing at the window of the ward in Pontefract General Infirmary when I saw Derek approaching, obviously just back from Brussels or Strasbourg. I saw him bend down and pick some daffodils from the flower-bed. In minutes he was up on the ward, presenting Sarah with the blooms. I walked with him down the corridor to the exit. "They were lovely flowers," I said, "where did you get them?" He didn't pause, "Duty free," he replied.

Apart from the sorrow of the occasion, saying goodbye to a dear friend and colleague, it was one of the most impressive events of my life and in hindsight, whilst I was apprehensive of performing this duty, as I later told Derek's mother when she very kindly thanked me for my address, I had found it very easy because I was able to be totally sincere. Every word I uttered about him was the truth. I continue to miss him.

* * * * *

I was completely bowled over when in April 1995 I received a letter from the then Prime Minister John Major informing me he was "mindful of recommending to Her Majesty The Queen that she should bestow on me a Knighthood for my service in public life." He requested I should inform him if I would accept such an honour. It took a day or two to sink in. Having always hoped to continue in my public life in the Upper Chamber when the day came for me to leave the House of Commons, I wondered whether if I accepted the honour of a Knighthood, it would jeopardise the chances of me fulfilling this desire. I found some difficulty in making a decision. I was unable to discuss it with trusted colleagues because the invitation was private and confidential. I thought long and hard. I was not aware that any other previous Pontefract MP had ever received a knighthood, certainly not from the Labour side of politics. I gave serious consideration to the past history of this famous market town of Pontefract. I genuinely thought that if I accepted it would not only be an honour for myself and my family but an honour for the whole town. Bearing all this in mind and after discussing it with my beloved daughter, Lynne, who like her late mum was never keen on the limelight of public life, and with my great colleague and friend, Betty Boothroyd, I decided I would accept the great honour and duly informed John Major of my decision.

I did not hear anything further until I received a letter from Buckingham Palace informing me that Her Majesty was to honour me by bestowing on me the title of Knight Bachelor. This was to be announced in the *London Gazette* at midnight on 16 June 1995. The letter was delivered to me by one of the attendants in the House of Commons. These people are mostly former service personnel who become very expert on the proceedings of the House and act as doorkeepers and generally look after the needs of the House of Commons when the House is sitting. I have often wondered if the attendant who delivered the letter, or his colleagues, were aware of its content. Since they must have delivered similar letters previously to other people I was suspicious of their knowledge. This was aroused when, on my way to take the Chair, one of them said, "Good morning Sir." It was not unusual to address me as "Sir", because all the attendants addressed me in this way. This was probably arising out of their military training. However, my suspicions were really aroused when one of them said to me with a mischievous smile, "Does my colleague know something we don't, sir?" If this was the case I knew that these men would never leak any information of this nature.

When the 1995 Queen's Birthday Honours List was announced at midnight on 16 June 1995, there commenced a very hectic weekend. The telephone never stopped ringing. After fifty years in public life, one way or another, I thought I could cope with most things, but I was not prepared for the reception the announcement created. People from all parts of my past life contacted me and my emotions became so affected they overwhelmed me. I spent the weekend on cloud nine. The following few days I had a massive postbag and I found great pleasure hearing from close friends, some of whom I had not seen or heard from for many years. What a pleasure I found in replying to them all.

When I arrived at the House of Commons on the following Monday, it was a usual Monday morning. I arrived in my office at about 10 am. I began the day's work looking through correspondence and considering applications from Members requesting to speak in that day's debate. At about 11.30 am, I received a message from Tony Blair's office saying he would like to see me in the Shadow Cabinet Room at 6.30 pm. I thought Tony would want to offer me his congratulations and I did not give the message any further thought, but to my amazement when I arrived the room was full. All the Shadow Cabinet were present including John Prescott, Gordon

Brown, Robin Cook, Jack Cunningham, the full team along with the former Deputy Leader of the Labour Party, Roy Hattersley, and a host of my parliamentary colleagues. Unknown to me, Ann Taylor had organised a party in my honour and had kept it secret from me. I must confess I was overwhelmed. All Members present offered their congratulations. Tony then made a congratulatory speech which really touched my emotions. He referred to my work for the Party both in the House of Commons and not least my work as Deputy Speaker. He went on to say he thought Members present would agree that I was probably the most respected Member of the House and he thought this view was held on both sides of the House. This caused my emotions to flow and I did not find it easy to reply to Tony's speech, although I think I just about managed. The following few days I received about 200 letters from colleagues of all sides of the House. I then had the task of personally replying to them in my own hand.

The day the Queen bestowed on me the honour of Knight Bachelor was 29 July 1995. I had investigated the procedures and found that the Queen, and occasionally another member of the Royal family on her behalf, confers knighthoods in Britain. The knight-elect can be knighted at a public investiture or privately. After his name is announced the knight-elect kneels on a knighting stool in front of the Queen who then lays the sword blade on the knight's right and then left shoulder. After he has been dubbed, the new knight stands up. Contrary to popular belief, the words "Arise, Sir Geoffrey..." are not used. The Queen then invests the knight with the insignia of the Order to which he has been appointed, a star or badge depending on the Order. By tradition, clergy receiving a knighthood are not dubbed, as the use of a sword is thought inappropriate for their calling.

I had been advised by the Palace that I would only be allowed three members of my family to accompany me. Of course, there was no difficulty in deciding who the three would be, my daughter Lynne and my two grandchildren, Thomas and Eleanor. This unfortunately left out my son-in-law. However, he did accompany us and waited in the Courtyard of Buckingham Palace while we went inside for the ceremony. I was very proud when I saw Lynne and Eleanor dressed in their Sunday best and Thomas and Tim, my son-in-law, dressed in morning suits and toppers. While Lynne and the children took their seats in the Ballroom where the investiture took place. Lieutenant Colonel Malcolm Ross, Comptroller, Lord Chamberlain's Office explained the ceremony and what we should do when approaching Her Majesty to me and the other eight people receiving knighthoods. I will never forget the pride I felt in having Lynne, my grandchildren and son-in-law with me to share this wonderful occasion.

I never really became used to being called Sir Geoffrey. Some of my friends would say to me, "What do we call you now?"

My stock answer would always be, "My mother called me Geoff and she never gave me permission to change it."

In early April 1997 I received a letter from the then Prime Minister John Major, telling me that he was to recommend to Her Majesty that she should honour me by offering me the opportunity of becoming a Peer of the Realm.

The knowledge that a peerage was being offered brought problems. I had decided that I would not contest the 1997 General Election. An antagonising decision for me, for I had no intention of retiring until a few weeks before the election.

In 1996 I had been challenged through the re-selection procedure by Norman Kennedy, Deputy Leader of Wakefield MDC. He sought nominations against me but failed to receive the required number of nominations to enable him to be considered. In fact he only received the nominations of two branches; Ferry Fryston and the Transport and General Workers. I received the rest. I took all the nominations from the Party branches and organisations entitled to nominate. Norman realised this and one Sunday afternoon called to see me and told me he was pulling out of the contest. Of course, having not received sufficient nominations, he had no alternative. I was pleased at the confidence the nominating bodies had shown in me and I was looking forward to the election and to continuing to be the MP for Pontefract and Castleford, and to my position as Deputy Speaker.

As the General Election approached, I was not feeling too well. This was probably the forerunner of the heart attack I suffered in September 1997. I began to wonder whether I should stand for election. I thought, "Will I be able to stand the pace of another five

149

years in the Chair and the ever-increasing constituency workload?"
However, my mind was made up for me when I read an article in *The
Times* newspaper which suggested that I was to stand down in favour
of Alan Howarth, the former Conservative Member who had crossed
the floor of the House. It was rumoured that the Party hierarchy were
keen to find him a Labour seat. However, at that point I had not at any
time seriously considered standing down, and in the circumstances
referred to in the newspaper report, I would never allow this to
happen. I knew that my constituents, not least my miner colleagues,
would never forgive me. And more importantly, I would never forgive
myself. I made a protest to *The Times* and requested an apology and
denial, which they very kindly agreed to give to cover my costs. That
was the end of it as far as I was concerned.

Then I read reports that Alan Howarth had been selected for a Welsh
seat, so I had no need to bother. I was beginning to feel very tired and
feeling unwell. Everything seemed to be an effort and I wondered if I
was being fair to myself and my family and, indeed, to my
constituents if I carried on. I wondered, would my health stand up to
another five years. I had reached seventy. For once I was beginning to
feel very low and uncertain. I was also under pressure from my
daughter and many friends not to stand for re-election. At that point I
approached my friend Ann Taylor about my dilemma, after receiving
medical advice that it may be wise for me to ease my workload. If I
were to retire, I would want a categorical assurance that members of
my own local Party would be considered for nomination. Ann
suggested that I should discuss it with Tony Blair. I took her advice
and met Tony and told him how I felt. I thought it would be better,
both for myself and the constituency, if I stood down and allowed a
younger Member to take over from me. However, I made it clear to
both the Leader and Ann that I would not consider standing down if
the Party imposed a candidate on the constituency without giving the
local constituency members a chance to offer themselves for
consideration and, indeed, to select the candidate in a democratic way,
One Member - One Vote. Tony was happy to give me that assurance
and indeed said he would do so in writing, which he did.

Notwithstanding this assurance, I was still agonising. I knew Betty
Boothroyd did not want me to retire and I arranged a meeting with

her before I made my decision. Betty recognised my difficulty, but she was very upset that I was considering leaving the House of Commons. We had developed a sound and trusting working partnership and, of course, had great affection for each other. This had grown over many years. She requested me not to make a hasty decision, but recognised that if my health was suspect, that must come first. After further discussion with my daughter, family and close political friends, including some senior members of the Constituency Party, I finally decided not to stand for re-election to Parliament as MP for Pontefract and Castleford.

When the news broke it certainly caused a stir within the constituency. There were all sorts of rumours as to why I had taken the decision, which was understandable seeing that my decision had come so close to the General Election. But as always on such occasions most of these rumours were very wide off the mark. *The Times* newspaper was understandably concerned after they had given me an apology for the article I have previously referred to. I could well understand that. The day I made my decision was on Thursday 27 March 1997 at about 12 pm.

Now many aspiring candidates threw their cap in the ring. I had travelled back home from London and arrived about 4.30 pm. By 6 pm a man knocked on my door. He had travelled from London and he called to seek my support for the nomination. This type of approach continued right up to the time of the selection meeting.

The Party machinery was set in motion. Eventually eleven candidates who had been nominated were placed on a long list. This included four members of the Pontefract and Castleford Constituency Labour Party. These were interviewed by the appropriate Selection Panel in London. Unfortunately, none of the four were shortlisted.

Five people were eventually set down to come before the Party nine days after my resignation and, with one exception, they all paid me a visit. There was a lot of activity. I was also continually pressurised by the press and the media requesting me to inform them who I would be supporting. They seemed to have the mistaken impression that I would have some influence on the final decision. This could not have been further from the truth. I had no influence whatsoever. However,

151

I was pleased to see the candidates who called to see me. I am sure that it was purely a matter of courtesy on their part that they thought it was right they should call. After their visits I would have found great difficulty in deciding who to support because I formed the view that they were all excellent candidates. On the occasion of some visits a television crew must have followed their cars, because when the candidates were in my home, the cameras were outside in my garden peering into my window.

In that week there was a knock on the door and as I opened it I found a fresh-faced young lady standing there. My very first impression was that she was one of the teenagers who always pass my garden on their way from Carleton High School. I thought, "Another one. Some boy or other will have thrown her hat over my garden and she is requesting my permission to retrieve it." She certainly did look as young as that. She wasn't.

"I'm Yvette Cooper and I am on the shortlist to be considered for the Parliamentary Candidate for Pontefract and Castleford." I immediately invited her in. I think probably for the first few minutes of our discussions I may have acted in a patronising, grandfatherly way, but not for long, for I soon realised here was a special young lady.

I thought, "She certainly knows her way about." This was before I had studied her background. I was amazed at the knowledge she had of the constituency, even though she had only been around for a few days. My immediate thought, although I did not tell her, was that I thought her age and inexperience in the life of constituencies like Pontefract and Castleford, a mining stronghold, would go against her, that she would have some difficulty in convincing the delegates to the Selection Conference that she was ready to take over as Member of Parliament for Pontefract and Castleford. But there was something about her that made me think that the time had come for the constituency to change.

Like many other coalmining constituencies, Pontefract and Castleford had only had three MPs over the past 50 years, all Labour. Mr George Sylvester, Mr Joe Harper and myself were all former miners but now the influence of the mining unions in the constituency had diminished. As she left my home, I thought, "Well if she wins the nomination, there will be a minor earthquake in the political scene of Pontefract and Castleford." It will be a miracle if this very pleasant young lady pulls it off.

I investigated her background. I found she was aged 28, had been educated at Balliol College, Oxford (BA Honours PPE First Class), Harvard University (Kennedy Scholar 1991) and London School of Economics (MSc Economics). She was a professional economics journalist, had been an economic researcher for John Smith, had worked on Bill Clinton's presidential campaign in 1992, had been advisor to Labour Treasury teams, an economic columnist and leader writer for the *Independent*. Impressive by any standards. I thought, "What a change she would be from the previous Members of Parliament of a constituency over the last 50 years; all had left school at the age of 14, but had great experience in the constituency."

In his famous speech on South Africa Harold Macmillan had talked of the Winds of Change blowing through a continent, now that wind might have arrived in Pontefract. However, it was still somewhat of a surprise to me and, indeed, I think many others in the constituency, when at the Selection Meeting, she was elected as candidate to contest the Pontefract and Castleford Constituency as the Labour candidate by the majority vote of about 250 delegates. I was later told by many delegates that she had taken the meeting by storm and she had performed brilliantly.

She very kindly paid me an immediate visit after her success and I was delighted. Indeed it was with great confidence that I went to assist her with the election campaign. This she carried out brilliantly. I never ceased to be amazed how she immediately grasped the problems of the constituency and how the constituency warmed to her. It was of no surprise to me that she achieved a 25,000 majority. I shall never forget my feelings at the count when she achieved this success. I felt no regret that I had retired, for I had a feeling of great comfort that I was being replaced by this exceptional young lady. I later gazed down with pride from the Visitors Gallery in the House of Commons when Yvette made her maiden speech. In all the years I have been in the House of Commons, both as a back-bencher and

Deputy Speaker, I have never heard a maiden speech given more confidently. The content was first class and learned. Her knowledge of the constituency was impressive. I gained great comfort that I had left the Pontefract and Castleford Constituency in safe hands. *(Appendix R)*

Two other young ladies in fact had gained seats in industrial strongholds; Rosie Winterton who took over from Harold Walker, former Deputy Speaker, at Doncaster and Caroline Flint had taken over from my dear and late colleague, Martin Redman at Don Valley. All three ladies came from the South. If anyone had tried to convince me no more than two years before their election that this was possible within our Party system, I would have thought there was something radically wrong with their thinking. This certainly indicated to me we had witnessed the wind of change sweeping through Tony Blair's Labour Party. This wind of change had obviously influenced the electorate, resulting in the massive vote of confidence the electorate gave to the New Labour Party at the 1997 General Election.

Women clearly have a major contribution to make to Parliament and whilst it has only been since the election of 1992 and 1997 that there has been a significant increase of women Members, I recognise that the success Labour achieved in the 1997 General Election meant that some young women who had fought seats they would in normal circumstances be expected not to win, in fact did so. Of course this does not only apply to women Members, but also to young men. However, whilst recognising the rights of women to become MPs if they so wished, I believe they will always find themselves at a disadvantage. It has always been acknowledged that women are the main foundation for stability in the home and they are the ones the children mainly turn to for comfort and love especially when small. Most women have a natural desire to be with their babies and small children.

This was brought home to me on one occasion in the House. One early evening, in that period when Members first started using electronic pagers - a device which makes a bleeping noise to alert the Member there is a phone message for them - I heard one go off. I had on a few occasions in the previous few days warned Members not to bring them into the Chamber because it tended to be a distraction on the debate. A lady Member realised I was not pleased following my previous warning so immediately left the Chamber. When she returned about ten minutes later she came to the Chair and apologised, "That was my six year old phoning to tell me he had just been sick and wanted me." It was clear where she would prefer to be. I noticed that the child had rung his mum, not his dad.

I also regret there appears to be evidence emerging that there are casualties arising from women being parted from their husbands and children to attend Parliament. Since 1997 I know of two ladies whose marriages have collapsed and I fear that there may be more. The risks may not be greater than the present rate of failed marriages in all walks of life.

I hope these reflections do not seem to come from an old man reflecting on the past, who has enjoyed a stable, traditional family life. I lost my father when I was aged four, but I have always valued the love, comfort and security my mother and extended family gave to me. They were always there whatever minor need I might have required at the time. I am convinced the need of a child for its mother is paramount and will never change. If a child is denied this, then I am sure it will be to the child's loss. Of course, it might well be that attitudes have changed and my views are obsolete and this situation created by the advancement of equal opportunities for women might not be a problem. When I emphasise my views on a woman's place being with her children, it may be that the young women of today may find the answer to balancing their interests and careers without affecting the normal bonding with their children through their absence. I certainly hope so.

During the period from 1992 there had been an attempt to re-organise and modernise the proceedings which would be more convenient for Members, not least for the women. Ann Taylor has played a leading part in this quiet revolution. There has been the introduction of Wednesday morning sittings which replaced a procedure which was called "Debating the consolidating Fund". This meant that Members could make application for a debate of a particular subject of their own interests which would take place throughout the whole of the night prior to a recess. I always thought this was a crazy idea having been a victim of it myself on several occasions. The debates now take place on Wednesday mornings. More recently, the House has begun to sit at 11.30 am on Thursday mornings and rise at 7.30 pm. This enables Members to return to their constituencies on a Thursday evening and so gives people whose constituencies are remote from London an extra day to work in their constituency.

Some older Members express concern that some of the young Members, both male and female, have not had sufficient experience in the rough and tumble of working in industry or the outside world in general. They complain that while they have experience in academic life and the public services, they have not received the experience which would benefit them in the work as a Member of Parliament. I have heard many experienced MPs say, "We used to have a trade union group of about 100 Members in the House and, indeed, a miners group of about 40 strong," and express concern that the membership has got so out of balance that the horny-handed sons of toil have about vanished. They feel that this is not to the benefit of Parliament. I have heard people say it is like a Sixth Form College. I do not believe this to be the case. I think some of the remarks are just those of old men basking in nostalgia.

I have been responsible for such thoughts myself, but now I accept things can never stand still and I feel great pride and pleasure that my own generation have been responsible, through the Labour movement, in giving the young people the opportunities of higher education which were denied to thousands of young working class people of my generation.

I don't call these young MPs Blair Babes but rather the Wilson Babes. Their opportunity was the result of the white-hot heat of technological change and the comprehensive system of education which that Prime Minister introduced. Now whilst I recognise that not all the children of that generation were educated in the comprehensive system, many were. Whatever system they were educated in, it is a fact that many of these are children given the opportunity of further education previously denied to their parents. When I look and listen to some of these young MPs I feel how fortunate the Labour Party is to have such bright young people representing them in Parliament. I look on with pride that the Party has produced what I believe are the two outstanding politicians of the day, Tony Blair and Gordon Brown. I also know that there are many more waiting in the wings, not least the women.

When listening to speeches from newcomers after the 1992 election, I would frequently jot down names, guessing who will eventually become Ministers. I identified Tessa Jowell, Estelle Morris, Barbara Roche, Janet Anderson, Kate Hoey and Glenda Jackson. When they first made their early speeches, like everyone else, their nervousness was apparent. I have always considered that there is a confidence barrier in the Chamber of the House of Commons and that barrier has to be surmounted before the Member becomes really effective. In my years in the Commons I always took a great deal of pleasure when I saw a Member break through the barrier. If they had delivered their first speech with command of detail, I knew their next speech would also be delivered with confidence. There were also newcomers amongst the men I identified as future stars: John Denham, Alan Millburn, Geoffrey Hoon, Stephen Byers, Alistair Darling and Michael O'Brien. All of these men along with the women have now achieved ministerial rank.

One minor change which arises because of the influx of women I find less welcome. Prior to 1997, the House of Commons barber was Mr Stephen Silverman. I always enjoyed visiting his salon. I found him to be a wit, but some Members did not enjoy a continued conversation whilst their locks were being doctored. There was one story that when the late Enoch Powell visited him, Stephen requested how Mr Powell would like his hair cutting. Enoch replied, "In silence."

I personally miss Stephen for a trim which cost between £3 and £5. When I last visited the unisex salon that has replaced Stephen's establishment, I found it cost me £14. This was a great shock to my system and whilst I show no disrespect to the present proprietors, I now visit my local barber in Pontefract with my pensioner's pass and for £3 I think I get a good job done.

When my illness compelled my retirement from the House of Commons at the start of the General Election campaign in March 1997, I had spent nineteen years in the House, in a job I loved, working for the good of the people of the Pontefract and Castleford Constituency. I had made many good friends amongst colleagues and staff in the Palace of Westminster and for the last five years of my career in the Commons, I had been honoured to be appointed Deputy Speaker, someone with a substantial say in the conduct, order and good name of the House. I had had a better run than many, but I know from my days as a young miner that neither bodies nor careers last for ever, and now my number had been called. I found consolation in the prospect of seeing much more of family and friends at home, and I was more than willing to place my experience at the disposal of my former constituency in whatever capacity might be deemed appropriate by whoever wished to take advantage of it. I wanted to keep myself as active as my health would permit.

I had spent all but nine months of my parliamentary career in opposition, and being aware that there was a strong possibility that Labour would win the 1997 General Election, I knew it would be a tremendous pleasure for me to be present at Westminster as a member of the ruling party. I would be able to carry on working as part of a government whose freshness and vigour would be in such a startling contrast to the staleness and sleaziness of the Major years, and I would have a position which I could use to advance the interests of Pontefract and Castleford, taking care not to infringe the prerogatives of my successor as Member of Parliament. I do not think I will ever be able to describe adequately my amazement when I received that letter from the then Prime Minister John Major in early April, 1997 telling me that he was to recommend to Her Majesty that she should honour me by offering me the opportunity of becoming a Peer of the Realm. This recommendation was probably made to the Prime Minister by Tony Blair. He obviously wished that I be appointed to the House of Lords as a Member of his new creation of working Peers, men and women charged with reforming its composition, role and function. My knighthood had been enough of a surprise. I have always very strongly disapproved of the hereditary Peers having a role in the government of this country. Simply that one of their ancestors had been a successful crook a century or three ago, or just a dedicated brown-noser, didn't give them a right to make laws. I am much happier with the system of life peerages, whereby those who have distinguished themselves in their chosen field of endeavour, and in doing so have enriched the life and the finances of the country, are recognised. They then put their intelligence and experience at the nation's service through their membership of the Lords.

With this in mind, I had no hesitation informing the then Prime Minister, John Major, that I would be delighted to accept a peerage if Her Majesty was mindful of offering me such an honour. I did not have to wait long. On the Sunday morning prior to the 1997 election, I received a telephone message from Donald Dewar, the Labour Opposition Chief Whip. Donald informed me that a list was about to be announced of the names of people who Her Majesty was to appoint as Peers. He informed me that there were six Labour nominations on the list and my name was one of them. I was very pleased when the list was announced, for among the six Labour nominations were my former colleagues in the House of Commons, Don Dixon, Peter Hardy, Stan Orm, John Evans and Roy and Bob Hughes. We would go in as a team. I was really looking forward to continuing working with them.

On the day before I was introduced to the House of Lords, 12 June 1997, I had visited both Black Rod's office and the Clerk of Parliament's office, to be briefed on the procedures of the House of Lords. I decided that I would go and enjoy a bit of nostalgia by going onto the public gallery in the House of Commons. What a shock I got. As I looked down into the Chamber there were very few people I recognised. It was obvious that most of the new Members were keen to be in the Chamber. I thought to myself what a job I would have had if I had remained in the Chair getting to know the names of all these new faces. The swearing-in at the House of Lords was a great relief. There I saw many faces I had known in the House of Commons over many years. In fact, I felt really at home.

* * * * *

159

Prior to my introduction to the House of Lords I had to approach two Peers to be my supporters or sponsors. I approached my life-long colleague, Lord Mason of Barnsley and my great friend, Viscount Tonypandy. Both were delighted to accept. However, Viscount Tonypandy was not of my own rank and may be he would not be allowed to be my sponsor, although he was keen to do so. However, regrettably on the day was unable to attend the ceremony owing to illness and another close friend, Lord Gregson, took his place. The ceremony used for the introduction of newly created Peers into the House of Lords today dates from 1621. It incorporates elements from two older ceremonies, the investiture of Peers by the Sovereign on first creation and the placing of a Peer, whether on creation or on succession, in his seat in Parliament by Garter King of Arms.

It seemed odd that an ex-coal miner from Featherstone helped by a coal miner from Barnsley should be standing in the centre of the Queen's Robing Room in the Palace of Westminster putting on the ermine robes and cocked hat. I had done something similar thirty years before in 1967 when I was Mayor of Pontefract but this was an altogether more splendid setting. Appreciating the setting I wondered how a person from my background had got here. Suddenly it didn't seem so remote for I recalled that it was in this very room that the Sankey Committee sat in 1917 and recommended the nationalisation of the coal mines. Yes, the setting was not altogether alien to my aspirations. It had also another association with the Pontefract area. William Joyce, "Lord Haw-Haw", the traitor who had broadcast propaganda from Germany over the radio during the Second World War, had attended Ackworth School not four miles from where I live. He was tried for treason in this very room.

The setting is grand. The room is about the size of a tennis court and it is dominated at one end by a portrait of Christ surrounded by knights and their ladies. Christ dominates my philosophy and my life. I learnt his teaching at my mother's knee and every Sunday without fail I worship at All Saint's Church, Pontefract. I was a choirboy at six years old at North Featherstone attending Church three times a day, and acts of worship have continued throughout my life. In my time I have been a Sidesman, I have spoken from the pulpit on many an occasion and have addressed the Pontefract and District Synod. It

160

gives me great satisfaction that two of my sister Daisy's grandsons are Anglican priests and the wife of one is also an Anglican priest. Like their love, my love of Christ knows no bounds because I believe what my mother taught me, and my faith has never floundered throughout my life. I have never experienced an occasion when I have prayed for His help that it has not been delivered. Man born perfect, Christ, for me is not only the saviour of mankind. He was a man born perfect and other human beings are not, they crucified him when he was 33.

It is wholly appropriate that the image of Christ is hung in the Lords - wherever an image of Christ occurs it is appropriate - for it reminds all of his sacrifice. I believe that Christ came to Earth and lived amongst us as a carpenter and a craftsman. The images in the Robing Room depicting him surrounded by lords and kings, some of them drawing swords, is not my image of gentle Jesus. However, one aspect of Jesus' presence is clearly evident, for when I look at the ornamentation of the room I see beyond the opulence of gold to the craftsmanship of individual workmen whose names are not recorded. Even in the early days of my life, when my mother and us five small children were in dire need, Christ was never absent. Whether it is in the Lords or on the 45's face at Ackton Hall Pit, Christ is ever-present.

He looks over me putting on the robes of a Peer of the Realm and putting on a pit helmet, for all are connected through Christ. Christ does not recognise that one is far greater than the other. There are other images of Christ throughout the Palace but it is not its main galleries that I feel most clearly reflect the religious side of my personality but the Crypt. This has been the setting not only of quiet meditation following arduous debates, but was also the place where my daughter Lynne's two children were christened. It leads off Westminster Hall and there is a wonderful feeling of tranquillity. It is sometimes known as Chapel of the Martyrs, for there, rising up to the apex, are carvings showing scenes of Christian martyrdom. The room is relatively small. The guides taking visitors through the crypt tell a story about the seats ranging along each wall. It is said that in previous times the centre was open so that priests offering Christian charity and succour to the weak and disabled could say, "The sick and infirm to the wall," thus allowing them to sit and await His ministry. The origin of the phrase "weakest to the wall" is found in this place.

161

I will frequently attend services there, especially mass in the crypt and also memorial services, although the majority of memorial services take place in St Margaret's Church across the road which is a parish church of Westminster. I also go to the crypt frequently alone and I find, although it is within the Palace of Westminster, whenever I visit I always feel miles away from the hurly burly of Parliament.

The throne at the end of the Robing Room is the Queen's throne and I owe her sworn allegiance: I am no republican. In this room I move to I witness her annually at the opening of Parliament enact the powers of a constitutional monarch. In England the monarch enacts the rule of Parliament, and moving along into that chamber I see pictures of the monarchs who have ruled during my lifetime.

I was born in 1925 during the rule of George V. In Featherstone although I knew his name he was remote from me and from us all, some great mystery. I recall that his son Edward VIII visited the town during the Depression. I stood on the steps of the Hippodrome and waved a union jack. His stay in our town was brief. That Edward didn't last long and his activities since that time are well recorded. The next monarch I knew a little more about. I never saw George VI in the flesh, although I identified him through the news media in the war years. With his wife, Queen Elizabeth, he visited bombed cities and indeed saw Buckingham Palace bombed. We liked him, for he identified much more closely with people like me and my family. I have met Elizabeth II on a few occasions. I met her on visits to the Palace, at garden parties and evening receptions and of course I met her when I received my Knighthood and when I was being honoured.

I have met most of the other royals on different occasions and I always enjoyed chats with Princess Anne. She is a down to earth woman and very easy to converse with.

I always enjoyed meeting Di. She was and is my favourite. Probably the most beautiful woman I have ever met, her social concern and the refreshing image she brought to royalty is much appreciated. I shall never forget my telephone awakening me about 7am on Sunday 31 August 1997. It was my friend, Alice Walton, informing me that she had just heard that Princess Diana had been involved in a car accident in France and it was reported she had died. I was still very drowsy and

I thought I must be dreaming. Then shock took over; like most of the country I felt emotionally drained. My mind went back to an occasion which I will always cherish, the first time I met Princess Diana.

I had, much to my surprise, been invited to an evening reception at Buckingham Palace in early 1982. This I gladly accepted. I was accompanied by my late wife, Sarah. At the time the Princess was heavily pregnant with William. I will never forget that meeting. Her beauty was stunning. She was dressed in a long white silk gown. Her condition of carrying a future monarch added to her natural beauty. She was like a live oil painting and it was like seeing a living doll.

My affections for her from that day never faulted and during my period as Deputy Speaker, which coincided with the period of her troubles, I took the liberty to correspond with her. My letters were always immediately replied to, always personally signed. The contents are private to me and are still in my possession. They will never be made public and I have instructions to my daughter, Lynne, that they must be destroyed on my death. Like the rest of the country, I was devastated by Diana's death. I always thought she had so much to offer the country and her family. At the time of writing I fully support the thousands of people who are campaigning for a permanent memorial to Princess Diana.

Yet although royal portraits hang on the wall the object in the room which I always drew people's attention to when constituents toured the Palace of Westminster was not these royal pictures but a piece of wood which lay, seemingly accidentally, close to the long picture of the Duke of Wellington at the Battle of Waterloo. This timber was part of the jetty at Dunkirk.

Dunkirk was particularly important to me, for I remember when France caved in we had to evacuate our troops from that French seaside town. Every boat owner in our nation - people with steamers to those with rowing boats - went to their aid. It seems appropriate in a time when Government is seeking to heal eighteen years of divisive Tory rule - government and philosophy which set class against class and made money God - we should remember how, as a nation, we can pull together for the common good, not only for our own country but for mankind.

I have memories of soldiers arriving at the Pontefract railway station in 1940, then filthy and ill equipped, marching to Pontefract Barracks to be recycled into a fighting force which would ultimately invade Normandy and, in association with Russia and America, defeat fascism.

On the other side of the room is a small display case containing documents which are also pertinent to the development of our democracy. One in particular always interested me. It was a petition sent by women demanding the vote.

Two long pictures dominate the Gallery the one on the right shows the meeting of the Duke of Wellington and the Leader Blücher at the Battle of Waterloo in 1815. The one on the left depicts the death of Nelson at the Battle of Trafalgar. These paintings can be controversial. France is a proud nation, I do not think the present young generation should find the painting offensive. We must look forward to a united Europe which is going to be so essential for the future economic wealth of the European communities, and while history has a major part to play it should not be allowed to be the whole story.

The Death of Nelson highlights the presence of women tending to the injured on the HMS Victory. Because ships were out at sea for many months, children were born and it is suggested that the saying "son of a gun" originated from that. Whether this is true or not, that is the story I heard and I am sticking to it.

As I walk through the room I recall a close affinity with that picture and the bas-relief which is found in my own Town Hall. The base of Nelson's Column in Trafalgar Square has on it four big bronzes. When the square was opened one of the plasters from which the bronzes were made was offered to Pontefract Corporation by the artist. Pontefract, ever anxious to get something for nothing, accepted the gift. By the time the artist's bill arrived it was comfortably ensconced in the old Magistrates' Court. The argy bargy about payment went on for decades and I believe the bill was honoured. Now the Death of Nelson not only graces the wall in the Royal Gallery, it also dominates the room in which flea markets are held on Wednesdays. During the Miners' Strike this room was the soup kitchen, so the inscription which reads, "England expects every man this day to do his duty," was in those days especially appropriate. From the Royal Gallery via a corridor depicting scenes from the English Civil War and also the departure for New England of the Pilgrim Fathers the procession goes into the Chamber of the House of Lords.

When you reach the Chamber all is formality, so it is perhaps appropriate that I do not use my own words to describe the ceremony but I will resort to the formal language of that House to capture its grandeur:

"A procession in single file forms up outside the Chamber, led by two officers of the Order of the Garter. The Gentleman Usher of the Black Rod with his black rod in his right hand and Garter King of Arms wearing his tabard, with his silver gilt rod or sceptre of office in his right hand and the vellum scroll, representing the new Peer's patent of creation, in his left. There then follows the new Peer with two Peers of his own rank as supporters or sponsors, the junior in front and the senior behind him. The new Peer and his supporters carry cocked hats in their left hands and wear their parliamentary robes. Women Peers wear tricorn hats with a gold cockade on the left side. The new Peer carries his Writ of Summons in his right hand. On reaching the Bar of the House, each member of the procession bows to the Cloth of Estate which marks the position which the Sovereign, if present, would occupy. The procession then passes up the temporal side of the House and bows are repeated at the table and again at the Judge's Woolsack. At the Woolsack, the new Peer kneels and present his Writ to the Lord Chancellor, while Garter King of Arms presents the new Peer's Patent. All then return to the table where the Reading Clerk reads the Patent and Writ and the new Peer takes the oath of allegiance or makes a solemn affirmation and signs the Test Roll. This was the oath:

"I, Geoffrey Lofthouse, Baron of Pontefract, Knight, do swear by Almighty God that I will be faithful and bear true allegiance to Her Majesty Queen Elizabeth, her heirs and successors according to Law, so help me God."

The procession then moves on and each member of it as they cross the Chamber turns and bows to the Cloth of Estate.

Garter King of Arms then conducts the new Peer and his supporters to the bench appropriate to their degree, where on Garter's direction they sit, put on their hats, rise, and bow to the Chancellor three times, which the Chancellor, seated on the Woolsack, acknowledges. (Women Peers do not remove their hats). The procession then once more passes up the temporal side of the House. Each member of it bowing at the appointed places, as before. The Lord Chancellor shakes hands with the new Peer from the Woolsack and the procession leaves the Chamber."

I enjoyed the ceremony, not least because my beloved daughter Lynne, her husband and my grandson were present. My granddaughter Eleanor was heavily committed to taking exams at school and got her priorities right. I really thought some of the ceremony wasn't quite necessary, others felt the same. I certainly did not think we should have to put hats on, rise and bow to the Chancellor three times. Indeed the Select Committee on the Ceremony of Introductions, shortly after my own introduction, investigated the ceremonial proceedings and recommended a new procedure:

Following the procession into the Chamber, each member of the party bows once on reaching the bar. The new member then proceeds directly to the Table of the House, where the Reading Clerk reads the Letters Patent. The new member takes the oath or makes the solemn affirmation and signs the Test Roll.

Led by Black Rod and accompanied by his supporters, the new member processes behind the Clerks' chairs. Stopping at the cross-benches the Peer and his supporters bow their heads to the Cloth of Estate.

The procession then proceeds along the spiritual side of the House. On reaching the Woolsack, the new Peer shakes hands with the Lord Chancellor before leaving.

This procedure is now in practice and is, in my view, a benefit to the House. It is much shorter and cuts out the hat raising and bowing.

Having taken my seat, I found the procedures rather different to the House of Commons. Peers are self disciplined so the duty of the

Chancellor and the Deputy Speakers are quite different to those of the Speaker and Deputy Speaker in the House of Commons. Their only duty appears to be reading out the motion to be debated, putting the motion and calling Divisions at the end of debate, then announcing the result.

A few days after my introduction I was surprised and flattered when the Deputy Chief Whip, Lord Mackintosh of Harringay, approached me and asked me if I would consider becoming Lord in Waiting to Her Majesty The Queen. I asked for time to consider and for information as to what in fact the duties would be. Lord Mackintosh arranged for Lieutenant Colonel Malcolm Ross of Her Majesty's Household to come and see me and explain the duties. I had met Lieutenant Colonel Ross previously at the Palace when I received my Knighthood. The duties included meeting foreign dignitaries at airports and representing Her Majesty. I could be called upon at any time, probably at weekends, to get to airports and perform this duty. My duties would also include presenting messages from the Queen to the House of Lords. After giving it great consideration and recognising what a great honour it was to have been offered such a post, travelling to airports up and down the country, especially at weekends, was less than attractive. I decided that with my health not as robust as it had been previously, I probably would not be able to fulfil the duties satisfactorily, not least to myself. But the main reason that swayed my decision was it would have necessitated me moving to the cross-benches. This I could not consider. My wish was and is to remain on the Labour benches for the rest of my political career.

* * * * *

Following presentation to the House of Lords I was summoned by Garter King of Arms to discuss my armorial bearings. He also asked me if I would like a coat of arms. I weighed this up carefully. As far as I could ascertain there had been no previous Lord Pontefract and so I decided that it would be appropriate that our town should be represented in this way and asked for details. He then asked me what I thought should be its key design features. I said, "Life in the mines, my sporting interests and something about my personal life." It is very unusual for the College of Heralds to allow total freedom of design. Over the centuries they have developed something like a house style. However, I needed help so I took my ideas to Pontefract's Museum Curator, Richard Van Riel. A great asset to the town, he has developed the museum to a high standard. He very kindly talked with me and did some drawings. These were the basis of the discussion which later took place in London and evolved into the final design.

On the top is a canary holding a miner's safety lamp. This is a reference to the days when canaries were relied upon to test for methane gas. Beneath that, coming off a knight's helmet which sits inside a coronet, are some cloth flourishes. One of my colleagues points out that the dominant colours are blue and white, rather than red, as would be expected from a Labour man, but as I explained, blue and white are the Featherstone Rovers colours. Two moles with Yorkshire roses in their mouths support the central shield. This indicates my life as a coal miner. The shield carries an image of three rugby balls coming up a mine shaft. This illustrates the popular belief that if Featherstone Rovers ever needed a player on a Saturday, all they needed to do was to shout down and one would come up in the next cage. Underneath is my motto "Stick and Lift".

"Stick and lift" is a common saying down the mine. It means, "Never give up." I think it originates from moments when men were buried by large stones and their mates would lift and not let go. On the order "Stick and lift" the rescuers were encouraged to lift the stone away, but stick with the lift until the injured man was free. I knew the phrase from experience. When I was thirty I was buried under a roof fall at Ackton Hall Colliery and pinned down by a large stone across the back - the marks are still there. I could have died, but I was fortunate. The ground we had been working in was under fractured strata. For this reason, the "bug dust" - small coal and dust - had been left following the previous shift's coal cutting. The existence of this small rubble saved my life. When the roof came down I went face forward into this dust. As I lay there under a piece of rock I could hear voices which started close to me but seemed to be gradually fading away. I heard my brother Vic shouting, "Our young'un is under that lot." I have very little memory of what happened next apart

On duty with Speaker Betty Boothroyd.

STICK · AND · LIFT

The Armorial Ensigns of
GEOFFREY
BARON LOFTHOUSE OF PONTEFRACT
of Pontefract in the County of West Yorkshire, Knight

College of Arms
London

Garter Principal King of Arms

Coat of Arms

from the stone being eased from my back and my breathing becoming easier. Vic, my brother, Freddy Greenaway, Dick Windmill, Clarry Ogley and Jack Oldroyd had taken hold of the stone, they knew how to "stick and lift".

A few weeks later on the same coal face I was part of the rescue team when a very experienced collier, Edgar Jukes, died in a similar roof fall. Poor Edgar had not been as fortunate as me, there was no bug dust to prevent his face being crushed in the hard stone floor.

Few outside the mining community would recognise the meaning of this motto, but then few in the mining communities would understand the Latin mottos which hereditary lords use to embellish their coat of arms. No one outside immediate family however would recognise the hidden message which has a great personal significance which rests in those three words. "Stick And Lift" - S A L - are there prominently displayed on the coat of arms, for they are prominent in my life. S stands for Sarah, A stands for Alice and L stands for Lynne; the three women who have had the most influence in my adult life.

* * * * *

Little was I aware, when my mother's brother, my Uncle Jim, took me to see Featherstone Rovers play in 1931, that his actions would be crucial to the remainder of my life and would cumulate in my being privileged to sit in the Royal Box at Wembley since 1997. In 1998 I had the honour to go onto the pitch at this famous old stadium and be presented to the players. Since that first time in 1931, my love for this great game has never waned, it has been my passion and has filled a major leisure and recreational part of my life. I am sure my uncle, long-since dead, could never have appreciated what he introduced into my life that afternoon. Apart from supporting my beloved Featherstone Rovers, I was to enjoy 20 years of my life playing the game. The friends and, indeed, the comradeship found in those years have remained with me through all my life.

In those days the Featherstone Rovers Club existed in our small mining town with a population about 15,000 people. The town's

169

economy rested on the local coal mine and on the hard working miners whose main sporting activities and interests went little farther than the Rovers. Like many communities during the 30s and 40s and into the 50s, transport to the town from other areas was limited. There were very few people who owned cars and apart from an occasional visit to the adjacent towns of Pontefract and Castleford, most of my neighbours were confined to Featherstone for recreation. Of course the town had the usual working men's clubs, one cinema and two dance halls, but this was the limit and in many ways an advantage, for it created a family community where everyone knew each other. Rugby league was a major part of the town's life.

The game was played in local schools so there was the usual rivalry between schools, both in Featherstone and surrounding areas. The greatest ambition of boys of my generation was to play in the school team, it meant you were really someone. When the school team was playing away at another school on Saturday morning, the players were allowed to take the school shirt home after school on Friday. You would put the shirt over your shoulders and tie the arms around your neck. This told the town that you were in the team and meant much more to most of the boys than any academic achievement. Most of the boys considered that whatever they achieved at their desk would be somewhat irrelevant to most of them because they knew that when they were fourteen they would be going down the coal mine. This resulted in their sole ambition to succeed as a rugby league player and eventually play for the Rovers. If this was achieved they would work in the pits and would also earn a small amount of money over and above their wages from the colliery by playing at Post Office Road. It made them the aristocrats of Featherstone.

In the early days of my association with the Club the league and cup results were mostly unsuccessful. They were competing with clubs from larger towns whose finances were far greater so they could offer to pay higher wages and consequently attract star players. There was progress though. Featherstone Rugby League Club was accepted into the Rugby Football League in 1927/28. Prior to that the Club, along with other clubs in Featherstone, had played as amateurs and though they had always been successful on the playing field, they struggled financially, a problem which continues to this day.

When I was fourteen I first saw Featherstone Rovers win a trophy in the 1939/40 season, just before the Second World War. They played Wakefield Trinity in the Yorkshire Cup Final at Odsal Stadium Bradford, and Rovers won 12 points to 9. This was a real tonic for the town, its whole family celebrated. The captain of the Featherstone team that day was Wilfred Pearson and it was reported that he made a speech at the celebrations in which he said he hoped to see the day when Featherstone Rovers would carry off the Rugby League Challenge Cup. I do not suppose Will Pearson would in his wildest dreams think they would have the success which they were eventually to achieve.

I was also present when the New Zealand tourists toured this country in the early part of the 1939 season. They played their first match at Featherstone, but only one more game before returning home because of the outbreak of the war. There were no competition games played in wartime, just a few friendly matches. After the war people in Featherstone started to become more affluent; the colliery was working to capacity, women who had gone out to work in the war years continued to do so, so things improved. At that point the Club started on a more secure financial basis, although it was never wealthy, and began to produce a host of star players, some seasoned internationals. The first break into the big time was in 1952 when they reached the Rugby League Challenge Cup Final played at Wembley, but unfortunately lost to Workington Town 18-10. I had the privilege of being at Wembley on that occasion to support the Rovers. They could quite easily have won the game. All hung on an intercepted pass secured by the Workington wing man. If his interception had failed, Featherstone would have scored and, I am sure, won the Challenge Cup.

This started a period between 1959 to 1993, when the club appeared in 18 finals in all, including the Yorkshire Cup and the Rugby League Challenge Cup. A small town of 15,000 people sent a team to play in the Challenge Cup Final at Wembley five times and won it on three occasions. It also won the championship of the Rugby Football League First Division 1976/77, mostly playing players who were born in Featherstone and the immediate surrounding district. I have taken great pride in the fact that my nephew Vince Farrar captained the Rovers in their championship season and that both Vince and another nephew, Barry Hollis, played in the 1972/73 Final when Featherstone beat Bradford Northern 33-14. I was Mayor of Pontefract the year the Rovers first won the cup at Wembley in 1966/7. My very good friend Malcolm Dixon, a great forward, was captain. What a thrill he gave me when he turned up at my Mayor-making and instead of bringing champagne presented me with the Rugby League Challenge Cup.

During that period, the Club produced many great players who achieved the game's highest honours as county, international, test match and touring team players. They certainly put Featherstone on the map. Each time a player was selected for an honour, the town was filled with pride. When I first went to Parliament, some MPs from the South would ask, "Where do you come from?" and when I replied, "Featherstone," they would immediately say, "Featherstone, the rugby town?" They had not forgotten the Wembley appearances.

This may not mean much to people outside the Featherstone Town area, but I will attempt to select the best team of players who I have seen play for the Rovers over the last 67 years. I believe this team would take some beating:

FULL BACK
Jack Fennel

RIGHT WING	*RIGHT CENTRE*	*LEFT CENTRE*	*LEFT WING*
Eric Batten	Paul Newlove	Walter Tennent	Albany Longley

STAND OFF   *SCRUM HALF*
Joe Mullaney   Don Fox

FIELDSIDE PROP	*HOOKER*	*BLIND SIDE PROP*
Jimmy Thompson	Keith Bridges	Vince Farrar

SECOND ROW
Terry Clawson   Peter Smith

LOOSE FORWARD
Harry Street

On the bench: Freddie Miller, Steve Nash, Steve Quinn, Cliff Lambert.

The great thrill of small clubs like Featherstone was playing top successful teams and occasionally beating them. In Featherstone this became a frequent habit. In earlier times star players would be spread across the league but in general they would remain in one club. Of course there were occasions when the smaller clubs had to sell their star players to maintain financial viability but Featherstone survived because they could always produce new stars to take their place.

I have outlined this brief history of Featherstone Rovers and indicated what the team meant to the local community and to other rugby league communities like Featherstone, because I want to highlight the near fatal blow dealt by the News International (Murdoch) deal.

All rugby league clubs had a burning desire to play in the Cup Final at Wembley. The BBC had always, through the radio and later television, broadcast the Final and over the years this programme had become a national occasion greatly appreciated by the southerners, who recognised the good behaviour of the northern visitors. I was very appreciative of the coverage the BBC gave the game, not least the finals, because it gave many passionate supporters of the game, who were unable to travel through age or infirmity - miners suffering from chest diseases - a chance to be in touch with the game.

It was, therefore, with experience and emotion that I examined the funding of an advisory group, set up by the Department of Culture, Media and Sport to consider the sporting occasions that should be protected for terrestrial television. There was an attempt to take the event over by Sky Television, owned by Rupert Murdoch. If this was allowed to happen, I believed that many rugby league supporters would lose the opportunity of seeing the Final in the comfort of their own homes. Sky Television was expensive. When the group, chaired by my colleague Lord Gordon of Strathblane, produced their report they stated to my great concern that although they recognised that this event had great significance in certain parts of the country, they did not feel either there were compelling reasons to see it as of great national importance or as meaningful as the international matches of the Great Britain team. They recommended that the Rugby Football League should be at liberty to sell the rights to televise the Challenge

Cup Final to either terrestrial or subscription broadcasters and they saw no reason to hamper its ability to do this. Accordingly, they did not recommend that the Rugby League Challenge Cup Final should be added to the prescribed list. I was very upset. I took the view that the Advisory Group, which had amongst its members such distinguished sports personalities as Jack Charlton, member of the England 1996 World Cup winning team, and Steve Cram, the international athlete, had missed the point. It appeared to me they had made the judgement on a commercial basis without recognising the social consequences to the rugby league communities. I was so concerned I corresponded with Chris Smith, the Secretary of State at the Department of Heritage, requesting him not to accept the recommendations and I made an application for a Debate in the House of Lords to enable me to present my case. I was successful in obtaining a debate which took place on 2 December 1998. *(Appendix N)*

Following my speech I corresponded and had meetings with Chris Smith. I emphasised the importance of the Rugby League Challenge Cup Final being available for all television viewers and drew his attention to the contents of my speech. I was delighted at a later date that the Secretary of State announced that he would not accept the recommendations of the Advisory Group, that the Rugby League Challenge Cup Final should be protected from the commercial market and that it should be protected to remain on terrestrial television. Following this announcement it was reported that the Super League through its Chairman, Mr Chris Caisley, made strong objections to the Secretary of State's decision. It appeared it was their wish to have an open market, which they believed would assist them with their negotiations to get the best financial deal. I can understand their argument on a financial basis and I recognise the need for clubs to be financially viable. However, that should not be the only criterion and supporters of the game should also be given serious consideration.

I take great satisfaction that my arguments seem to have won the day; rugby league supporters - many of them elderly and unable to travel to the Challenge Cup Final or afford commercial television - will be able to continue to watch the Final on the BBC. This proved to me that debates in the House of Lords can be effective.

It was a great shock when it was announced in 1995 that the Rugby Football League had accepted a deal with News International (Rupert Murdoch). The deal gave the Murdoch organisation the right to televise rugby league for the payment of £87 million. This caused great concern because the announcement was so sudden. There had been no pre-warnings that such an offer had been made. One of the main concerns was, it was suggested, that some of the old established clubs would have to merge to meet the conditions of the agreement. It was in fact recommended that Wakefield, Featherstone and Castleford should merge and form a team called 'Calder'. Considering the healthy rivalry between these clubs for a century, it is not difficult to understand the reaction of the supporters. They were concerned that many of the clubs' chairmen had been bounced into the decision through financial difficulties. They understandably took the view that this vast amount of money could solve the games financial problems. Regrettably, as I write, this does not appear to have been the case.

Maurice Lindsay, the then Chief Executive of the Rugby Football League, has explained to me the reasons why the deal appeared to have been done in haste. He informed me that on 4 April 1995, he received a phone call from Sam Chisholm, Chief Executive of BSkyB telling Maurice Lindsay he wanted to do a deal to allow Sky to sponsor rugby league. He said there was some urgency about it owing to a situation which had developed in Australia where there was some competition between News International and the Packer Organisation. Maurice said he told Chisholm he would put the request to the Council meeting which happened to be the next day, 5 April. At that meeting, Maurice informed me, he was instructed to meet Chisholm. Maurice said that on Thursday 6 April 1995, he went to London on the 5 am train and met Mr Chisholm at the Sky office. First he made an offer to Maurice of £50 million for television rights. However, he said he told Chisholm it was not sufficient and by 11.30 am he had managed to increase the offer to £75 million. At that point Chisholm informed Maurice that he would expect a league of ten clubs to match the Australian League but that the offer was on condition they could have an early answer because of the situation in Australia. Maurice informed me that following the meeting he went straight to see Sir Rodney Walker, a Wakefield businessman, at the Sports Council office. When he informed him of the offer, Rodney expressed the view that it was a fantastic deal and they both agreed to speak to the clubs. On Saturday 8 April 1995 they arranged a meeting of club representatives at Central Park, Wigan.

In the meantime Maurice had received a fax from Ken Arthurson, President of the Australian Rugby League, advising the British Rugby Football League not to accept the Murdoch money. Maurice informed me that he read the fax out to the meeting of club representatives on 8 April 1995. Maurice also informed me that the representatives of 18 clubs met on 7 April 1995 at Huddersfield where the meeting went on until 2am the following day. The clubs all agreed to the suggested mergers and the following Saturday, representatives of the 32 clubs met at Wigan where, and by unanimous vote, they agreed to accept the deal. In an effort to bring down the league to the required 10 clubs, the representatives recommended mergers. This included the Wakefield, Featherstone and Castleford teams. It was all tied up, with the minimum of consultation or long term thought, in six days.

When the news broke it sent shock waves through the rugby league world. There was a spontaneous reaction. The majority of supporters, myself included, objected. We could not believe our ears. To think of merging these famous clubs was bordering on treachery as far as the supporters were concerned. The popular revulsion created an uprising in people's passion and loyalty for the clubs. For supporters of my generation sell-out was unthinkable. I felt so strongly myself that at the next Featherstone match - possibly the last time I would see Featherstone play - I led a peaceful demonstration of supporters. We marched from Pontefract Town Hall to the Featherstone ground, a distance of almost three miles. When I looked back I saw that the march stretched for about a mile. We were cheered all the way. At half time Eddie Ashton, a personal friend of mine and Chairman of the Castleford Rugby League Football Club, tried to explain the deal. Even though Eddie was using a powerful microphone, he could not make himself heard above the roars of objection. He eventually gave up. The crowd continued to occupy the pitch and sat in total silence until the players returned for the second half. I later made representations to the club officials and impressed on them that following such a genuine demonstration, they must never agree to the conditions in the deal that meant merging these famous historical clubs. I was aware that the Featherstone and Castleford officials were not happy but had been caught in an impossible position; it was a large amount of money to ignore. I had watched the reaction of Featherstone Rovers Chairman Steve Wagner throughout the match. I knew he was agonising and he felt the same way as the supporters. Following this great reaction of support, which included the production by the Yorkshire Art Circus of a small book within a few days, it was finally agreed to drop the merger idea. Representations made by Steve Wagner, and others like him, had a great influence on the decision.

Out of this deal the Super League under the jurisdiction of the Rugby Football League was formed. The twelve clubs who met the criteria were admitted. The remaining clubs formed the first and second Divisions and their own organisation, FASDA. The Super League later formed its own marketing organisation. I was sceptical about this development. It appeared to me that this was a breakaway from the Rugby Football League administration and what followed supported my views.

I was informed that Mr Chris Caisley, Chairman of Bradford Bulls, later had a meeting with Sir Rodney Walker, the Chairman of the Rugby Football League, and R Wardby, a Director of the Rugby Football League and informed them that the Super League would be forming a limited company on the lines of the FA Premier League. Of course they always denied that this was a breakaway, but I believe it was. They now have their own administration and a separate headquarters from the Rugby Football League. They have their own Chairman and Chief Executive and have, in fact, now negotiated their own deal with News International. This does not include any money for the clubs outside the Super League.

What financial difficulty these clubs will face in the year 2000 when the money for the first Murdoch deal runs out is very difficult to ascertain. I think it is a fair assessment to say that probably all the clubs, both Super League and the rest, are no stronger financially than they were before the Murdoch deal. The Rugby Football League have received £87 million, but there has been very little capital investment or financial support for the amateur game. It is an indictment on the Rugby League that the Murdoch money appears to have gone on players' contracts with very little benefit to the structure and the game in general. I believe that the Murdoch money should have been shared out more equally, with at least 10% into an emergency fund and 10% to BARLA for the amateur game. The Rugby Football League would still have been left with £60 million. Some of this should have been set aside for improvement of facilities at the clubs. I do not begrudge players their rightful rewards but I do not think it has been for the benefit of the game that most of the Murdoch millions has been spent on players' contracts.

Great concern regarding the Murdoch deal was expressed in the House of Commons. The debate was led by David Hinchliffe, Member of Parliament for Wakefield and Secretary of the All Party Rugby League Group and Ian McCartney, the then Chairman of the All Party Rugby League Group in the House of Commons. Since this was an Adjournment Debate I had the privilege to chair. This was the first time that rugby league had been debated in the House of Commons throughout its history. The debate lasted 90 minutes and nine Members had informed me they hoped to catch my eye. There were also others who were interested in speaking if time permitted. At its commencement there were forty Members present. This was the largest number I have seen attend an Adjournment Debate all my time in Parliament.

It was a stormy debate. During my dealings with Sir Rodney Walker since that time, I have never found any evidence that he would compromise the Rugby Football League arising out of other positions he has held. To the contrary, I have found him to deal very fairly with all sporting organisations and from my early days as President of BARLA, he has played a leading part in bringing the professional and amateur code together after many, many years of hostility between these sections. The agreement "Partnerships through Progress" was mainly achieved by his leadership. I think it would be wrong to point a finger at any one individual for accepting the Murdoch contract. One must appreciate what a major decision it was for all people involved. The opportunity for the vast amount of money to be injected into rugby league football would have been very difficult not to accept. However, the worst fears pointed out during the debate are appearing to materialise. The concerns so strongly made by David Hinchliffe and Ian McCartney were supported by other Members, including Doug Hoyle (Warrington North), Gary Waller (Keighley), Alice Mahon (Halifax), Liz Lynne (Rochdale), the late Derek Enright (Hemsworth), Norman A Godman (Grennock and Port Glasgow) and Kevin Hughes (Doncaster North).

* * * * *

When in 1995 Maurice Oldroyd, Chief Executive of the British Amateur Rugby League Association - BARLA - informed me that some BARLA members were to nominate me for the position of President of BARLA I was somewhat hesitant. I was very committed as Deputy Speaker and had little time available for any other major commitments. Maurice informed me that there would be very little involvement of a practical nature and the post would not be time consuming. My life-long love of the game, not least the amateur section, made the offer very appealing and after serious consideration I decided to accept. As time has progressed I am very pleased that I did. I found that my collective life experience in local government, at Westminster, in both the House of Commons and the Lords, certainly stood me in good stead and even opened my eyes on more than one occasion to the intensity of politics in sport, and in particular my own game of rugby league football.

It was as a member of the All Party Parliamentary Rugby League Group, founded in 1988, that I first became involved in the politics of the game's two governing bodies: The British Amateur Rugby League Association and the Rugby Football League.

The All Party Group came about because of the drive and initiative of my parliamentary colleagues, David Hinchliffe and Ian McCartney of Ashton-in-Makerfield, near Wigan - a tenacious Scott, who is at present climbing the ladder in the Tony Blair Government. The aim of the group is to assist all sections of the rugby league game and to promote it in the best possible light. To this end, we invite guest speakers to our monthly meetings from all sections of the game, who in turn update our members with first hand knowledge of the workings of the sport and its politics. As a consequence the group has become more knowledgeable and stronger and it has now grown to 90 members. During the early days, it was quite natural that our members received invites to various functions at both professional and amateur levels and were received with open arms and warm hospitality, as one would expect from our great family of sport. I find my position as BARLA President, and by now Chairman of the All Party Rugby League Group, has provided me with great, pleasurable occasions.

Attendance at the Yorkshire Junior League Presentation Evening in 1996 was an occasion that was typical of the warm family spirit of the game. The occasion actually spread over three evenings, because of the sheer size of the League, which represents over 200 teams from Under 8 to Under 15, the largest league in this age group in the game. This annual gala evening was held at the Painthorpe Country Club near Wakefield. The parents of the young children, who were there to receive their annual prizes, were bursting with pride as their little ones received their trophies. It was really one of the most stimulating and moving sporting functions I have attended. It warmed my heart to see these young charges, both boys and girls, with their beaming faces, representing their clubs; Smawthorne, Normanton, Crigglestone and many others, all community based, voluntary youth clubs, proudly providing organised competitive sport at an amateur level to benefit the community at large, as well as the young players themselves.

There are almost a thousand teams playing in youth and junior rugby throughout BARLA. These statistics will surprise many people. When one considers that the cost of running a team can be as much as £3,000 per annum, it is clear that over £3 million is invested in the grass roots of the sport at this crucial level. This excludes the capital investment of many progressive clubs. Lock Lane, Shawcross, Hillsborough Hawks and Featherstone Lions to name but a few, in my own immediate area have built their own substantial facilities and club houses, in many cases, thanks to grant aid from the Lottery, the Foundation of Sport and the Arts and local authorities. They all recognise the contribution that such clubs make to the quality of life, particularly in the many areas of urban depravation. I think Sir Rodney Walker may have been influential in obtaining capital investment for many of these facilities.

BARLA has been one of the sporting success stories of modern times. The Association was formed in Huddersfield in 1973 as a breakaway from the Rugby Football League. At that time the RFL was controlled by thirty professional clubs, with the amateurs having no vote or say in their own destiny. The sport was in serious decline. There were fewer than 150 amateur teams, with youth rugby teams down to as little as thirty sides. The 'breakaway' was acrimonious and was strongly contested by the professional game. However, thanks to the rugby league senior statesman, the late Tom Mitchell of Workington, who was a visionary and a colossus in the professional game, a vote 29-1 against recognising BARLA was turned round within twelve months to an unanimous vote of approval for the newly born 'BARLA baby'. When I took over the presidency, Tom would frequently telephone me with words of wisdom and advice; I was always grateful.

Twenty-six years later there are more than 1,400 teams, and 900 youth and junior rugby sections, a truly remarkable record. Few other sports, or indeed businesses, could boast such an impressive growth record. I must pay tribute to all who have voluntarily worked so hard to achieve this for very little reward apart from their love of the game and their interest in youth and young children. Maurice Oldroyd, the Chief Executive of BARLA for 22 years, has worked relentlessly in his own special manner. The whole of the rugby league world, both professional and amateur, should be indebted to him.

After becoming President I found it surprising, in view of BARLA's success, that all was not sweetness and light; the amateurs and professionals were at each others throats. The major rift appeared to be over youth rugby. There was hostility between the two codes, but I also found that the BARLA officials were concerned that the professional game, in its search for more junior stars, began to encroach on this growth section of the amateur game. It was a problem which many people considered complex, whereas I thought it was quite simple. BARLA believed in mass participation and 'Sport for All', in providing healthy feeder leagues into the professional game which enhanced the routes. This method of increasing the number of young players taking up our sport through a development strategy was supported by the Sports Council. However most big teams believed in the professional philosophy with its 'one team syndrome' mentality; that having one super team in a town at each age group was the best strategy. These philosophies are diametrically opposed. When a super team is formed the result is often the demise of the other clubs; naturally the better players gravitate to the 'super team' as a consequence, a contract policy evolves and the amateur clubs suffer. The slow developers and the young people there to play the game for fun go to the wall.

I found the BARLA system was very similar to that in Australia. There they encourage their junior leagues to have as many as 100 teams in the region, which in turn feed their premier clubs. During the years of strife between the two bodies the Sports Council had encouraged and guided BARLA, and supported the amateurs when the professional clubs tried to set up their own junior amateur teams. When friction arose as in 1981, Dick Jeeps, Chairman of the Sports Council, had insisted that the Rugby Football League honoured the agreement which transferred all amateur rugby league to BARLA. Consequently, Rugby Football League was prevented from forming an Under 17 League in direct opposition to BARLA. I was informed that when a similar situation arose again in 1992, the then Chairman of the Sports Council, Sir Peter Yarinton, took a similar stance. Again BARLA believed that the Rugby Football League was steered in the right direction by the Sports Council.

BARLA was grateful to both Jeeps and Yarinton, who were former Presidents of the Rugby Football Union, for having shown an evenhanded approach to BARLA and recognised that the Sports Council had supported them from day one through such august Chairmen as Sir Roger Bannister, Sir Robin Brook and later Sir John Smith of Liverpool Football Club. In 1987 Sir John Smith, aided by Dudley Wood, Secretary of the Rugby Union, helped to bring about the end of 'rugby apartheid' which had existed between rugby union and rugby league at amateur level since the last century, and brought about the 'free gangway' at amateur level between the two codes.

This event was truly a piece of rugby history and especially attractive to BARLA, for with its amateur ethos it had always endeavoured to cultivate a working relationship with the Rugby Football Union.

On the international scene, BARLA have made a major impact on the expansion of the game. In the pre-BARLA days, amateur international games were limited solely to annual exchanges with France. In 1977 all this changed. BARLA extended its boundaries 12,000 miles to take in Australia and New Zealand. In that year BARLA Young Lions made their historic inaugural tour. This was just the beginning. BARLA then became honorary members of the International Board. They have never really looked back since.

I think progress can be measured in simplistic terms. Over the following 20 years no less than 31 tours have been made to the southern hemisphere. These include pioneer visits to Fiji, Western Samoa, Conga, the Cook Islands and South Africa. In the northern hemisphere games have been played against Moldavia, Russia, Morocco and the USA. Indeed, in one 12 month period, BARLA played international games in no less than 13 countries. The International Board was delighted with BARLA's role in the international expansion of the game. It therefore gave me great pleasure, along with members of the All Party Rugby League Group, to be able to host the dinner for the International Board members at the House of Commons in Rugby League Centenary Year. It really was a very special occasion, more special because I formed a lasting friendship with Ken Arthurson, President of the Australian Rugby League, a man who I very much admire.

The highlight of BARLA's short history occurred in 1990, with the opening of its new offices in Huddersfield - the birthplace of the game - by Her Majesty, Queen Elizabeth II. It was another wonderful piece of rugby league history, for above all this gave the royal seal of approval to the 100,000 enthusiasts who are involved in the sport every week of the season and who give so willingly of their time and efforts in a voluntary capacity to promote the game of rugby league at grass roots level among our young people.

Having painted such a rosy picture of BARLA's growth it seems strange that I inherited such a mass of politics that made even an old war horse like me raise my eyebrows from time to time. June 1996 when I was elected President of BARLA at its Annual General Meeting, was 'D-Day' for me. Having had a lifetime's experience of rugby league football, little did I realise that my education was only just beginning as I placed my foot into the wider arena of the politics of sport which existed between BARLA and the Rugby Football League. From the first I was determined to take an evenhanded approach as I must, being Chairman of the Rugby League All Party Group in the House of Commons, but it was not easy. My experience in the House itself was certainly a background which proved to be invaluable to me as I proceeded to tip-toe gently through the mine fields of the game.

The introduction of the 'Super League' through News Limited and the Rupert Murdoch empire certainly added another dimension to the sport by bringing about the introduction of summer rugby. With the investment of £87 million over a 5 year period, potentially there was a terrific boost to the game. This relationship heralded the cultural change to the traditional rugby league game as it began to celebrate its Centenary Year in 1995. The first committee I was welcomed onto, as an observer, was the BARLA Negotiating Committee. This met on a regular basis with the Rugby Football League, under the umbrella of the Sports Council. The latter were doing all in their power to bring the two together. I found these early meetings acrimonious and full of passion. It was obvious that much work would need to be done to bring harmony, for little existed. I found that Members from each side had very rigid views and some Members, certainly from the professional game, were not keen that the two sectors of the game, professional and amateur, should operate together for the general good. It was clear that the major problem between the two governing bodies was that of youth rugby, as I understand it had been since BARLA's inception, almost a quarter of a century earlier. The fact that the game had two coaching schemes was another challenge to be met.

The Chairman of BARLA's Negotiating Team at that time was Billy Gill. He had played for Huddersfield in the halcyon days of the 50s and 60s. Also on the committee was BARLA's Chief Executive Maurice Oldroyd, a founder member of the association, together with the Cumbrian stalwart Jackie Reid MBE. I found Jackie to be rock

Explaining Rugby League to Tony Blair.

With Tony Blair, John Smith and Margaret Beckett at the Pioneer factory.

Picture by kind permission of Pontefract and Castleford Express.

My agent Kathryn Stainburn, Lynne and myself, after my last election victory in 1992.

Pictured here with Councillor Roy Hirst, Chief Whip, Wakefield MDC.

solid in his genuine love of the game, a very wise and fair man who had no time for petty jealousies. Leading the League party were their Chairman Sir Rodney Walker, Chairman of the Sports Council and Maurice Lindsay, the professional games Chief Executive, a former Chairman of Wigan.

I recognised from the start that Sir Rodney Walker as Chairman of the Rugby Football League was walking a tight rope between the two sides, but was genuinely keen, unlike some of his colleagues, to bring the two arms of the game together. The success later achieved is much to the credit of Sir Rodney Walker, whose guidance and whose desire to put past pettiness and personalities behind and look to the future were inspiring. It also came as a pleasant surprise to me when I was informed that the respective chairmen and chief executives of the two bodies had come very close to a solution in 1994 following the first such meeting of the game's senior officers for many years. There was also a belief that the 'Two Maurices', Maurice Lindsay, Chief Executive of the Rugby Football League and Maurice Oldroyd, Chief Executive of BARLA, were so opposed to each other's views there would never be any progress while they occupied their respective positions. For my part I never found any evidence that this rift was as serious as suggested. If there was serious friction between them it was receding when I arrived.

Sitting as an observer at the negotiating meetings allowed me to take a wider view. The first major positive action taken with the Sports Council was to form a Working Party as a prelude to a 'Youth Commission'. It was established that the Chair of the Working Party be given to David Oxley, the former Chief Executive of the Rugby Football League. The Working Party, along with BARLA representatives, was made up of representatives from English schools, student rugby and the Rugby Football League. It was agreed that when the commission became a reality BARLA representatives would be equal in total to the collective delegation of the other parties. Following twelve months of hard work, and many hours of burning the midnight oil, David Oxley presented his final report. This became the basis of the official formation of the Youth Commission. Quickly the Working Party agreed that there should be a neutral person to act as co-ordinator for a six month period to bring the commission together. I was honoured to be invited to be Chairman for this prestigious and important post, and accepted willingly. During this short period, much hard work was put in by all parties to ensure that the foundation stones were well and truly laid. With my six month mission successful I handed power to my successor and Chair of the Youth Commission, John Cornwell, a former Leader of the Sheffield City Council. He was one of the driving forces behind the formation of the Sheffield Eagles and of the Club's amateur development association. As in the final, Sheffield certainly got it right - they had a magnificent win against Wigan in the 1998 Challenge Cup Final, ending Wigan's record breaking run of eight successive Challenge Cup victories. The Youth Commission is now serving all sections of the game as the sport plans together to meet the challenge of the new millennium.

In my mind, the biggest step forward was the formation of the Joint Policy Board which came about through the early meetings of the respective negotiating teams. The catalyst for this monumental step forward came from two new rugby league officials, Bob McDermott of Dewsbury and Bob Scott of Huddersfield, Chairman and Manager respectively of FASDA, the Rugby Football League's First and Second Division Association. Theirs was an open-minded approach. Sir Rodney Walker sent a letter to Maurice Oldroyd, the BARLA Chief Executive, suggesting a meeting and this was quickly accepted. The rest is a piece of rugby league history. This exploratory meeting was held on 13 May 1997, at the new Crown Flatts Stadium, the home of Dewsbury Rugby League. Attending the meeting, along with myself, were the two top officers of both governing bodies; a master stroke for what was to come. Within six months the partnership agreement was formulated and an official launch took place at the Trust House Forte Hotel, Brighouse. The way forward was clear, we even had a motto 'Progress Through Partnership'.

* * * * *

When I eventually joined the Labour Party in 1950 I joined an enthusiastic mass party. All over the country the Party consisted of small ward units which fed into city, borough, urban and rural district councils. Pontefract for instance had eighteen councillors and six Aldermen representing six wards. Central Ward was usually won by the Conservatives, but I won it in 1962 and from then on it was mostly Labour. Baghill, Castle and Tanshelf were our real strongholds. Park Ward fluctuated but was usually Labour, and Carleton was always won by the Conservatives. At that time each of the councillors and Aldermen made quite sure their families and friends were members of the Party. They also linked in with local working men's clubs, bowling clubs, allotments clubs and their unions and in that way were known by hundreds of people. They maintained this membership to give them some form of security in maintaining their seats. They weren't in it for the money, for there was no official financial gain apart from small expenses in coppers for travelling. Why did they do it? They did it mainly for the interests of the town and the feeling that it gave them: power to make decisions on the town's future. I well recall in my early days leaving the Council Chamber after a meeting feeling we had achieved something. It might have been we had agreed to build housing estates or to clear a slum. At that time we had the power to do things, we were not controlled by central government funding but by the rate payer. We produced our programme in the election manifesto - quite long documents - for each year. We then costed the programme and fixed a rate to meet the budget. If that meant fixing a rate which was not acceptable to the people, they had the opportunity of slinging sections of the Council out each year and sometimes did so. This, I always believed, was local democracy.

In the 1960s the Council officials did not change so often. The Town Clerk in my early days lived in a somewhat superior council house built for him, with the Chief Librarian living next door. Once a man became the Town Clerk he had a job which he hung onto and carried through to his retirement. Town Clerks were important but in every way elected members were masters of their own households.

The re-organisation of local government in 1973 took the word "local" out of local government. Instead of 26 representatives in Pontefract we were represented by six councillors in Wakefield, a city which is 11 miles away and not much visited by Pontefract people.

Pontefract people when they go shopping usually go to Leeds and Castleford people always go there. From then on local people could not know the officers, or the officers know the towns. Increasing they lived outside the district. Pontefract councillors became more isolated from their grass root support because they only had a voice in the larger authority when previously they were all speaking and decision making for Pontefract. They ceased to be active decision makers.

The old system of eighteen councillors plus Aldermen impacted on the Party. I well remember the local branches were asked for nominations for the candidate to represent Labour following the death of Joe Harper MP. Pontefract South Ward met in the Pontefract Labour Club to nominate their candidate to go forward to the Constituency Party for consideration. At that meeting there were two candidates proposed, myself and the late Derek Enright. The voting on that occasion was 86-24 in my favour. What is noticeable is that 110 voted. A similar meeting of the North Ward would perhaps not have produced quite as big a meeting, but even then it would be well over 80. Using these statistics you see that in 1978 at least 170 were active in two wards in my home town.

Today it would be an exceptional meeting which would attract twenty and indeed there are occasions when the wards have found difficulty being quorate. Since the Blair success there has been a massive increase in membership. There are something like 550 members, but few of these people are attending meetings. This is partly because they do not feel involved in decision making.

Similar enthusiasm was found in the Pontefract and Castleford Constituency Party. When its Management Committee met in the Nelson Room at Pontefract Town Hall in the early 1970s, there were complaints there wasn't sufficient seating capacity, and in fact people were unable to get into the meeting. There was a request that future meetings should be held in a larger hall. I estimate that that room held 150 seats. That is some indication of Party strength. Now the meetings are open and rarely contain more than forty delegates.

Why this should be so when two years ago the Party enjoyed its biggest electoral success since 1945 and has become increasingly stronger, when both middle and working class people are joining because they believe that there are ways to re-invigorate the country, is a mystery. The country is experiencing, it is suggested, the most popular Labour Prime Minister and yet very few of these new people are actively becoming involved in debate or in decision making. Very few are putting themselves up as candidates. The infrastructure has gone.

When I was first on Pontefract Council there were the usual grumbles about corruption but it appeared that alleged corruption was relatively small and related to council house lettings and council jobs for Party members. Most councillors were not corruptible. As in Parliament the vast majority were sound and honourable people whose only wish was to do their possible best for the town and the people they represented. I recall from my early years some councillors I thought to be local government giants; people I looked up to when I first entered local government in Pontefract. These included men like Aldermen George Poppleton, Tommy Hill, Frank Lane and Jim Rhodes. They knew the job inside out. I learnt more about local government finance from Alderman Rhodes, an ex-railway man, than I have ever learnt from anyone else. Led by former Pontefract miner Joe Frain, who lived in a council house opposite Willow Park Club, this strong group of local men turned Pontefract from a Conservative market town into a Labour stronghold. His political base came from the Prince of Wales and from club membership. They were the people who I looked up to as a young man when I entered the council. They were much respected.

Today local politicians are not respected in the same way. This is a pity because most of them are of the calibre of these earlier men. Times have changed and the environment which cherished them has been eroded. The Local Government Act of 1972 not only altered where councillors met but when they met. Up to that point meetings were held on an evening. This enabled interested people to offer themselves to the electorate to become local councillors. Members of the professions or any other occupations became local representatives. But because of the large area covered by the council the meetings were held in the day time; this was also partly to accommodate officer involvement. This change unfortunately ruled out many people. Release from work increasingly became a real problem. This diluted the council membership so that only the retired, unemployed and small business people could offer themselves as representatives. School teachers, lecturers or anyone working for a large authority could not apply. People living, for example, within the Pontefract area and working for another council such as Castleford could stand for council election in their own town in earlier time. When you had a much larger authority it limited this opportunity for anyone working for the authority, for these groups were effectively removed from the scene.

In my early days it was always the elected members who controlled the authority. Officers would work within the elected members' policy not make it. A chairman would control his department. Of course a wise chairman would make quite sure that the officer under his control was capable of producing the information and the plans for the department which the chairman required and he also would listen. He was bound by the council's reputation resting on the officer. Yet the unpaid councillor was the ultimate decision maker.

I was very fortunate when I was Chairman of Housing for Wakefield. I had an exceptional young officer in Edward "Ted" Cantle - he was later to become both Secretary of the Association of Metropolitan District Councils and the Chief Executive of Nottingham County Council. In every way an exceptional man, Ted had to listen to me; but I was wise enough to also listen to him.

Ted Cantle once took me to a field - not 200 yards from where I lived on the Circle - which was occupied by prefabricated bungalows placed there as an emergency housing solution directly after the war. Ted was somewhat of a visionary so he said to me, "We ought to knock these down and give local people the opportunity of using their skills to build their own houses and become home owners which they had never previously thought they would." He recognised that in every working population there are labourers, plasterers, builders, roofers, plumbers who will come together and in a collective way build an estate if they are given the opportunity. This idea was well before its time. I was convinced, I made the decision, I argued it through council and I proposed the resolution. Again Ted needed me and I needed him.

Dilution of the quality of councillors has not only led to incidents of corruption, such as at Donnygate, but also increased the power of officers. People will not be fooled for when they recognise that local voting does not produce decisions they stay away on polling day and I cannot see any of the solutions on offer altering that. People have got out of the habit of thinking that they vote to make their wants known.

I honestly do not think that the new Cabinet notion of local government control, initiated by central government, will change things or lead to a healthy democratic system of local government. Today the Wakefield MDC is more or less controlled by nine councillors who are members of the Cabinet, and whilst I am not fully aware of the details of the participation of the rest of the elected members, I have never liked power being in a few hands. It suggests that the remaining 57 councillors only have limited input and therefore I remain unconvinced that there is increased efficiency. If people do not have direct access to policy making via their elected representatives, they will turn their back on elections altogether. I sometimes think that Cabinet government will achieve exactly what I believe Mrs Thatcher set out to achieve; that is the removal of choice at a local level or in other words, the end of popular local democracy.

It appears to me that there will be much less input and more importantly, influence by back-bench councillors, and increasingly by new councillors - make no mistake, those in power will hold to power. Officers in their town halls will get closer and closer to their cousins the civil servants. At every step local democracy loses and the people become apathetic.

I watched Nelson Mandela being helped down the steps of Westminster Hall by Betty Boothroyd. He had been elected to a difficult role in South African society by voters who had queued all night to place their crosses on ballot papers and yet in Pontefract, the English town which first used the secret ballot in 1874, only 19% voted at this year's local government election. It may well be that people will come out and vote at a general election but I see no evidence that people will ever come out and vote in significant numbers for local cabinet government.

I have been assured by Hilary Armstrong, Minister for Local Government and very much the architect of this system, that back-bench councillors will have an input on scrutiny committees. I am not aware what these committees will scrutinise. If it is post-decision scrutiny, then it is not worth much. If it is to be parallel to the Select Committee System, I mistrust it. Hours and hours of work for back-bench councillors will be called for, then like the majority of House of Commons Select Committee Reports the findings will be pigeon holed to gather dust. There will be a few days' publicity on report, then they will be forgotten and mainly ignored by Government, the Cabinet and senior officers. That sort of scrutiny will have little effect on policy. The intention may be admirable but as an input into policy and decision making nothing will be achieved.

* * * * *

Following the run-down of the mining industry I was very keen to support the Wakefield MDC. The general economic decline in and around Wakefield presented two major problems. Thousands of jobs were lost and secondly there was a blight on the landscape created by redundant colliery sites. Wakefield's response was swift and decisive so I tried to be equally swift to support their efforts. In the late 1980s they created a new department, Economic Development, later to be re-organised as Regeneration Department. This was under the Chairmanship of Councillor Peter Box, now Leader of the Council, and its Chief Officer was Annie Faulder. She was an outstanding officer in this field and I was very sorry when later she left the Authority to take a post in Kirklees. This was certainly Wakefield's loss. I always thought Wakefield should have appointed her Chief Executive when the post became vacant, but they didn't. Both Peter Box and Annie Faulder worked very closely with local MPs in the early days and were successful. They tackled land reclamation and retraining. A network of resource centres was established in the district with two flagship buildings at the Five Towns Resource and Technology Centre in Castleford and the Westfield Resource and Enterprise Centre in South Elmsall. Using European grants, these

192

At a reception in the House of Lords with Anne Taylor.

Opening of the extension of Streethouse Cricket Club.

On the Featherstone Memorial March, followed by my colleague Dave Hinchliffe.

On the Isle of Iona at John Smith's grave.

centres provided training opportunities, assistance and premises to those wishing to establish new businesses.

Their first major success was in persuading the Japanese company Pioneer to establish its European base manufacturing laser discs at Whitwood. Peter Box and Annie Faulder worked very hard in presenting the Council's case and eventually the Japanese company was keen to obtain a European base in our district. As MP I was aware that there was competition from other European countries, as well as from the northeast. We had advantages. The motorway network especially attracted the Japanese company, but I think the success in getting them here can be traced back to Peter and Annie's determination to succeed. They never knew when to give up. Sometimes they went beyond midnight, sitting on the Planning Committee, working to exclude the chosen site from the Green Belt restrictions.

I was in constant contact from my office in London with Councillor John Pearman, the Leader of the Council. During the latter days of negotiations in particular, various problems arose as the directors of Pioneer became very cautious. There were many conditions on which the company wanted to satisfy themselves. The infrastructure, the roadworks necessary for access to the site all produced difficulties.

Eventually all these problems had been settled and the Pioneer directors seemed satisfied and were prepared to sign the agreement the next day when a crisis occurred. At 11.45 pm my phone rang in my office in London. It was John Pearman, he was very upset. He said, "We have problems with the purchase of the land. If it is not cleared by tomorrow, the Pioneer Company will pull out and go to Barcelona."

John explained the problem to me. He said the land was owned by a local farmer who was away on holiday in Spain. However, the farmer had given a legally binding assurance to a land speculator that he would have first option on purchasing the land. John said the appropriate council officers had met the speculator that day. He was aware that the Pioneer company were keen to settle, would not consider any further delay and so was now asking a price for the land which was too high for the Council. On hearing this news, to say I was less than pleased would be an understatement. I obtained the speculator's phone number from John Pearman and phoned him at his home at twelve midnight. I knew this gentleman very well. I expressed my anger at the information I had been given by John. I told him that if we lost the Pioneer development arising out of this, I would let the public know why. He, in his turn, informed me that there had never been any intention to hold the Council to ransom. As a local man, he was keen that this investment should come to the area and assured me that the land would be sold to the Council the next day at the previously agreed price. The Pioneer development was the first inward investment for manufacturing industry in the area following the miners' strike. The rest is history.

The Council's brief was to attract more inward investment into the district and to ensure that the now redundant workforce of ex-miners were retrained and school leavers given a better chance. Job creation for manufacturing industry was not as rapid as I would have liked. There have been other minor successes since the Pioneer development, but I am afraid Wakefield do not appear to have been as successful as some of the neighbouring authorities in creating a manufacturing industry.

On 19 October 1992 Michael Heseltine, then President of the Board of Trade, made a statement to the House of Commons that he would close thirty-one pits with a loss of 30,000 jobs. He tried to soften the blow by offering new money to the affected areas, about £165 million. I immediately thought, "I am having some of that!" He went on to say that the programmes would be carried out by a number of separate agencies, each of them with established expertise and a track record of achievement in their own field. This, he said, would ensure that the programmes would mesh together properly, creating neither wasteful overlaps nor damaging gaps. Lord Walker would act as co-ordinator and facilitator at national level.

I knew Lord Walker and put much of my energy in a campaign to get British Rail to site the European Freight Depot in our area. I had pushed Wakefield's case strongly by corresponding and meeting with the then Transport Minister, Roger Freeman, and Sir Bob Reid, Chairman of British Rail. As I was doing this I was aware that my colleagues, the late Martin Redman, Member for Don Valley Doncaster and Merlyn Rees - now Lord Rees - were pushing for their own areas, Doncaster and Leeds.

On my own initiative I invited Roger Freeman, the Transport Minister, to visit the site and was able to show him the motorway network in the immediate vicinity. He was very helpful and commented to me that if he had said to one of his officials, "Go out and prepare me a perfect site for a European freight depot," they would not have been able to produce one more suitable than the Whitwood site. This was encouraging and I was very grateful for his support. Following my many meetings with Sir Bob Reid I had also invited him to visit the site. He later told me that he was satisfied that the Wakefield site was the most suitable in the area and it had British Rail's backing. I was also very grateful that Jon Trickett, now Member of Parliament for Hemsworth, who was at that time Leader of Leeds City Council and also interested in obtaining the site for Stourton, always dealt very fairly and, in fact, was very supportive.

I was over the moon when the announcement was made that the Whitwood site had been chosen. I had been informed it was expected the depot would probably attract thousands of jobs to the area; manufacturing industry would be keen to manufacture near the depot and this development would go a long way to replace jobs lost through the closure of local pits. Knowing that the development would attract European funding, I visited Brussels to meet Bruce Millan, European Commissioner for Regional Development. Bruce was an old friend and colleague of mine from the days when he was a Member of Parliament. I impressed on him the importance of the development to an area which had suffered job losses in the mining industry. Bruce, as always a very courteous and understanding man with obvious sympathy for the mining communities, gave me a very fair hearing. As I expected he would not commit himself and give me any guarantee that the grant would be forthcoming but he was not negative. I readily understood though that there were bids from other local authorities which had to be considered along with Wakefield.

As time passed and there appeared to be no decision on the Wakefield application I grew apprehensive. I was less than pleased

195

when I was informed that it had not been possible to consider the Wakefield bid because it had arrived too late. When I asked the Wakefield MDC for the reason I was told that the young officer who was responsible for dealing with this matter had left the Authority's service and had failed to send the application forward.

This error delayed the commencement of the work for twelve months. During this time Doncaster, who had not been chosen as an official site, pressed forward with private capital to produce a depot in Doncaster. Even though it did not have British Rail's backing, they made an application for European funding which meant the bid was considered along with Wakefield's. The result was that the grant was split two ways. I think it more than likely that if Wakefield had sent its previous application within the time limit, they would have received the full grant.

During this period, another major setback to the development of the Europort occurred: AMEC, the company which was to have developed the scheme, pulled out. I do not know the reason, for it still maintains an interest in land surrounding the port. This decision put the Council in a near impossible situation - they found great difficulty in attracting another developer to fund the scheme. The Council had major decisions to make, they had to find sufficient capital to continue with the development. At this point they made a very courageous decision. They decided they would sell the interests in the Ridings Scheme, the shopping centre in Wakefield Town centre, to fund the Europort scheme. This shopping area was earning a yearly income which was not unsubstantial. They took the decision and the Wakefield Europort was built. I applaud the Council for their courage.

Fortunately the Europort is now turning into a success story as we all hoped it would, bringing jobs to the area.

On a recent visit to the site I was informed that it was not anticipated that there would be the large number of manufacturing jobs created that had previously been expected. However after seven years of completing the major infrastructure there are now very encouraging signs over the last three years that the distribution and manufacturing industry are now developing the site and I am told that one train per day is now leaving the Europort for Europe. It appears that the development is creating many jobs even though not in manufacturing industry. The reason for Europort's slow start is difficult to ascertain. Some may take the view that the Doncaster development, probably by greater marketing, has beaten Wakefield's efforts, or that the price which is being asked for the land surrounding the port was unattractive to manufacturers. It appears every effort has been made to make the depot and land adjacent to the area viable, so that we can provide an economic uplift for the local economy and produce jobs.

On 10 November 1993, following Michael Heseltine's pit closure programme, John Gummer, Secretary of State for the Environment, and Lord Walker launched English Partnerships, a new body to promote regeneration with Lord Walker as Chairman. English Partnerships was set up by statute as an Urban Regeneration Agency. One aspect of its work was to develop vacant derelict and contaminated land throughout England and bring land and buildings back into productive use. It was also to stimulate local enterprise, create job opportunities and improve the environment. English Partnerships would immediately take over city grant development, a scheme previously operated by the Department of the Environment. The Secretary of State at that time, John Gummer, said English Partnerships would build on the success of existing programmes and put the Government's private finance initiative into practice in this key area of national development by forging a new spirit of partnership with all those involved in regeneration. He said the announcement demonstrated the Government's commitment to regeneration and the environmental improvement of our towns, cities and rural areas. Lord Walker said it was creating a body with the ability to promote regeneration on a wider scale than ever before. He said they would always be ready to listen to imaginative new ideas for development through partnership with public, private and voluntary sectors, they would make every pound count, paying for early pump priming which could unlock schemes and bring in private sectors and EC money into the equation. In June 1993 Lord Walker announced that David Taylor had been appointed Chief Executive Officer of English Partnerships.

I knew David Taylor very well. He had held a senior position with AMEC, the company which was to build the Europort at Wakefield.

This appointment gave me new hope, for I saw a chance to solve a major problem I had been trying to solve within my then constituency for several years. The site of the former Glasshoughton Colliery which closed in 1986 and the coke ovens adjacent to the Colliery which closed in 1974 had produced an environmental disaster for the area. The derelict land was a major eyesore, there were fears that the ground where the coke ovens had operated were toxic. I immediately wrote to Lord Walker requesting him to give serious consideration to support a scheme for the regeneration of both these sites. He very kindly replied that he would call at my office in the House of Commons and discuss the scheme. When he did a few days later, he informed me he was keen to help and assured me that the scheme would be one of the first to be considered. He was true to his word. By 1996 British Coal was required by Government to dispose of its property holdings in Glasshoughton. As part of this process, English Partnerships negotiated a national portfolio of sites which transferred from British Coal to them in December 1996. This included the Glasshoughton sites. After this British Coal were no longer involved on that site.

I thought, "We are on our way." By this time, Waystone had been shortlisted as a preferred developer and in March 1996 the Board of English Partnerships approved the joint venture between themselves and Waystone. Waystone would undertake an agreed reclamation site project and English Partnerships would fund. Following that, Waystone would fund the infrastructure works and arrangements for sharing downstream receipts from the sale of any surplus land to third party developers. Waystone also invited public consultation and organised an exhibition at the Glasshoughton Cricket Pavilion. The plans the company displayed were very impressive and I found the people who attended were enthusiastic about the scheme. There was some scepticism, quite understandably, following the experience of previous proposals for the sites, but the company were very confident they would deliver the scheme and local people and I fell in behind.

Planning permission for the site reclamation works was applied for in September 1995 and granted in February 1996, alongside outline planning consent for change of use from a colliery to a site for a range of mixed users, including factory retail, leisure, housing, offices and industrial, as well as public open space. The detailed consent for the first phase of the site - servicing works, motorway junction improvements, a new junction to Park Lane and the first phase of a new road to open up the site together with associated services - were quickly submitted and approved but not before Wakefield MDC Planning Authority called a meeting of business people in Castleford to discuss the plans with them. The Chairman of the Planning Committee, Councillor Denise Jeffery, and the Planning Officer attended the meeting when natural fear was expressed that the scheme may have an effect on their businesses. I also attended the meeting and heard assurances given to the local business people that there would be no normal retail trading on the site. I spoke in support of the business people because I was convinced if there was normal retail trading on the site, it would have a catastrophic effect on both the town centres of Castleford and Pontefract. I was very pleased that when planning permission was granted, it included the condition that there would be no retail trade apart from factory outlets.

A headline in the *Pontefract and Castleford Express* read, "Snowdomia Unveiled!" and it announced that after years of anticipation and speculation, the multi-million pound winter wonderland plans for Glasshoughton have become much more than a dream. The report announced that work on a giant leisure mountain will commence in a few months' time bringing hundreds of jobs to the area. The major attraction will be a year-round ski slope and toboggan run with real snow, there will be a multiplex cinema, a bowling alley, virtual reality games and restaurants. The report suggests that the construction of the 21st Century complex will create an outstanding landmark dominating the local skyline and challenging London's Millennium Dome. The 150 foot high building will be visible for miles around and will incorporate a multiplex cinema and restaurant. Mr Stuart McLoughlin of Waystone has suggested that it will quickly complement the nearby retail outlet centre at Glasshoughton which is set to start trading in September 1999. The developers have said the site will bring in around 1,700 jobs.

This was becoming very exciting and I found that the general public was enthusiastic in support of the scheme.

Following the granting of outline planning consent for change of use, the Pearl Insurance Company - owners of the Carlton Lanes Shopping Centre - belatedly complained about the factory retail outlet proposals and sought a judicial review through the courts. This was fought by the Council who won the case. A detailed planning application was then submitted in respect of the factory retail development, which was approved. As I write, this development is well on its way, indeed it has now opened, and it has turned out to be beyond my wildest dreams.

I have always been a little concerned that the factory retail outlet may have an effect on the Pontefract and Castleford town centres, but arising out of assurances I received, I decided I could live with the decision. Provided we keep out supermarkets it will be a real asset for the area. However if we allow supermarkets to become part of this development then it will have a devastating effect and Castleford and Pontefract. I believe the development has a place in our post-coal economy. The developers estimate these facilities will attract over 1.5 million visitors per annum to the site and the developers have informed me that local bus service operators are already keen to run services from the site to Pontefract and Castleford town centres.

I was very pleased when David Taylor visited the site. He gave a statement to the *Pontefract and Castleford Express* which said, "Without the efforts of Geoff Lofthouse, the scheme could never have got off the ground." This was gracious but I must recognise that other people had worked very hard over many years in an attempt to bring the regeneration about, not least Norman Kennedy, former Deputy Leader of the Wakefield MDC and the local community committee, led by a formidable lady named Mrs Hilda Burton.

I believe this project has been an example of how English Partnerships and its partners can help tackle the problems faced in colliery closure areas. They have addressed difficult levels of contamination on these sites, but also shown how a public and private sector partnership can work to tackle reclamation and redevelopment. Glasshoughton also demonstrates how the immediate local community can be involved in such a project. They have negotiated the provision of improved landscaping and parking arrangements for

Picture by kind permission of Charles Green, Middlesex.

My daughter Lynne and family after I received my Knighthood at Buckingham Palace.

Picture by kind permission of Universal Pictorial Press.

My daughter Lynne, her husband and son with Black Rod and Garter King of Arms, after my introduction to the House of Lords.

some houses closest to the site. Local schools have also been involved in the project through information packs and site visits.

However, there is, as I write, a further worry. A piece of land on the extreme perimeter of the site has been fenced off. I am told that this small portion of land was not included in the original planning application and in recent months ASDA, the supermarket chain, has made a planning application to build a superstore. I can well understand why. It is directly on the perimeter of the M62 motorway, with access to the site through the improved road network which has recently been completed. I strongly believe that if this development is to go forward, whilst it may be of benefit for the Glasshoughton development, it would have a devastating effect on the trading of both Pontefract and Castleford town centres and I am very surprised that Wakefield MDC have in fact given their blessing to the scheme and forwarded the application to the Secretary of State for a decision on the planning application. I found this decision rather strange, considering that not too many months before Tesco had applied to build a supermarket on a site on Park Road, Pontefract, which is less than a mile from the proposed ASDA development and probably roughly the same distance between the proposed ASDA development and Castleford town centre. After the Public Inquiry on the Tesco development the Inspector was reported as saying that the Tesco appeal was turned down because of the effect it would have on Pontefract town centre. I find it difficult to understand the difference between these schemes and why the Council thought it necessary to turn down the Tesco scheme whilst supporting the ASDA scheme.

When I look at the site at this time, even in its present state it gives me a great thrill that I was able to play a leading part in securing this development. I will always recall the day Lord Walker knocked on my office door in London and gave me his support for the scheme. Whilst our political opinions were always miles apart I shall be extremely grateful, on behalf of all mining communities, for the efforts he made to cushion the traumatic situation arising out of the rapid run down of the coal industry, and to regenerate the areas.

As I walk round the centre of Pontefract and I see the results of the Local Authority's efforts to refurbish the centre of our historical town,

I feel very proud that I have been able to have an input into the scheme and I feel privileged and pleased to have worked alongside local business, community and amenity groups, particularly Alan Blaza and Peter Dewes of the Civic Trust, to achieve something special. I am also grateful to Councillor Denise Jeffery, Chair of the WMDC Planning Committee, whose enthusiasm and support for the scheme was paramount but I would also like to make special reference to Councillor Jack Kershaw. His drive and tireless effort for the scheme is only matched by his overall work in Pontefract during the short time he has been a councillor in the town.

When I walk around and admire the frontage of the Market Place and the Museum and Court House and, not least, the repaired Buttercross, I feel a great satisfaction. The Town Centre Partnership has produced a magnificent refurbished historical town centre, of which the area can be justifiably proud. When I took the Salute at the Armistice Parade in 1998 at the March Past in the Market Place, my eyes wandered to the cobbled streets and I experienced great personal pleasure. The first scheme which was considered seemed to me rather cheapskate. The materials to be used for the roads, streets and ginnels was similar to that which had been used in the Wakefield town centre scheme. Whilst I was aware that that scheme had been satisfactory to many Wakefield people, it was not good enough for Pontefract people. At their urging Councillor Jack Kershaw and myself made representations both to the Council and to English Heritage, pointing out that Yorkshire stone and cobbles were more appropriate for the historical town of Pontefract. Fortunately English Heritage shared our view and informed me if stone cobbles were not used, it might jeopardise the grant. On that I telephoned Councillor Denise Jeffery, who I knew supported my view. She advised me to speak to Councillor Wayne Jenkins, Chairman of the Highways Committee. I had previously been informed that Councillor Jenkins did not support stone cobbles but I took Councillor Jeffery's advice and telephoned him. He recognised that the English Heritage threat was real and he gave his support. As a result Pontefract Town Centre has maintained its character.

Currently, I am very concerned that the application to the Heritage Lottery Fund for a grant sufficient to regenerate the Grade II* Listed

Building of Pontefract Town Hall may not be forthcoming. The initial bid was not successful but it is absolutely essential for the Council's Heritage and Tourism Strategy that the Council makes further bids to regenerate the historical building. Built in 1785 it was for many years the site of the local government for Pontefract. Today it houses a life-size model of one of the faces of Nelsons Column in Trafalgar Square. In 1872, it was one of the two polling places in Pontefract for the first-ever English election by secret ballot, so it has worldwide significance. The Assembly Rooms, added 1881, provided more office space and a large function room in keeping with the growing importance of Pontefract as a thriving market town. The largest historic public building in the town centre, it needs reinstating to its former splendour so that it can become an attraction in its own right and a welcome addition to the regeneration programme.

Of course I know there are problems. Like everyone else I very much regret that over recent years the structural problems of Pontefract Town Hall have worsened but neglect it and the town will not be forgiving. Closure and sale to the private sector is not a happy alternative. Councillors representing Pontefract must never allow this to happen.

During the last twenty years new schools have been built. Some I have been privileged to open, not least the Love Lane Junior and Infants School, now re-christened Halfpenny Lane following its removal from the top to the bottom of the hill. I was a Governor there for 32 years and the Chairman for 29 years. I presided over the negotiations, had the privilege of cutting the first sod and opened it on completion. There have also been improved facilities to the King's High School and Carleton High School. I have seen the Sixth Form College - which was formerly the Pontefract Girls High School - play a leading part in the education of the Wakefield District. All this has given me great satisfaction.

* * * * *

In the 1960s Joe Blackburn was Mister Pontefract, a powerful politician, but a very caring man. A radiographer at Pontefract Infirmary, he had a particular interest in elderly people. I remember him saying, "When you get old you end up in side streets, behind lace curtains and nobody outside your immediate family knows your name. It is important, Geoff, that we give thought to these people. Many of them are proud but they are also lonely and as time passes and families move out from the town, that loneliness will increase."

I had seen this myself: I had lived in this type of community all my life but was particularly aware of it when elections came around and a whole gang of us went out canvassing. In those days, the Tanshelf Ward contained a lot of terraced housing. Close to Tickle Cock Bridge in Railway Avenue lived an elderly couple. I knew the man from his time in the mines. He was a bit of a character when younger but always well turned out. So it was a great surprise when I knocked on his door to see if he wanted a lift to the polling station and experienced a long wait on the doorstep. When it was opened it was immediately apparent that neither of them could cope. I still remember that day forty years later, for it upset me. In the days when canvassing took place at every election and we went around door by door knocking out, I was often surprised to discover that none of them refused to be taken to vote, indeed they often sat outside waiting for us, our visit was the first they had experienced that month.

My commitment to old people from my very early days as a politician was always strong. Of course, well before Joe Blackburn spoke to me, I was aware that there was a system of social care for the elderly in our town. Almshouses had been there from ancient times, but by the time I joined the committee, apart from building and repairs little was done to support the occupants. They got a box of chocolates at Christmas; indeed the annual debate seemed to be about whether the box should be a pound or half a pound in weight.

Then there was the workhouse on Northgate. By the sixties this was a caring place but the nineteenth century tradition continued and "being sent to the workhouse" was a dreaded term.

Two types of care were by this time coming into operation. There were sheltered housing schemes being set up in which a warden was

Picture by kind permission of Harold Lacey, Ackworth.

With Yvette Cooper MP, Jack Kershaw and other dignitaries at Pontefract War Memorial.

My home as a boy.

The garden I enjoy at my present home.

appointed and a community centre built. There was also accommodation for people who were more at risk. This was administered by Social Services. Here the intervention of outside carers was more direct. Under the control of the County Council, under the guidance of a Pontefract politician, Bob Egan, it was doing an excellent job. It was responsive and initiated common-sense strategies. One comes to mind: Pontefract Council found that one-bedroom bungalows were no good to a family whose carer was an unmarried son or daughter so at Eastbourne we built two-bedroom accommodation for elderly people.

Sometime in 1962 there was a massive thunderstorm and Sarah and I stood on the doorstep looking out across Chequerfield Circle to the shops on the other side. The complete area was covered in builder's rubble and clay, for the practice had evolved that any rubbish coming off the various building schemes in Chequerfield and Willow Park was dumped on that massive green circle.

Sarah looked across and I can hear her now, "Look at that lot, it's time you and some of the others got some old people's accommodation built there. You shove them into quiet corners where the only people they see are other pensioners and the only topic of conversation is, who died last week and who is about to die next. Why don't you put these elderly folk among the people? Build houses where they can look out and see the Church, see the pubs and the shops." She was having a go at me, I can hear her now, but she was right.

That same evening I telephoned Joe Blackburn and Bob Egan and put Sarah's view to them. Bob in particular was a great champion of "constant care" and, to his credit, he was very enthusiastic. Within two years he had got a complete complex built opposite our house and between us and the shops. It was a real triumph. Bob opened part of the development and got the Prime Minister, Harold Wilson, to come in and open the other. Labour's commitment to the care of the elderly within the public sector was absolute.

I was upset when in the early 1990s local politicians abandoned public sector care without much of a fight. The first hint I got that anything was afoot was when Tony Dean, one of my ward councillors but also Chair of the Social Services Committee, approached me in the Labour Club one Sunday. He told me that Wakefield was contemplating closing six of its old people's homes. I told him that I would oppose this move with all the energy I had.

As the story unravelled it appeared that not only were they preparing to force elderly people into private accommodation, but they were shipping some out of the district to places as far off as Selby. In a town like ours, where extended families still exist, such a move seems especially offensive. For although many people have cars, some do not and our public transport system to the east is notoriously bad. It was becoming clear that the private sector was a gold mine for anyone who wanted to make money, and the system of private nursing homes was mushrooming under Thatcher. Licences were even being requested for individuals to be accommodated in semi-detached houses. What inspection there was, was underdeveloped and, as far as the small units were concerned, amounted to no inspection at all.

Regretfully my opposition to this change did not alter policy. But in self-defence I would say this was to a large extent because councillors chose to ignore information which I supplied. When I first approached the officers and the councillors on this matter I was told that there was no option but to pass Council Community Services - effectively the care of the elderly - to the private sector. Wakefield said that it was Conservative Government policy that 85% of the financial allocation to run homes must be used in the independent sector. I was sure that there was a serious loop hole in this legislation and therefore discussed a strategy with Roy Widdowson, the Chair of the Wakefield and Pontefract Community Health Trust.

I argued that the Trust was not part of local government, therefore it could act as an independent agency, that in effect Wakefield Council could pay the Trust for services. Roy - a Featherstone man - and I have a long history going back years. So his commitment resembled mine and we agreed that what I was proposing was feasible and, if applicable, would receive his backing. I passed this information on to Wakefield arguing that if our plan was implemented we could protect the community from high charges and at the same time ensure that elderly people in our area got the best care on offer. Looking longer-term I argued that when a Labour Government was returned to power it would be easy if the accommodation was controlled by one major body rather than a lot of little entrepreneurs.

When this was put to Tony Dean and his officers, both said that it could not be done, for my strategy lay outside Conservative Government policy. My position in the House of Commons as Deputy Speaker placed me on a par with a Minister and this meant that I could approach the relevant Minister of State, in this case John Bowis, and ask him if my view was correct. When he heard my argument, he not only verbally agreed that it could be done, but wrote to me to that effect. What he said was that he saw no impediment to regarding community trusts as part of the independent sector rather than the public sector. The letter seemed to me decisive. Wakefield did not have to go private.

I forwarded it to the Council anticipating a change of policy. With such a letter I was right to anticipate success. What I had not calculated was that the letter would be ignored, not only by the Chair and his officer, but also by my own constituency councillors. My terms of reference as an MP mean that I can only communicate with councillors in my constituency and so I sent each a letter indicating John Bowis' opinion. This letter was ignored and at the relevant meeting those who sat in the Committee did not present my case. I never expected such a rebuff and find it difficult to forgive. Councils, not landlords, should look after the elderly.

* * * * *

In 1995 the Wakefield Health Authority published its Health Strategy for the following five years. I realised this could possibly have effects on the services that were provided in Pontefract and the probable outcome would be centralising services. I recognise Pontefract is no different to many other towns and I was aware that many health authorities in the country were undertaking work to close traditional general hospitals and develop services on a single site serving a much larger population. Naturally people worry about access to services that they had traditionally found available close to their homes. While I realise that technology has moved on and that the skills of doctors need to be used to best effect I was worried over the balance between the availability of services and the travelling time that members of the public would increasingly have to face.

On investigation I became aware that the British Medical Association/Royal Colleges had issued a consultation paper which stated that the effective size to provide most acute services for medicine and surgery is one serving a population of 250,000 to 350,000. The consultation paper also said the ideal unit for fully comprehensive medicine and surgery is a hospital or integrated group of hospitals serving a population of 450,000 to 500,000. I was not impressed by these figures. There was a strong feeling in the Pontefract district, which I shared, that the hospital services may be getting too big. Locals have a loyalty and love for their own hospital. They feared that the suggested new units would become so distant and inconvenient to reach by public transport that the average person would not be able to associate with them. On the other hand others - not least amongst the clinicians - realised that better outcomes could be achieved by travelling further to receive specialist services. I believed in a balance and that the immediate availability of advice, support and treatment traditionally provided through Accident and Emergency Services needed to be sustained through services near to people's homes.

When the Wakefield Health Authority published their strategy, the alarm bells began to ring throughout the district, for many of my local constituents saw this as the beginning of centralisation and a diminishing of local services. The Health Strategy document emphasised that change would be necessary because existing services were not sustainable under a Tory Government policy which emphasised competition.

Prior to the Health Authority publishing the Health Strategy the Wakefield Area Health Hospitals were managed by two separate trusts, the Pinderfields Trust and the Pontefract General Infirmary Trust. The question arose as to whether services should be changed first or whether the merger of the two Trusts should take place. The document which was put out for consultation mainly emphasised the merger of the two Trusts and not the reconfiguration of services. Both Trusts decided to recommend merger so it was agreed that the Chairman of the Pinderfields Trust and the Chief Executive of the Pontefract Trust should be the project leaders.

When they delivered the document people realised this was the first step on the road to losing the local hospital services, and people in my constituency grew angry. I shared that view and led a campaign opposing the merger. I spoke at several public meetings, many of them well attended, and heard views both for and against. At every meeting I attended there was overwhelming opposition to the recommended merger. It was following one such meeting that it was recognised that the authorities had not acted correctly before commencing the consultation period, that their action was 'ultra vires'. This discovery delayed the consultation period by several months.

During this period of uncertainty there was a real sense of outrage. People believed that the mergers were being steamrollered through, that members of the hierarchy had made their mind up over-early. There were grounds for these suspicions: even after 60,000 letters from individuals opposing the mergers were presented to the House of Commons by Jon Trickett, MP for Hemsworth, the then Secretary of State agreed to the merger. There was a great deal of disillusionment throughout the area, most believed that the consultation period was nothing but a myth. I was to recognise this disillusionment when campaigning to maintain the services at both ends of the Wakefield District.

In May 1998 the Wakefield Health Authority issued both a Green and White Paper prepared by the Pinderfields and Pontefract Hospitals Trust on the reconfiguration of acute health services for the area. They informed the Secretary of State that both the Health Authority and Trusts unequivocally believed that the problems of the area needed urgent resolution if local services were to remain viable, affordable, and of sufficiently high quality. They said the scenario without investment was one of crisis management, failing services and ultimately a loss of acute hospital provision for the local population. The proposal for the capital investment put forward in the bid was for a new acute specialist centre. They said this would enable centralisation and integration of all acute and complex in-patient activity, critical care services, including Intensive Care Unit and A&E, and high-tech ambulance care. The bid said that the acute specialist centre was not a traditional district general hospital, but a high technology hospital. They said that the configuration and capacity of the centre had been based on new models of care and challenging performance targets, and that these had the full support of the Trust clinicians.

I believe when submitting their case, they made a major blunder, for they identified a preferred site for building the new facility if the bid was successful. That site was at Pinderfields Hospital. This caused outrage at the eastern side of the district, especially in the Pontefract area. The Community Health Council expressed their great concern that they had not been consulted prior to the bid being put in nor prior to the consultation period. The CHC accused Wakefield Health Authority of having prejudged the outcome before the end of the consultation period and in these circumstances sought legal advice on whether or not they could go forward with a judicial review. The legal advice they received was that, in fact, there was a case for judicial review so they decided to take such a course. Following this decision a series of meetings was held between the CHC and the Chief Executive of the Wakefield Health Authority. Arising out of these meetings the CHC agreed to withdraw their request for a judicial review on condition that the Wakefield Health Authority withdraw its decision to support a preferred site and set up a working group to consider the reconfiguration of services and the possible siting of a new hospital. This working group was formed under my Chairmanship.

Following the submission of the Strategic Outline Case to the Secretary of State, the Wakefield district became split on parochial lines. The MPs were split, the councillors were split. The Chairman of the Health Authority resigned (though not because of controversy, but because he was leaving the district). This meant that the Wakefield Health Authority was without its captain at a crucial period. It was at

210

this time when I was first approached by some of my political and non-political colleagues. They asked if I would consider being nominated to take over the Chair of the Wakefield Health Authority.

It was a major decision, as I had retired from the House of Commons and was looking forward to a more relaxed life. I was 73, my health wasn't as robust as previously but I was aware the National Health Service which we inherited from the previous Government was run down and shabby. I decided to give it a go. I did not inherit a happy situation. Much of its investment in information technology had been an expensive failure. Much of its equipment was unreliable and let down both patients and staff. The priority of the new Government was to modernise the NHS, build new hospitals, replace outdated and unreliable equipment and give patients quicker, easier and more modern access to NHS services. This was not easily done in our area.

The new Government had already committed an investment of an extra £21 billion in the NHS over the next three years. The biggest hospital building programme in the history of the NHS was already under way. The coming year at least £350 million was to be invested in upgrading and replacing outdated equipment. I was keen to be a part of this and my excitement was such that after giving it very serious consideration, and after receiving advice and opinions from various colleagues, I decided I would probably be able to perform a useful service in guiding the Health Authority through this difficult period. I informed colleagues who had requested me to consider being nominated, that I was prepared to stand up and be counted.

During the period after nomination it crossed my mind that the Secretary of State for Health might wonder if I was the right person for the job. Understandably he might think that my involvement with the local Pontefract General Infirmary over many years might influence my judgement. So I decided I would make a speech in the House of Lords to make my position quite clear. I thought it was right that the Secretary of State should be in possession of my views and I could think of no better way of doing so. *(Appendix K)*

On 14 December 1998 the Secretary of State for Health announced that he had appointed me Chairman of the Wakefield Area Health Authority.

The decision on Wakefield's bid for capital monies was eventually received in July 1999. As I anticipated the Health Minister was not able to support the proposals from the Trust. However he did give a clear indication that the case of need for investment in the district was acknowledged but further work was necessary.

Clearly mistakes had been made in the approach added to which was confirmation that Leeds had been accepted as the Number One priority in the Region. Interestingly, Leeds had been turned down some twelve months previously and it is therefore understandable that their revised approach was accepted this time round.

The optimism contained within the Health Minister's letter to me required Wakefield to amend its proposals to include clearer references to the important part that primary care would play in the future, together with Wakefield being adopted as a Health Action Zone. Wakefield Health Authority had gained national recognition for their primary care work and had piloted a national approach based on the Primary Care Groups that have subsequently become part of the NHS infrastructure. In addition, because of the levels of deprivation and need in the Wakefield district, the Government had included Wakefield as one of the Health Action Zones in the country. This attracted additional finances to use in a range of schemes and was intended to co-ordinate the work of the health organisations with the Local Authority and voluntary groups. The Minister expected Wakefield to use the HAZ status innovatively in its revised plan.

The timing of the revised bid became particularly important. With the delays in notification of schemes that had occurred and that would be undertaken using the Private Finance Initiative it was not known when or if a further round of bids would be expected. There was the possibility that because of the strength of Wakefield's need approval would be given outside of the normal capital bidding round and it was with this in mind that "due haste" was applied in completing the additional work.

There was an acknowledgement by most people that change needed to happen and that the district did not have sufficient finances to maintain the current level of services over two hospitals. This option was included in the review that I chaired together with further consideration to the use of the two sites under a different pattern of care and also the potential of a new acute specialist centre supported by ancillary accommodation. This option was the basis of the Strategic Outline Case that had been submitted by the Trust, and subsequently turned down. The final option involved the building of a new district general hospital to serve the entire district, which would see the closure of existing facilities at Pinderfields General Hospital and Pontefract General Infirmary.

The intention is to write up the revised approach in the form of a consultation document and to gauge people's views on what is affordable and what will demonstrate the means by which improved levels of health care can be provided for the people. Wakefield now stands at the crossroads with the potential to move forward in a positive way, or alternatively the inability to secure support for a way forward will detract from the Government's ability to support Wakefield through investment. If not successful the result of this scenario will no doubt see services move from within the district to Leeds and other surrounding areas. The decline that had been feared would become real and for this reason we need to meet the challenge and succeed.

* * * * *

I have served 40 years in public life as a trade union official, councillor, Member of Parliament and Peer of the Realm. As I ride around the area I have been privileged to represent over those years, I experience great satisfaction when I see the regeneration of the area and I feel what a great honour it has been to have been able to play my part in producing it. Whilst it has been slower than I would have liked, the area is now showing signs that rising from the ashes of the mining industry, there is appearing a future more environmentally friendly. I see the former colliery sites and spoil heaps being reclaimed. I think of the wonderful days of my childhood, growing up in the mining community of Featherstone. We knew nothing else but dirt and grime, created by the colliery. Many of us were housed in accommodation that had mostly been provided by the former colliery

213

owners. Some of the miners of past generations would say they used to dig a big hole in the ground and then build houses around it, which they called stables for colliers. Of course the miners and their wives turned these into homes to bring up their families. They were clean and cared for. They were mostly homes with love in them. The children were taught standards to live by. The whole community was one large family who shared both happy and sad times together. On the death of a member of the community, many of whom were killed in the pits, the community would mourn. I recall as a boy when a funeral cortege was passing through Featherstone, people would stop and doff their caps in silence while the cortege passed. It would move slowly and all the town paid its respects.

In happier times they would rejoice together. In Featherstone when the rugby team were doing well the town rejoiced. Of course the community became more of a family through marriage. Owing to limited transport provision, few partnerships were formed outside the community and neighbouring areas. Lots of lifetime loving partnerships began in school days. The greatest privilege I have been fortunate to experience is being born and living all my life in one of these communities. Nothing can ever surpass the memories of that period of my life.

This was brought home to me recently when I heard of the death of a lifelong friend who I had attended school with and enjoyed both our adolescence and adulthood with as friends. We both worked in the local mine and also enjoyed many recreation hours together. Men of our generation who were born in the mining communities were more than friends, we were brothers. This particular friend was Edward (Ned) Roberts. As I left my home one Friday morning to attend Ned's funeral, I had arranged to call and pick up another lifelong friend, Derek Gray, to accompany me to Ned's funeral. As I drove from Pontefract to Featherstone I passed the school that Ned and I attended. This school was called South Featherstone Modern School. We always called it "the new school"; it had been built in about the 1930s to accommodate children from age 11 to 14. As I passed the school the memories came flooding back. I could see the scenes when we were arriving and leaving school. I recall the fun we used to share at lunchtime running from the school to the Regent Street School in

Station Lane, which would be about one mile. Children from poorer families would attend for free school meals. The fastest runner would get there first and get the pick of the food. I recall the Friday afternoons when the school rugby team was playing away at another local school when we took great pride in displaying the football shirts, which were then called 'jerseys'.

I recalled vividly the Friday when along with my classmates we left school at the age of 14 and met each other to go down the local colliery the following Monday. We sat in a classroom at school together on a Friday and then were committed to begin work in the bowels of the earth the following Monday and for most of these boys there they would remain for the rest of their working lives. My own experience in the pits provided a comradeship and loyalty to each other that I have never seen surpassed in any other form of employment.

As we drove past South Featherstone Modern School - now Featherstone High - with my friend Derek Gray on the way to Ned Robert's funeral, I said to Derek, "Another one of us gone, we are a dwindling band. When I visit Featherstone now, I recall some words my grandfather used to say, 'The trouble with getting old is you do not know anybody.' I did not appreciate what he meant at the time, but I do now. It is getting very depressing, these funerals come too often. Each one I attend, I feel emotionally naked, it is like a part of your life coming to an end and I realise I will not always be following. But for all that I thank God that He gave me the privilege to be part of this community.

When we arrived at the Methodist Chapel in Featherstone, a chapel I was familiar with and which I had attended on many occasions, I found it full to capacity. This was no surprise to me because I was aware of Ned's popularity in the town. As I looked around the Church I knew in a direct way what my grandfather meant. Most of the mourners were children and grandchildren of my contemporaries I recognised because of a likeness to their parents. This was a new age but I got the feeling that they had not altered much from their parents. They were better dressed these days and had more modern homes, but basically they are the same good people, though facing modern

215

difficulties of life, such as drugs, broken marriages and the disruption of family life, possibly greater problems than my generation ever faced.

When I had settled I saw we had not all passed on and felt great joy in seeing people from my own generation and from my school days. Just behind me was Joan Cording, she had married a close friend of mine, Austin Rollason. Joan, along with her sister Kath, were two of the many beautiful Featherstone girls I had enjoyed my recreational hours with in my teens, dancing at the Featherstone Miners Welfare and the Featherstone Baths. Jack Fennel, another lifelong friend, was just across the aisle. A distinguished Featherstone Rovers rugby player, he was a few years younger and I had known him since he was about five years old; one of the safest tacklers I ever saw.

After the service I followed Ned to the crematorium at Pontefract. Here again the place was so full. I only just managed to get a seat beside a lady who I sort of knew but could not place. She said, "Have you forgotten me?"

I replied, "I am afraid I do not recognise you, but your face is familiar."

She said, "I am Rita Bradley."

I remembered her immediately. She was Bernard Bradley's daughter. Joan, Jack and Rita, all three brought home to me the real price of coalmining. Each of them had a father killed at Ackton Hall Colliery when I was working there in my teens. Then they would have been men in their 40s and early 50s, killed working in conditions that would not be tolerated today. In my small way I had been placed to fight to change these conditions.

I realised what I suppose I have always known: I was at home amongst the family of Featherstone. Standing there close to the coffin, I thought, "Thanks Ned, at the end of your life, you have given me the opportunity to realise that the greatest privilege of my life was to have been born into the family of a mining community and whilst I certainly do not wish to denigrate the great privileges I have enjoyed at Westminster, this is a very special occasion. I bid you, Ned, my last goodbyes in the belief that the Lord decides who meets Him next and we will meet again in a better world."

As I left the crematorium friends of a lifetime - men who I had worked in the pits with - came to congratulate me on my efforts in obtaining compensation for miners suffering from bronchitis and emphysema. They said, "You have done us proud." Yet I did not feel that way but humbled I thought, "How lucky I am. Thank you God for placing me in a position where I could fight for the rights of miners, fight for others and these, my lifetime friends. No one can have had a greater privilege than to be in a position to help one's fellow men. I am so fortunate. I am sure if it had not been me, it would have been someone else from the community who would have carried out the same work, but I was the fortunate one. It has been a good life. I have been given great personal satisfaction. I have been favoured by the people of the Pontefract and Castleford Constituency, for they elected me to represent them in Parliament. What a good job it is."

I recall an incident which is a footnote to the day of Ned's funeral. It was getting very late one evening in Westminster, I had just left the Chair and went to the Tea Room for a drink of tea. All around were groups grumbling about the House sitting to this late hour. One MP said to me, "Mr Deputy Speaker, how long are you going to let this go on? It is stupid legislating in the early hours of the morning."

I replied, "Yes, but we have got a good roof, a good floor, there is very little dust, but unfortunately plenty of hot air." He looked at me in amazement, for clearly he did not have a clue what I meant. But I did and I knew that my own people in the mining communities would know.

* * * * *

It is now fifteen years since the death of my wife Sarah. In the final lines of *A Very Miner MP*, written as a tribute to her and the major part she had played in my life for over forty years - as sweetheart, wife, mother and grandmother - I said she was always my wise mate. She was more concerned about her role as wife, mother and grandmother and the wellbeing of all her family than her role as a politician's wife.

217

She was supportive and protective of me and after her death I wondered and worried how I would manage without the stability she brought into our lives. As I commenced my life without her, experiencing a loneliness in my private and personal life, I felt I was alone. I had not experienced such vulnerability since having lost both my parents by the time I was aged sixteen. Again I found myself living alone and whilst I had a demanding and interesting job and plenty of interests to fill the time, I wondered how I would cope.

I need not have really worried because my beloved daughter Lynne stepped into her place. She has been the real strength and cornerstone that I have been able to cling to. She has maintained the stability of the family life Sarah always provided. I also have had the support of her husband and my beloved grandchildren, Thomas and Eleanor. All have always shown great love for me and enable me to understand in some way the views of their generation. They experienced the great loss when their grandma died, for they were aged four and two. They are now teenagers, both in higher education. I have always had the love and affection of my sisters, Daisy and Annie and sisters-in-law, Violet and Margaret and I have had a real pal in my brother-in-law Cliff. I recognise how fortunate and privileged I have been to be part of a family life, the true foundation of society.

The main cornerstone of my life has been my Christian belief which has always sustained and guided me. I have tried to base my judgement on the Christian teaching I learned at my mother's knee. Through this I have always found the strength, security and faith throughout a life which continues beyond the period this book covers. As I have looked over the period I realise what a happy and privileged life I have experienced and what a major part God's guidance has played.

Of course the last fifteen years have brought highs and lows. As in all families some members die. I felt a great deal of sadness when my much-loved sister-in-law Lily died. Since Sarah's death she had been an angel to me, looking after my home and my domestic needs with great love and affection. Her death left a great void in my life which was widened when her beloved husband, Albert, died a few weeks after her. In the short period after their deaths I also lost my brother-in-law, Bill Ward (Sarah's sister Margaret's husband), and my friend and spiritual guide, Reverend Eric Fowkes. I had known Eric for all of 37 years. He was the Vicar of All Saints' Church, Pontefract and I relied on him for support in my times of need, which he invariably provided. I have continued to miss him greatly

Following this sad period of loneliness after Sarah's death there has been a period of great happiness. The most significant thing that has happened to me in my personal life is my re-meeting with Alice. Alice is the widow of Roy Walton, a local businessman and professional cricketer, who died two years prior to Sarah. No autobiography of my life could be possible without the story of Alice and I.

I recall as a boy aged twelve whilst at the school which Alice also attended, I always had a schoolboy crush on her. At that time boys and girls were separated at school and invariably kept apart. However, during our leisure time at home, along with my friends I used to play rugby and cricket on the green in the immediate vicinity of our homes in Little Lane, Purston. I suppose I had just about reached puberty and my mind was beginning to give some thought to girls. I have very close recollections of a beautiful girl about two years my junior. She was the daughter of a local butcher, so she would arrive twice weekly riding her bicycle to deliver meat to some of our neighbours. Of course I recognised Alice from school and I know that on many occasions that my eyes and mind would wander in her direction although she never gave me a second glance. Of course - she was the local butcher's daughter and businessmen's daughters got on with carrying out their duties. Mind, this did not diminish my interest. I would always look forward to Alice arriving on her delivery days and, indeed, would organise our matches to coincide, but we never spoke.

I left school and started work at the pit the day I was fourteen, and our games on the green became less frequent. When Alice left school and commenced work, I did not see very much of her. I have since learnt that she joined the WAAF and left the area. Our paths did not cross for many years.

In about 1981/2 I attended Morning Service at All Saints' Pontefract, which was rather unusual for me because it was my practice to attend Evensong. On leaving my pew, I cast my eyes on this beautiful lady sat towards the back of the Church. I immediately recognised her and spontaneously went to her and said, "You are Alice." Considering it was well in excess of forty years that our paths had crossed, I suppose I could be forgiven for being mistaken, but I knew I was not. She said, "Yes, and you are Geoff Lofthouse." I did not know whether she recognised me as a local public figure or from my boyhood. She introduced me to her daughter Susan. The next time I saw Alice was in less pleasant circumstances. Sarah and I were leaving a local supermarket one day towards the end of 1983. I saw Alice and went to speak to her. During our conversation Alice said, "Did you know I had lost Roy?" I did not know what to say. I said I did not, and expressed my usual condolences. I was upset for her and when I arrived home Sarah suggested I should call and see her. This was not unusual because in my position as local Member of Parliament I would occasionally visit people who had lost loved ones.

The next time I saw Alice was in mid-April 1985. Our paths had not crossed at Church because I had continued to attend Evensong and Alice the Morning Service. Sarah had undergone an operation in mid-March 1985 for what I believed was a minor complaint but turned out to be very serious. I was told by the consultant her life expectation was about three months, but it turned out to be only six weeks. The only time I left Sarah's side during that period was towards the end of her life. I had to visit the bank in Pontefract to arrange Sarah's financial affairs. I think during that period I must have been in a very poor state. My mind was in a whirl and I must have looked like a zombie. As I was leaving the bank the person I came face to face with was Alice. I told her of my bad news. I think it was the first time I had seen her since she told me about the death of her husband Roy. I could see the shock on her face and she appeared to be lost for words. Sarah died on the 4 May 1985.

After that I threw myself into my work in Parliament and spent my weekends in my surgery, paying visits to elderly and disabled constituents, and also spent not a little time with Reverend Eric Fowkes. He had been preaching the Christian message at All Saints' for in excess of thirty years, at the time of his death he had completed 37 years at the Church. I started returning to London on Sunday evenings and so I decided to attend Church on Sunday mornings.

Here with Eric Fowkes after a Service at All Saint's Church, Pontefract.

With Alice in her garden.

This, of course, coincided with Alice's attendance. From then on we would chat and over a period of ten years, we would always leave Church together and exchange pleasantries.

Over these years I realised that my affection for Alice was growing. I never declared this to her and I was certainly never aware she was experiencing similar affection for me and so the years rolled by. I think Eric Fowkes must have been aware of our feelings because he invited me to assist him and give the address at Alice's daughter's wedding. Alice informed me later that he had approached her with the idea. We gradually realised that we both looked forward to our Sunday morning meeting even though it was just a few minutes when we were leaving Church. This continued and if it had been left to our own devices, it is possible that it would have stayed that way. In 1995 Eric Fowkes died. I had visited him in hospital after the Morning Service, three days before he died. He seemed very tired and said to me, "I am having an operation tomorrow. Andrew (Mr Andrew Broughton the Consultant) is going to perform the operation. He is a good lad is Andrew - but I have told him not to bother too much, I am ready to meet my Maker." When I left him I had the feeling I would not see him again.

After Eric's death the Church struggled on with small congregations, but the few regular worshippers, with the assistance of Reverend Eric Brown from South Kirkby, kept the Church operating. After a spell without an incumbent at All Saints, the Reverend Kevin Partington was appointed. This was a very happy occasion for all the regulars at All Saints. When he was installed by the Bishop of Wakefield I was privileged to be invited to say a few words of welcome during the service. I informed both Kevin and the full Church that I had been at the service when Eric Fowkes was installed. That was thirty-seven years previous. I apologised and said that if he stayed as long I could not promise to be at his side for all of the period.

Eric Fowkes was very proud when I was elected Member of Parliament and I was particularly conscious of this pride when I arrived at Church on Sunday morning to find a brass plate had been fixed on the seat at the front of the Church I had occupied for many years. It said *Member of Parliament*. I was uneasy about this because

I have never believed that there should be reserved places in the House of God. I did not make my feelings known to Eric for fear of upsetting him, so the seat remained reserved for the MP up to Eric's death and into the early months of Kevin's arrival.

The congregation had begun to grow and Kevin introduced some of his own practices, one being christenings during Sunday Morning Services. To that end, one Sunday morning, Kevin requested that I leave the seat on the front to allow families attending the christenings to sit at the front of the Church. This he said would be more convenient for him when performing the act of christening and I gladly agreed. I moved and without hesitation walked to the back of the Church and joined Alice. I do not know if I received spiritual guidance to the pew, but I did not even think about sitting elsewhere. From that day our affection for each other began to grow apace. Since that time we have spent all our free time together and it is my hope that this will continue until our Lord decides that one of us joins him in his Holy Kingdom.

APPENDICES

APPENDIX A - Conclusion of The Select Committee on Energy (28 January 1987)

"Conclusion - For many years coal will continue to be the electricity supply industry's dominant primary fuel. Even on pessimistic estimates, coal will also continue to form a major part of the industrial steam-raising market; and there are still a substantial number of households which use coal. For the foreseeable future, therefore, coal will be vital to the country's energy needs. The Government have told the Committee that their "first energy policy objective..... is that there should be adequate and secure supplies of energy available to the people of this country." Indifference to the future of the British coal industry would be an abrogation of political responsibility, and we are pleased that the Secretary of State recognises the strategic needs for a British coal industry.

The dichotomy between a "market forces" and a "planning" approach is a false one. The common aim should be for a coal industry which is efficient and able to make a very substantial contribution to meeting present and future British energy demand. It is neither sensible to contemplate long-term subsidy nor realistic to deny the possibility that government assistance will occasionally be necessary to help this basic industry cope with future disruptions caused by short-term market factors. The industry's future is much more likely to be assured by continued productivity improvement than by a return to production targets which are not related to productivity achievements. However, as it is not possible to "fine tune" mining capacity and difficult to ensure an inflow of new jobs into mining areas to offset mining redundancies, the coal industry's future cannot be left wholly in the invisible hand of market forces.

When the transformation which it is at present undergoing nears completion, the coal industry will be in a far better position to face market conditions in the 1990s and to ensure that indigenous coal has a growing rather than contracting market. This transformation, meanwhile, is placing a heavy burden in terms of unemployment and social decline upon the coalmining communities, and our recommendations to lessen the burden through more effective policies to bring new jobs to these areas are among the more important recommendations of this Report.

The need for changes in the coal industry was unquestionable. But it would be a grave error of policy if the Government's pressure on BC to move in that direction resulted in an industry incapable of meeting the demands which the country might put upon it in the future, or in a legacy for the coalmining areas of stagnant communities, bereft of any prospect of the economic prosperity enjoyed by other parts of the nation."

APPENDIX B - Minority Report to Energy Select Committee (28 January 1987)

"Whether an industry is publicly or privately owned has no bearing on its efficiency. Sir Robert Haslam, most of whose life has been spent in the private sector, told us unequivocally, "The perception that somehow private industry has some great magic wand and can come in and do something which nationalised industries cannot do, has not got a great deal of validity." We believe that discussion of the privatisation of the coal industry is an unnecessary and potentially harmful sideshow - which the Chairman of BC called an "unfortunate diversion" and the General Secretary of the BACM described as "very destabilising". The structure of the industry is broadly acceptable as it is, and its ownership by the public brings real practical and strategic advantages. No case for alteration has been adequately made.

We are sure that at least some of those in government recognise this. The Government has on several occasions assured the Committee that there are no plans for the privatisation of BC, though sometimes we have been assured that there are "no plans" while on others we are told that there are no plans "at the present time". However, we are equally sure that some Ministers remain ideologically committed to privatisation. As far as coal is concerned, we set particular store by the Prime Minister's words on this matter since decisions about the privatisation programme are clearly taken at No 10 and the Treasury rather than in the sponsoring Departments for the industries concerned. Mrs Thatcher was asked a specific question about privatisation plans for the coal industry. However her answer was unclear:

"The Government has privatised one-fifth of the state sector of industries which they inherited in 1979, and will have transferred a further one-fifth to the private sector by the end of this parliamentary session. We have also announced our intention to return most of the remainder to the private sector in the next Parliament. However, there are no current plans for the privatisation of British Coal. The priority for the industry's management is to build on the enormous productivity gains that are now being achieved and to restore the industry to financial viability."

Do we infer from this answer that BC is not to be privatised by a future Conservative government? We recommend that the Government state categorically that BC will not be privatised.

We readily admit that part of our opposition to a privatised coal industry is based on the experience which this country had of a private coal industry before 1946. Sir Robert Haslam must be one of BC's few remaining employees who worked in the private industry, and he spoke graphically of some of the problems of the old private system. What the miner-poet, Idris Davies, described as the "ghosts of the slaves of The Successful Century" still stalk the mining villages of Great Britain, where memories of an exploitative system of ownership of coal assets are still vivid. The perils of failing to acknowledge that the present is bound up with the past are at least recognised by the Secretary of State. He told the Committee that privatisation of coal was not on a par with other privatisations because

225

of the "difference in social background in the coalmining communities."

However, it is not principally for historical reasons that we support public ownership of the coal industry. We believe first of all that the achievements of the nationalised industry in bettering the health and safety of the workforce would be jeopardised by a change to private ownership. The British safety record is the best in the world. This is despite the fact that some foreign statistics may not tell the whole story - for example we were told during our visit to the USA that the much worse accident figures were based only on incidents in unionised mines. The T&GWU gave evidence about the "cowboy" operators who at present work the private opencast sector, and who "make a mess of the communities; they leave muck all over the place; the accident rates are high." We believe that there would be a great increase in these problems if the industry were in the hands of those driven solely by the profit motive.

BC has argued that the steps it has taken to alleviate the problems of declining activity in particular locations "amount to the most comprehensive and substantial response made by any responsible employer in the United Kingdom." In our view, it has not done half enough, and in some of its actions - for example, the sale of its houses - has shown very little regard for its wider obligations to the communities which it has exploited in the past. However, we believe that even less would be done by private owners, driven only by profit motive and without the vestige of public obligation which remains in BC. As the Coalfield Communities Campaign argue, BC, as a nationalised industry, should be expected to "take a wider view of its responsibilities than a private company."

Our third principal argument for maintaining public ownership of BC is our belief that important strategic assets should remain in public control so that any temporary storms in the world energy markets can be ridden out, and our principal energy asset preserved for the country's future needs. The case for running down the coal industry is one based on short-term economic factors. A privately-owned industry would intensify the rape of the best coal assets if its short-term profits required it to do so. A state-owned industry should have a long view of the future. Again, we were heartened that Mr Walker seemed to go some way to meet this view: "I very much want to see the coal option as a form of energy to remain active and open ...we cannot predict the future supplies and cost of supply of energy and if you have such a resource you would be crazy to close off one industry for a long while or for ever." In times of "irredeemably unstable" oil prices, Mr Walker's statement implies state aid to help the coal industry. We believe that the public interest is best served by public ownership of an industry which receives substantial amounts of aid because of its crucial strategic importance. Moreover, we take exception to the anti-democratic view implicit in arguments like those of Professor Robinson about Ministers and Parliament "meddling" in the affairs of BC. Ministers and Members of Parliament have a duty to concern themselves with strategic energy needs just as much as with strategic defence needs.

The most commonly envisaged form of privatisation is one where individual pits are sold off or new licences to mine coal are offered to all comers. The result would be to have a number of medium-sized firms supposedly in competition. However, even the Government clearly recognises that these private sector firms would have scant regard for the national energy needs which are part of BC's duties to consider. If the industry were privatised, private sector firms would buy the most profitable mines and, recognising that their principal customer - the electricity supply industry - was a monopoly, sell their coal at a price which just undercut the prices at which the nationalised sector could produce coal. As Mr Walker said, "what that has done for competition and the good of the country, I do not know." We cannot improve on his words for this sort of system - "absurd, lunatic". We are also impressed by advice we received from a distinguished group of accountants that there would be dis-economies of scale implicit in any split up in the British coal industry and in Sir Robert Haslam's testimony to the problems for a mining engineer in operating in a system where different companies were jostling for coal in one geographical area.

We have no quarrel with the existence of small private deep mines in Great Britain, especially those operated on a family basis by fewer than half a dozen men. However, we see no need for a relaxation in the law which at present limits private deep mines to a workforce of

30, and we noted that no common argument on this point was advanced to us by the different constituent elements of the Federation of Small Mines of Great Britain in their evidence. A more rigorous argument was presented to us for allowing more private sector opencasting on bigger sites, and this argument had been backed by the Monopolies and Mergers Commission in 1983. We have argued elsewhere that there should be a limit on the quantity of coal extracted by opencast methods as a means of easing the pace and scale of the difficulties BC faces. A limit on opencast is precisely the sort of national energy policy need which BC could be required to fulfil because it is a nationalised industry, and for this reason we would resist any extension of private opencasting. We note that those who support the privatisation of opencasting would remove any restriction in the size of the opencast industry - despite opencast's adverse environmental and employment effects. The limits on private opencasting introduced by the then Conservative government in the Opencast Coal Act 1958 are reasonable - though we should like to know why the law is not being properly enforced - at present it appears that opencast sites of up to 35,000 tonnes are licensed to the private sector, though the law limits them to sites not greatly exceeding 25,000 tonnes.

We do not particularly defend the royalty system which imposes charges on the private sector on a royalty per tonne basis. However, as one advocate of privatisation conceded, private mine operators must be making a profit nevertheless. As Sir Kenneth Couzens pointed out, complaints about royalty levels are only natural. However, it may be that a fairer economic rent could be paid by the private sector through the taxation system. In addition, however, we believe it would be necessary for the private sector to compensate BC for the work it does on behalf of the industry as a whole, especially in licensing coal extraction.

That BC should issue licences, we regard as essential. BC advanced a sensible case for this in evidence to us. We note also that, despite claims about what has happened in the past, there is no evidence that licences are being rejected by BC on unfair grounds. We believe that the mining engineers the Board employs are best placed to decide whether geological conditions permit a licence to be granted, whether workings could cause subsidence or the sterilisation of workable reserves and whether the proposed operations would be safe. We also believe that BC is best placed to discharge several of the functions which it does under statute on behalf of the whole industry. These were listed in evidence. We believe, for example, that BC should provide the principal mines rescue service and that BC should take care of abandoned shafts. They have the best resources to do so. We do, however, recommend that BC's statutory duties on behalf of the whole industry should be separately accounted for by them, and directly reimbursed by the Government where they are undertaken on behalf of companies now out of business, and by the existing private sector where they can directly be attributed to current private operations.

In evidence to us, Professor Robinson listed three gains from what he described as the "liberalisation" of the industry. The second and third of these were "less politicisation of decision-taking" and "efficiency gains". As we have already argued, we see no advantage in the first and no evidence of the second. However, for Professor Robinson, the primary gain of privatisation would be "reduced monopoly power of labour". Although he says that he is not suggesting moves to break the power of labour in British mining, we regard this as disingenuous. The history of the last three years gives adequate evidence of the strong interest there has been at the highest levels in government and the industry in devaluing and undermining the great contribution which the trades unions have made to the British mining industry. For example, Sir Ian MacGregor's recent book made clear that the Miners' Strike of 1984-85 was fomented elsewhere than within the headquarters of the National Union of Mineworkers. We strongly believe that the coal industry can never be truly successful until management and unions work co-operatively together. For this reason we think it is alarming that we received evidence of "the deplorable state" of industrial relations which were at an all-time low for NACODS or based on a "confrontational policy for the NUM". We hope that the new management is trying to lift morale, but we are sceptical about their claims about how much has been achieved. We are quite sure that talk of privatisation only helps further to dispirit mineworkers.

229

We regret that it has been necessary to include any reference to privatisation in this report. Privatisation has been a means of providing quick profits to the affluent and is increasingly regarded by independent commentators as doing nothing to increase efficiency or to promote competition. The Energy Committee's scepticism about the whole programme must be apparent from our Report on the Regulation of the Gas Industry. In the case of coal we rest on Sir Robert Haslam's own words "there is no magical quality in private sector management which can instantly and dramatically improve the efficiency of our industry." As the NUM say, "it is ludicrous to treat the coal industry as a political football." In our view, the British coal industry must be allowed to get on with its business without being diverted by fashionable ideological nostrums." - (Mr Geoffrey Lofthouse)

APPENDIX C - Departmental Committees

Departmental Select Committees have to be very selective about the topics that they choose to investigate. MPs on committees have other calls upon their time, and the task of surveying the workings of departments of state is such a massive one that a committee cannot hope to investigate more than a small proportion of a department's work. Once a topic is selected, a committee has to set itself some sort of time scale in which to reach its conclusions. Normally most committees want to conclude each inquiry within a matter of months. Within that timetable, the committee has to receive evidence in either written or oral form, obtain detailed memoranda from the government department under examination, pay any visits which it thinks are essential and discuss and agree a report which would be published.

The first job is to decide who should be asked to give evidence. Anyone is free to offer advice which is formally called "evidence" to the committee and many people who have an interest will write in without an invitation. Committee will decide what viewpoints it wants to hear and will invite particular representatives of those viewpoints to submit evidence. Typically, representative pressure groups from different sides will be asked. Normally witnesses invited to give evidence are willing to do so. If they are not, the committee can then invoke its formal power to call for persons, papers and records. If a witness disobeyed an order of the committee the House would be asked to uphold the order. If the witness still disobeyed the House has the power to imprison him or her.

And also, as well as ordering individuals to give evidence, the power to send for papers and records allows committees to insist on being shown copies of documents that are relevant to their inquiries.

These formidable powers are restricted in one important area. Committees cannot demand the attendance of other MPs or Members of the House of Lords. Since all Government Ministers are members of one house or the other, this means that committees cannot insist that a particular Minister should give evidence to them, but in practice I know of no occasion when a Minister has refused. Normally the Government will send a Minister when requested, but should there be

231

controversy when the attendance of a particular Minister is demanded, ultimately it is the Prime Minister who decides which Minister should attend and not the committee. The second restriction in dealing with government is that committees powers to send for papers and records do not extend to papers and records held by government departments. However, Norman St John Stevas - now Lord St John of Fawsley - when launching this Select Committee system as Leader of the House in 1979 gave an undertaking that every Minister would do everything in his or her power to co-operate with the Select Committees, and this has very largely been observed.

If there is time, witnesses are frequently asked to submit a written memorandum before they give their oral evidence. On the basis of this as well as other information that they had, the committee's staff will prepare a brief for MPs on the committee which suggests what the oral evidence session should be used for. The oral session may then last for 3 hours or so with witnesses asked to express their opinions and then tested on them. It can on some occasions be a harrowing experience. The witnesses are interrogated by politicians under the gaze of the press and public, and cannot refuse to answer or just get up and leave. Of course, witnesses are often politicians, senior civil servants or senior officials of private industries. Some of them, not least the civil servants, are experts on giving "non answers" - giving the minimum amount of information consistent with not lying. They can certainly hold their own and can sometimes get away with saying very little or with escaping really probing questions on the views that they are putting across. There are many occasions when the politicians on the committee can get very frustrated with what is sometimes deliberate evasion of answering the question. Sometimes they vent their anger on the witness, which I have personally done on many occasions, certainly when interviewing Mr Ian McGregor and others who are deemed to be hostile witnesses.

The Committee in fact expressed its dissatisfaction with the fact that the Chairman of British Coal had twice failed to give full answers at Committee evidence sessions about British Coal's prospects, but had subsequently done so to the media. I always very much regretted that the Committee took the view that owing to the impending dissolution of Parliament, it was agreed to take no action on this. I thought the Committee were unwise to miss the opportunity of highlighting their concern and I think they should have sent for Mr McGregor to inform him of their concern.

After the evidence has been taken, the visits made, and the submitted papers studied, the committee meets in private to discuss the area it wants to cover in its report. Often the staff of the committee will provide a skeleton outline of the report as a basis of discussion. When agreement is reached on the opinions to be expressed, the staff is normally asked by the Chairman of the Committee to produce a draft report reflecting the committee's thinking. The Clerk to the Committee does this with the assistance of the specialist advisers, and the length of what is produced can vary greatly, usually reflecting the amount of time that the committee has spent on its deliberations. The Chairman will then study this draft report to see that it accurately reflects their opinion and that of the committee as they see it, and it will be submitted to a private meeting of the committee. It is discussed paragraph by paragraph and any member of the committee can suggest and, indeed, remove amendments to the report as highlighted in my minority report on the inquiry into the coal industry. A Chairman of a Commons Select Committees does not vote unless there is a tie, as was the case when voting on my minority report. When the report has been considered in this way there is an opportunity for a final vote before the report is formally made to the House. Officially there is no such thing as a minority report, but any member can propose a draft report to the committee as an alternative to the Chairman's and this is exactly what I did with the Energy Select Committee's investigation of the coal industry in 1987. Such a report is voted upon and incorporated into the minutes of the proceedings. When the report has been agreed, arrangements are made for it to be printed and published. In due course the Government is expected to respond, normally by means of a detailed memorandum, to the points made in the Committee's report.

APPENDIX D - House of Lords Debate - Industrial Illnesses (16 November 1998)

Lord Lofthouse of Pontefract - "My Lords, I am grateful that so many noble Lords have shown an interest in the debate, which is important to disabled miners. Your Lordships will be aware that on 25 November 1992 the Industrial Injuries Advisory Council report recommended that chronic bronchitis and emphysema should be listed as a prescribed disease in coal-miners. That recommendation was not implemented until 13 September 1993. There was great concern among disabled miners suffering from this disease that there was a deliberate policy by the then Government to delay the implementation because the longer it was delayed the more miners suffering from the disease would have died and this would of course have lessened the financial cost to the Government. This fear seemed to have foundation, when a leaked document came into my possession of 29 October 1992 from the Department of Social Security to the Department of Trade and Industry suggesting they delayed implementation of the recommendations of the report for as long as possible because the longer the delay the more miners would have died. I am sure noble Lords will appreciate how suspicious the miners are now. However, I want to assure miners that the present Government are not getting up to such tricks as did the previous government. I have satisfied myself through meetings with the Minister of State in another place, John Battle, that that is not the case.

However, since the awards by the Industrial Injuries Advisory Council many miners have placed claims against the British Coal Corporation for compensation. Arising from those claims I corresponded with the then Lord Chancellor, the noble and learned Lord, Lord Mackay of Clashfern, on Thursday 9 March 1995, and Mr Tim Eggar, Minister of State at the DTI, on Wednesday 22 March 1995. I expressed my concern that if the claims were to be heard by a High Court hearing it would cause long delays and, considering that many of the miners suffering from bronchitis and emphysema are elderly, infirm and in some instances terminally ill, any long delayed High Court hearings could deny them the immediate substantial compensation to which they are entitled. I requested that instead of

234

preparing for years of litigation, with trials of simple cases taking about eight weeks or more, I would consider it equitable and consensual for defendants to give earnest consideration to setting up a bronchitis/emphysema compensation scheme. This would avoid massive litigation expenditure on legal aid costs over the years.

I regret that my suggestions were not accepted. Had the previous Government taken on board my proposals, clearly the present Government would not have inherited a liability running into several billions of pounds. Arising out of this, the miners, as a last resort, pursued legislation with the utmost reluctance, supported only by the Legal Aid Board and the appropriate union. I was delighted that Mr Justice Turner, sitting in the Royal Courts of Justice in London on 21 January 1998, ruled in the miners' favour. In his summary, his Lordship was extremely critical of the British Coal Corporation both in respect of health and safety and, indeed, its defence of the litigation.

The present position, as I understand it, is that it has been agreed by the two sides that in principle there should be a single medical assessment process rather than either side proceeding on the conventional basis of separately obtaining medical evidence and then exchanging reports. The reason for this is that it removes the need for two examinations. They feel that this in turn will speed up the assessment of individual cases and the assessment of damages. I personally do not believe that it would speed it up sufficiently.

The speed of delivery of medical assessments is a key issue because there are now 60,000 claims, with a potential of 120,000 claims, and many of those people are elderly. The DTI is concerned that every single claimant who wishes to claim full damages under a handling scheme should, as part of the medical assessment, undergo a physical examination by an appropriately qualified physician. The medical advice I have received states that in a large number of cases this is not necessary and will delay assessments significantly.

Why will there be a delay? I am informed that there are approximately 500 appropriately qualified respiratory physicians available in the country. Your Lordships will readily identify that if all the 500 physicians were employed on this work alone, which is very unlikely, it would mean 1,200 cases for each physician. If there are to be 120,000 applications the number rises to 2,400 for each physician. One can imagine the delays that will occur.

Considering that I have received medical expert advice that it is both fair and reasonable to undertake paper assessments in a large number of cases, this would streamline the assessment process and ensure that compensation is paid as quickly as possible. I ask my noble friend the Minister to give consideration to that.

I also understand that there is a distance between the two sides as to how retrospectively to diagnose chronic bronchitis. I understand that the DTI is concerned that there must be some criteria. I can well understand that, but I feel that that is going to be difficult. Chronic bronchitis was so common in many mining communities that it was thought by the men not worthy of medical attention and some general practitioners who were faced with a patient with a condition often thought it not worthy of a note in their medical records.

I understand that the DTI is seeking a discount of 15 per cent from damages to reflect the benefits of handling agreements. The benefits are illusionary if the process is not as quick as it could be and if the medical assessment is full and comprehensive. The DTI has indicated that 15 per cent is not its final position. But if there is to be a full and fair medical assessment in all cases where full damages are claimed it is difficult to understand why any discount is justifiable.

It is fairly obvious that the present arrangements will cause considerable delay, which will mean that many miners suffering from the disease will have died while the negotiations are in progress. I ask your Lordships to bear in mind that it is calculated that since the judgement 10 months ago, 1,000 people have died, at an average of 20 per week.

I believe that the procedures could be speeded up. Noble Lords may recall that during Questions on 29 January of this year I put a suggestion to my noble friend Lord Clinton-Davies. It concerned the men who had already been certified in accordance with the Industrial Injuries Advisory Council's recommendations and where it had been proved that they had been suffering from bronchitis and emphysema. They had been medically examined and assessed and given a percentage assessment of disability. Those men then received industrial injuries benefits. Surely it is not beyond the bounds of possibility that those men could be accepted as suitable for the payment of compensation. They have gone through the medical routine; they have been examined; and they have been certified and awarded a pension. Surely it would be a simple exercise to pay compensation to those men without dragging them through the further procedures, if and when the examinations can be carried out. It seems simple to me. I appreciate that not all the claimants will have been examined, but the majority have been.

In conclusion I should tell the House that I have discussed the matter recently with the Minister of State in another place, Mr John Battle. He is in a unique position. It is not often that one finds a Minister who has money available without having to go dashing into the Treasury. I understand that he has about £2 billion at his disposal and he is keen to spend it and pay it out to those miners. However, he has been held up by arguments between lawyers.

Some heads must be knocked together. There is no doubt that those lawyers will be earning vast sums of money from the exercise. I have formed an opinion of the people whom I have met in my area. They seem quite genuine and they want to help the miners. However, others will be in it simply to see how much they can obtain for themselves. There will be a colossal bill. The Minister of State has given me assurances and I know that he is keen to recompense the miners. Surely a formula can be produced which will enable as many of those men as possible to be paid before they die of that terrible disease, as have many of their predecessors."

Lord Mason of Barnsley - "My Lords, I shall be brief. First, I pay tribute to my noble friend Lord Lofthouse of Pontefract. He made the first presentation of a Bill in another place which asked that emphysema should be recognised as an industrial disease qualifying for compensation. That was way back in October 1982. He has pursued that issue doggedly, with five Ten-Minute Rule Bills in another place, and, incidentally, his sponsors have been my noble friends, Lord Hardy of Wath and Lord Ashley of Stoke and myself.

My noble friend Lord Lofthouse also prepared learned papers on the subject and persuaded the Industrial Injuries Advisory Council to undertake the studies. He is undoubtedly the miners' champion in this cause. My noble friend is fully aware of this issue both from his experience of working underground and from observing some of his very ill and breathless constituents."

Lord Ezra - "My Lords, I should declare an interest having served for many years in the mining industry. I am still actively involved in the energy sector. We are much indebted to the noble Lord, Lord Lofthouse, who has for long been a strong advocate for the mining industry and the miners. I do not believe that in all that he has done anything is as important as his work in connection with the whole dread issue of bronchitis and emphysema. I was interested to learn that he had made the suggestion that the previous government should set up a fund to deal with these diseases that everyone recognises as one of the high prices of mining."

APPENDIX E - Press Responses to the Passing of the Emphysema Bill of Commons

Yorkshire Evening Post - "Victory for the miners' champion. Ever since he became MP for Pontefract in 1978, ex-miner Geoff Lofthouse has campaigned doggedly for a fair deal for miners crippled by industrial lung diseases like bronchitis, emphysema and pneumoconiosis. It has been a long, hard slog. But it has finally paid off, with the Government agreeing a £2 billion pay-out. That sounds a fortune, but it isn't. It will pay, on average, around £25,000 each to former miners and their widows. For tens of thousands of men, this settlement - so long resisted by governments - comes tragically too late. Lung disease, or 'the dust', has exacted its price through their breathless agonies and early deaths. Second only to asbestos workers, British miners suffered a cynical betrayal of their health and well-being. Only a very rare few ended a lifetime in the industry free of injury or impaired lung function. Yet for decades industry bosses were in denial about it, terrified of massive compensation claims. But men like Geoff Lofthouse - now Lord Lofthouse - knew the miners had an unanswerable case. Britain owes its miners a great deal. They in turn owe a debt of gratitude to men like Lord Lofthouse who fought their case with courage and faith, certain of the rightness of their cause."

Yorkshire Post - "The price of coal - Most men who worked down the pits knew the job was ruining their health. But they did it nevertheless. Sons followed fathers into the cramped and choking tunnels to hew coal from the narrow seams. Many thought they belonged to the aristocracy of the working class - highly paid, industrially powerful, often militant and tribally loyal, their union banners seemed the brightest and most splendid.

But the miners have had to pay a heavy price for their aristocracy. While fit young pit-men marched proudly to the annual gala, many of their older former colleagues were forced to stay at home, gasping for breath as they fell victim to bronchitis and emphysema. Many simply suffered in silence, accepting their illness with stoical dignity. But others rightly regarded these ailments as an outrage, and began to campaign for compensation from the Coal Board. Anyone who thinks that publicly owned industries are more kindly disposed to their workers than private industry should follow the history of this long struggle.

Winning compensation from government has been like hewing coal from the most stubborn of seams. Yet, MPs like Yorkshire's Sir Geoffrey Lofthouse and Mick Clapham have hacked and chipped away at their quarry. They have had their successes, most notably in ending many of the more humiliating and degrading tests that dying miners had to endure before being declared eligible for compensation.

But yesterday's £1.5 billion settlement between the Department of Trade and Industry and the miners is the most eloquent tribute to the campaigners' tenacity. Even so, the lawyers at Irwin Mitchell, who have been as dogged as the local MPs in prosecuting the miners' case, find their legal victory is tinged with regret. They know that as many as 15,000 former miners have already died of industry related illnesses, and an additional 25 former miners are dying every day.

Had the Coal Board been as receptive as John Battle's Energy Department, this scandal might have been ended years ago. Indeed, it is to his great credit that Mr Battle has fought to keep the issue on the political agenda when Treasury colleagues have been trying to prevent any additional government expenditure. He, along with Sir Geoffrey, Mick Clapham and the team at Irwin Mitchell, should be toasted in the pubs and clubs of Yorkshire this weekend."

Pontefract and Castleford Express (Thursday 1 April 1999 - "Geoff's Finest Triumph") - "A beaming Lord Lofthouse of Pontefract was celebrating this week after winning the greatest battle of his life. Thousands of ex-miners with lung disorders will receive a chunk of a £1.5 billion pay-out thanks to Geoff Lofthouse's unstinting 50 year struggle. He was forced to watch hundreds of men die from chronic bronchitis and emphysema while negotiations with the Department of Trade and Industry dragged on.

But this week the former Labour MP for Pontefract and Castleford was jubilant in victory. "I am absolutely delighted," he said. "But it is also tinged with sadness. So many have passed away without seeing a penny." Around 65,000 men will be compensated with payments of between £4,000 and £50,000 after being tested over the next six months. Around 30 special testing centres will be set up across the country, with the most acute cases given priority. "It is without doubt the highlight of my political career," he added as he toasted the momentous occasion with a cuppa at his semi-detached home in Carleton Crest, Pontefract. "I started fighting as a member of the National Union of Mineworkers and continued as an MP and in the House of Lords. The victory means so much to me. The greatest privilege I have had is not a knighthood or a peerage. It is to have been born into the mining community and that has always stayed with me."

His successor, Yvette Cooper, who continued his campaign in the Commons, promises to get the best deal for the constituency. She said, "I am pressing hard for one of the testing centres to be set up locally. The Five Towns have been at the heart of the coalmining industry for years. At one time nearly a third of men in the area worked in the pits. By my reckoning over 1,000 could be eligible for compensation, so it is only right we should be at the heart of the claims process."

The final settlement, made at the high court in Cardiff, was agreed between Ministers and solicitors representing ex-miners and makes provision for pay-outs to the widows of men who have already died."

Pontefract and Castleford Express - "What a great achievement for Lord Lofthouse of Pontefract. After 50 years of struggle he has won his battle with officialdom. Former miners, crippled with lung disease after a lifetime's toil in the pits, have got the compensation they deserve. But for hundreds, if not thousands, the jubilation has come too late. Untold billions mean nothing to the men who have died in the half century since Lord Geoff took up their cause.

Money cannot relieve their suffering as the coal dust took its toll and sent them to a premature grave. Westminster could not hear them fighting for breath. But Geoff could and he was determined that their sacrifice for the country's prosperity would be compensated. That day has come. Lord Lofthouse is a happy man."

Yorkshire Post - "Sir, - If anyone has to be honoured for the recognition of emphysema and bronchitis as an industrial disease it is my colleague Lord Lofthouse of Pontefract. He made a first presentation of a Bill in the House of Commons as long ago as October 1982, he pursued this doggedly with five Ten Minute Rule Bills year after year which persuaded the Industrial Injuries Advisory Council to undertake studies which eventually advised recognition. He even initiated a major debate in the House of Lords last November. Lord Lofthouse has been and still is a miners' champion."

APPENDIX F -Britain In Moral Crisis (Pontefract and Castleford Express, 1996)

"Britain faces a moral crisis. Its people have sensed for some time that violent crime was gnawing at the edge of the country's social fabric. But it has taken the brutal murder of the toddler James Bulger to crystallise the country's fears, and move people to ask aloud what kind of nation we are becoming.

They are painfully aware that there has been a marked growth in crime, more alcohol abuse, and a worrying rise in the number of drug addicts. Since the Second World War, murder has more than doubled, the reported rate is up sixteen fold and robbery has spiralled up fifty fold.

Things have got worse. for everybody; for those living in some housing estates in other parts of the country, they have got very much worse to a point where law and order, have in effect, broken down. Why this should be so is the subject of much debate. It must be significant that such institutions as the family, school and community, which once gave children regardless of background a sense of discipline and moral compass have declined in their ability to impart these values.

It was not always like this. Until recently most working class children, however deprived otherwise, were brought up in a wholesome environment. Their parents were poorer than today, their houses smaller and their schools not so modern. But they were brought up in a two-parent family which offered stability and discipline; they went to schools which reinforced that discipline; and they lived in communities of two parent families which shared the same values, including sending children to Sunday school.

There are so many people in the Pontefract and Castleford constituency who can remember when most parents could assume that most children were safe, most of the time, and when young girls and elderly women could walk the streets in safety. They also remember a childhood where they were left to play in fields and parks and streets for hours on end. Some people can recall heartbreaking times of dire poverty and deprivation. But they can also recall that as tiny children they could wander about the streets at all hours of the day and night without coming to any harm. Such criminal activity as existed was more a matter of thuggery between gangs, a culture of violence from which women and children were automatically excluded as targets.

To blame the British slide into lawlessness on bad housing, poverty, and unemployment makes sense, but there was far more of it in the 1920s and 1930s, but very little crime. We can see the responsibility in the decline of those three sources of traditional discipline - the family, the school and the community. I shall confine myself to the deterioration of the traditional family, though this has undoubtedly been exacerbated by the growth of long-term unemployment, which adds to the cycle of despair.

I can best illustrate by drawing on both my experience as a Member of the House of Commons and on my experience as Member of Parliament for Pontefract and Castleford. In Parliament, I have always sought the ethical context of my responsibilities and, where possible, the moral dimension. That is always my starting point, where possible. As a result I gave priority to the nurturing of the young, to

243

provision for the old; in short I gave priority to the well being of the family. In practice, I consistently probed and monitored the treatment of children in my constituency, before birth and after birth, the unborn as well as the born. I watched with growing concern the increasing assault on the mould of family life.

My casework in Pontefract and Castleford increasingly disposed me to see the connection between the swinging sixties and social disintegration, between sexual permissiveness and the decay of family life. Let me offer just one, if very disturbing, aspect of this trend. The social implications of single parenthood came to constitute a growing proportion of my constituency case load. Nationally, it is estimated that there are now more than 1.25 million such families, without a father. We should be glad that unmarried mothers are no longer stigmatised, but my constituency experience confirms weighty research and findings elsewhere, in the United States as well as Britain, that out-of-wedlock parenthood correlates with antisocial behaviour, bad neighbourliness, problem children, delinquency, low achievement, fraud and crime in short, with an emergent underclass.

Most single parents I encounter in the Pontefract and Castleford constituency say life is tough, but manageable, and they would not repeat the experience, given the choice. I honour them. Nearly all of them insisted that absent fathers should be dealt with much more firmly when they fail - as so many do - to pay the maintenance for the children.

So I am in no doubt that when the conventional two-parent family is threatened, our whole society is put at risk. Unhappily, the moral revolution during the last thirty years, starting with the swinging sixties, seems to have taken the family as its main target. Its more naïve supporters believed that the permissive society was going to bring a vast increase in human happiness. Men and women would no longer be trapped in marriage. They could liberate themselves from traditional constraints and pursue lives which combined maximum sexual fulfilment with maximum emotional honesty. What is the result?

Social trends show that the UK has more marriages, more illegitimate births, more divorces, and more prisoners - with some of the highest numbers in Yorkshire and Humberside - than almost anywhere else. More children are born to unmarried mothers in Yorkshire and Humberside than almost anywhere else in the country. More than 33% of new marriages are now ending in divorce. Last year 30.6% of all births in our region were illegitimate, nearly 3% above the national average. The latest figures released by the Office of Population Censuses and Surveys show yet more divorces, but fewer marriages.

Our region emerges equally badly from other recently published official figures. Schools in Yorkshire - notably in Barnsley - are the country's worst hit in a tide of vandalism, arson and theft. The Schools Minister reported a year ago that nationwide vandalism cost £60 million the previous year - two-thirds of the total cost of schoolbooks. There has been more reported agitation on the part of parents about the lack of schoolbooks than about the destruction of schools.

John Patten, now Secretary of State for Education, stated that when he was a Home Office Minister, 30% of all recorded crime was committed by youngsters of 16 or less. The roots of criminality are now to be found among the 10, 11 and 12 year olds. And they are not deterred by custodial sentences. 70 out of every 100 inmates have been in prison before. Attitudes that lead them to this are formed early in life, in the home, in an increasingly fatherless home.

Nearly 100,000 children are thought to go missing in Britain every year, and though more than half return home safely within 24 hours, some simply vanish. Not surprisingly, there are now to be heard on all sides calls for the restoration of family life.

One great advantage of the traditional family is that it involves a network of reciprocal obligations. These are not always honoured, but they offer the best hope that unwanted children or spouses or parents will not be cast aside. Like democracy, the traditional family has its weaknesses, but, like democracy, it is the best system yet devised for sustaining the individual.

A policy for the family, when it does emerge, will not only encompass such matters as child benefit, child care for working mothers, and the poverty of many single parent families. It will also not only seek to reconcile the traditional role of the family with the new idea of equal social and economic opportunities for women. It will also include such moral issues as divorce, the duties of absent fathers, and the vital need of the inculcation of a sense of guilt on the part of its members, in particular the young.

Dwindling belief in redemption and damnation has led to the loss of fear of the eternal consequences of goodness and badness - the religious sanction. It has had a profound effect in consequence on personal morality, especially on criminality. Everyone now has a view on the policy. But how many have yet seen what a hard time the police have in trying to enforce the law in a society that has jettisoned morality? Sir Peter Imbert, until recently Commissioner of the Metropolitan Police, sees us as a fragmented society, which indeed we are, each portion pursuing its own selfish interests, and thus imposing on the police a disparity and diversity of demands which they find impossible to meet. Morality has become subjective. Regardless of class or upbringing - though not of religion - it is how each man or woman chooses to define it, no more and no less. Inevitably, standards of human behaviour have declined, and lawlessness threatens to engulf us.

We will continue to hear those calls for the restoration of family life, but it will not be easy. Underlying the problem is the collapse of moral consensus in Britain today. Among the many corrupting things the permissive society brought us is complete freedom from guilt. But how can we not feel guilty about some things, notably the abandonment of vulnerable people who depend on us? Yet, one of the shocking disclosures about the Duchess of York and Woody Allen, when they were in the news last year, was that they expressed little or no contrition whatsoever. They stand as symbols of western society in a decadent phase.

Rock stars are the Messiahs of too many of today's young. Profanity, obscenity, blasphemy and worse is the message of too many of them. There are a great many reasons why selfishness, hooliganism, violence, greed and vulgarity have come to dominate public life. I do not ascribe all the blame to the tinsel heroes of the gullible. But anyone who fails to see the connection between the shameless behaviour of these "stars" and the decline of public standards has got his eyes shut. There are not positive moral influences any longer on the lives of many of our children. Where is the responsibility of the parents? Unhappily the parents themselves have grown up in the void, and it is no longer possible for religion to provide a framework of values and guidance.

But if there are no positive moral influences, there are plenty of negative ones, chief among which are those of television and, worse, video. The part these play in people's lives, and especially in the lives of children, can hardly be overestimated. The idea that there is nothing sacred, nothing that cannot be mocked (except the right to mock) has had a devastating effect on young and weak and unprepared minds. If neither values nor authority exist, then everything is permitted, no matter how socially and even personally destructive.

A former Lord Chief Justice, a former Lord Chancellor, and a former Archbishop of Canterbury have all agreed in recent years on the origins of the corrupting influences of modern society. The Lord Chief Justice, Lord Lane blamed the exaggerated freedoms of choice of the 1960s, specifying as the chief agents of degradation, easier divorce, broken homes, easy abortion, the Pill at 11 or 12, hard drug abuse, alcohol and unemployment. But most of all he blames the increase in horror and filth on the degrading film and television programmes, soft and hard porn "depicting scenes which we see faithfully acted out in the courts." Violence and obscenity are presented as an entertainment. "Very soon the weaker brethren accept them as a norm." That meant not just children; it included "adults with the mind of a child." Yet he lamented that society's falling standards were, "always someone else's problem." If the trend was to be reversed, he believed, the answer lay in Parliament, in schools, in homes - "preferably not single parent homes" - and also in the churches.

The nomination of the family and the church by Lord Lane is very significant. However imperfect he recognises with his vast experience that there is nothing else. They are both what the promptings of nature and the wisdom of civilisation have constructed to care for children.

247

They have been sustained by a Christianity whose second most important image is that of a mother and child.

So the Church must rise to the challenge, if Britain is to become civilised again. There is no other path available, not political ideology, not Members of Parliament, not local councillors, not the DSS, not the police. Let me explain in conclusion.

It is, to me, self-evident that we are all born with a sense of good and evil. It is also self-evident that as we grow up each individual chooses whether to be good or bad. Fear of eternal damnation was a message reinforced through weekly attendance at church. The loss of that fear meant that a critical motive has been lost to young people when they decide whether to try to be good citizens or criminals. Since World War II crime has risen. So has secularisation. Loss of faith is hard to measure. The best gauge of secularisation available to us statistically is church attendance. This is falling steadily throughout the United Kingdom. In a few areas church attendance remains relatively high. These are also areas with low crime figures. While peace and personal happiness are not necessarily evident in those places, there does seem to be a clear relationship between the retention of traditional values, church attendance and low crime figures.

Words cannot convey how beholden our generation is to Mother Teresa. She has given us a whole new vision of what being a Christian means; of the amazing power of love, and how in one dedicated soul it can burgeon to cover the whole world. No other value system, culture or ethos has thrown up a comparable figure. Her example can provide a role model to fill the moral vacuum at the heart of western civilisation."

APPENDIX G - Geoffrey Howe MP - Resignation Speech (13 November 1990)

"I find to my astonishment that a quarter of a century has passed since I last spoke from one of the back-benches. Fortunately, however, it has been my privilege to serve for the past 12 months of that time as Leader of the House of Commons, so I have been reminded quite recently of the traditional generosity and tolerance of this place. I hope that I may count on that today as I offer to the House a statement about my resignation from the Government.

It has been suggested even, indeed, by some of my Right Honourable and Honourable Friends, that I have resigned solely because of questions of style and not on matters of substance at all. Indeed, if some of my former colleagues are to be believed, I must be the first Minister in history who has resigned because he was in full agreement with Government policy. The truth is that, in many aspects of politics, style and substance complement each other. Very often, they are two sides of the same coin.

The Prime Minister and I have shared something like 700 meetings of Cabinet or Shadow Cabinet during the past 18 years, and some 400 hours alongside each other, at more than 30 international summit meetings. For both of us, I suspect, it is a pretty daunting record. The House might well feel that something more than simple matters of style would be necessary to rupture such a well trained relationship.

There was, or should have been, nothing novel about joining the ERM, it has been a long-standing commitment. For a quarter of a century after the Second World War, we found that the very similar Bretton Woods regime did serve as a useful discipline. Now as my Right Honourable Friend, the Prime Minister, had acknowledged two weeks ago, our entry into the ERM can be seen as an "extra discipline for keeping down inflation". However, it must be said that practical conclusions have been achieved only at the cost of substantial damage to her administration and, more serious still, to its inflation achievements. As my Right Honourable Friend for Blaby (Lord Lawson, former Chancellor) said, "The real tragedy is that we did not join the Exchange Rate Mechanism at least five years ago. As he also made clear, "This was not for the want of trying". Indeed, the so-called Madrid conditions came into existence only after the then Chancellor and I, as Foreign Secretary, made it clear that we could not continue in office unless a specific commitment to join the ERM was made. As the House will no doubt have observed, neither Member of that particular partnership now remains in office.

It is now alas, impossible to resist the conclusions that today's high rates of inflation could well have been avoided had the question of ERM Membership been properly considered and resolved at a much earlier stage. There are, I fear, developing grounds for similar anxiety of the handling, not just at and after the Rome Summit, of the wider, much more open question of economic and monetary union.

But it is crucially important that we should conduct these arguments upon the basis of a clear understanding of the true relationships between this Country, the community and our community partners. And it is here, I fear, that my Right Honourable Friend the Prime Minister increasingly risks leading herself and others astray in matters of substance as well as style.

The point was perhaps more sharply put by a British businessman trading in Brussels and elsewhere, who wrote to me last week stating: "People throughout Europe see our Prime Minister's finger wagging and hear her passionate, "No, No, No," much clearer than the content of the carefully worded formula texts". He went on, "It is too easy for them to believe that we all share her attitudes, for why else has she been our Prime Minister for so long." My correspondent concluded, "This is a desperately serious situation for our Country," and sadly, I have to agree. The tragedy is and it is for me personally, for my party, for our whole people and for my Right Honourable Friend herself, a very real tragedy, that the Prime Minister's perceived attitude towards Europe is running increasingly serious risks for the future of our own nation. It risks minimising our influence and maximising our chances of being once again shut out. We have paid heavily in the past for late starts and squandered opportunities in Europe. We dare not let that happen again. If we detach ourselves completely, as a Party or a nation from the middle ground of Europe, the effects will be incalculable and very hard to correct. In my letter of resignation which I tendered with the utmost sadness and dismay, I said, "Cabinet

Government is all about trying persuade one and another from within." That was my commitment to government by persuasion - persuading colleagues and the nation. I have tried to do that as Foreign Secretary and since, but I realise now that the task had become futile: trying to stretch the meaning of words beyond what was credible, and trying to pretend that there was a common policy when every step forward risked being subverted by some casual comment or impulsive answer.

The conflict of loyalty, of loyalty to my Right Honourable Friend the Prime Minister - and, after all, in two decades together that instinct of loyalty is still very real - and of loyalty to what I perceive to be the true interests of the nation, has become all too great. I no longer believe it possible to resolve that conflict from within this Government. That is why I have resigned. In doing so, I have done what I believe to be right for my party and my country. The time has come for others to consider their own response to the tragic conflict of loyalties with which I have myself wrestled for perhaps too long."

APPENDIX H - Norman Lamont MP - Resignation Speech (9 June 1993)

"To give up being Chancellor of the Exchequer in the circumstances in which I did is bound to be an uncomfortable experience, but I have also been a Treasury Minister for almost seven years, a longer continuous period than anyone else this century. Indeed, I have been the only person ever to have held the three offices of Financial Secretary, Chief Secretary and Chancellor of the Exchequer.

When the Prime Minister told me two weeks ago that he wished to make changes in his Government, I of course told him that I appreciated that he had a very difficult task. He generously offered me another position in his Cabinet, but, in my opinion, it would not have been right either for him or for myself if I had accepted. If he wishes to change his Chancellor, it was surely right that I should leave the Cabinet. Perhaps I can make it clear that I wish the Prime Minister well and hope that his changes will produce whatever advantage for him and the Government he intended.

It has not been easy being Chancellor of the Exchequer in this recession, continually and wrongly described as the longest and deepest since the war or, even more inaccurately, since the 1930s.

But it is a recession which has affected many areas which have not experienced such severe recession before; and that was bound to have an adverse effect on the fortunes and popularity of the Government.

But the recession is now behind us, and so I am able with confidence to wish every success to my Right Honourable and Learned Friend the new Chancellor.

When my resignation was announced 10 days ago, the reaction of many was that it was a delayed resignation, a resignation that should have happened on 16 September. On that day, and during the subsequent days, I did of course consider my position carefully with friends and colleagues. I was anxious to do what was right for the country and for the Government. Sir Stafford Cripps, who is rightly regarded as an honourable man, did not resign after devaluing the pound. On the other hand, Lord Callaghan, also an honourable man, did.

There are three principal reasons why I decided to stay in office. First, the events of last September were very different from those of 1967. They affected not just this country, but most of Europe. The Finance Ministers of no fewer than nine countries were forced to eat their words and either devalue or float. Five floated; four devalued; one both devalued and floated. In none did the Finance Minister resign or, to the best of my knowledge, come under any pressure to resign. Indeed, in one country the governor of the central bank was actually promoted: he became Prime Minister.

Secondly, membership of the exchange rate mechanism was the policy of the whole Government; and as the Prime Minister said, I was implementing Government policy. Our entry was not a decision in which I myself played any part. It was, however, a decision made after a whole decade of fierce public and private argument - a decision made by the previous Prime Minister, the present Prime Minister and the present Foreign Secretary.

Thirdly, I did not resign because that was not what the Prime Minister wanted. When the Prime Minister reappointed me after the general election, I told him two things: first, that I did not wish to remain Chancellor for very long; and, secondly, that he did not owe me any debt or any obligation. On 16 September he made it clear to me in writing that he had no intention of resigning himself, and that I should not do so either.

Of course, I discussed the question further with the Prime Minister subsequently. In all those discussions he emphasised that he regarded the attacks on me as coded attacks on himself, so I decided that my duty and loyalty was to the Prime Minister and that I should remain in office.

Two and a half years ago, I did play some part in helping the Prime Minister into the position that he occupies today. I have always believed, and still believe, that in supporting him then I made the right choice, and I now wish to say one thing to him; it goes to the heart of the way in which the Government conduct themselves.

There is something wrong with the way in which we make our decisions. The Government listen too much to the pollsters and the party managers. The trouble is that they are not even very good at politics, and they are entering too much into policy decisions. As a result, there is too much short termism, too much reacting to events, and not enough shaping of events. We give the impression of being in office but not in power.

Far too many important decisions are made for 36 hours' publicity. Yes, we are politicians as well as policy-makers; but we are also the trustees of the nation. I believe that in politics one should decide what is right and then decide the presentation, not the other way round. Unless this approach is changed, the Government will not survive, and will not deserve to survive."

APPENDIX I - Address to the Local Synod: The Christian in Politics of Commons (26 April 1995)

...render therefore unto Caesar the things which are Caesar's, and unto God the things that are God's.

(St Matthew Ch 22 v 21)

This text poses an age-old question. As living becomes difficult, as society becomes more fragmented and corrupting, as personal morality and individual responsibility becomes more elusive, so we are driven back again and again to the famous text of St Matthew.

What guidance does the Bible offer us today on those difficult ethical dilemmas that face modern society? All are challenging, even perplexing and, perhaps for some of us, personally tormenting questions. How do we separate those matters - increasingly nowadays - claimed for Caesar, from those which we believe are matters for God? What guidance does St Matthew's text offer us any longer, whether we are clergy, lay-people or Members of Parliament? Which, on the other hand, of any of today's moral issues can be kept clear of politics? Or do more and more of them call for political action, as well as moral judgements? Let me repeat, what guidance does St Matthew's text offer us, clergy, lay-people or Members of Parliament?

Jesus Christ himself lived in a culture in which religion was politics. The coming of God's kingdom was identified with the expulsion of the Romans. True, this was an aspiration in which he displayed remarkably little interest. But from the Book of Apocalypse onwards, the Church has had much to say about the wider community that surrounds it.

The Church of England has been mischievously likened to the Tory Party at prayer. Its approach to social questions, however, is to lay down general principles, and not to identify itself with particular parties or ideologies. But along with other churches, it has not found it easy since the onset of permissiveness to reconcile lasting Christian essentials with current political fashion. For example, the permissive society was going to bring - its more naïve supporters claimed in the "swinging sixties" - a vast increase in human happiness. What has been the result?

On all sides the churches see that those institutions such as the family, the school and the community, which once gave children, regardless of background, a sense of discipline and a moral compass, have now declined in their ability to impart traditional Christian values. The result has been the destabilisation of society, for the social consequences have become horrendous.

Allow me to offer a few, brief examples. The Police have an increasingly difficult time in trying to enforce the law in a society that has jettisoned personal morality and individual responsibility. People blame the police, and all too rarely nowadays look at themselves, much less examine their consciences.

Men Behaving Badly, the show that has done so much to inspire a new generation of lager louts, is the most popular light entertainment programme on TV, with weekly viewing figures approaching 12 million. The young male the show depicts, who feels no need to become "a responsible adult in a functioning community" has emerged in many ways as the very emblem of the post-Christian world. His conduct must stir within us concern for today's teenage girl. The programmes author by the way - Simon Nye - describes himself as "mild C of E". What is "mild C of E" ?

The City of London emerges no better from close inspection. The trader's word is no longer his bond. Precious few businessmen in the City and elsewhere are any longer prepared to seal a deal on it. They send for their lawyers.

Social trends continue to show that our country has fewer marriages, more divorces and more illegitimate births. Recorded crime is up. We even have child murderers, as well as children murdered. Doncaster is now ringed by new prisons.

Anyone who fails to see the connection between the decline in public standards and the shameless behaviour of rock stars and some other public figures - profanity, obscenity and blasphemy is the message of too many of them - have got their eyes shut. It must be touch and go whether we are going forward or backwards. The

Archbishop of Canterbury is so concerned about declining public morality, that he initiated an unprecedented full day debate in the House of Lords in July.

Dr George Carey warned that unless people return to old-fashioned Christian values society will crumble. Arguing that morality has been privatised, that individuals now feel no compunction to act for the benefit of the community, that they have become greedy and cynical, he stressed the need for a recall of society's moral and spiritual well-being and, in particular, for the restoration of the family. How far can we look to Parliament and Whitehall to bring about either? How far can we look to parents - to yourselves? How far can we look to the Churches?

To take the first question, the role of Parliament or, if you wish, Caesar. There is no doubt that Parliament is intervening more and more, if reluctantly and, in my experience and judgement, all too often, mistakenly. I can best illustrate and, incidentally, show how confused we have become about our Christian inheritance, by drawing on my experience as a Member of the House of Commons.

In Parliament I have always sought the ethical context of my responsibilities and, where possible, the moral dimension. Inevitably, I have given priority, for example, to the nurturing of the young, to provision for the old, to the probing and monitoring of the treatment of children, before and after birth, and to the growing assault on the mould of conventional family life. I was not alone.

I have become increasingly concerned throughout the 1970s and 1980s about the undermining of the institution of marriage and the lack of respect for human life. Yet I have also become aware throughout these years that any MP who actively concerns himself with such ethical questions and their implications for society, such as divorce, child-care, absent fathers, single parent families and abortion, finds himself venturing down a stony path. The frightening issue of euthanasia has yet to come before Parliament. Increasingly I have found myself living dangerously, politically speaking, even though my constituency casework pointed conclusively to the connection between sexual permissiveness and the decay of family life and public morality, generally.

256

How far is that view shared by my constituents? It is significant that during the same period I receive far and away most letters of concern about abortion and animal welfare. I readily see the connection. People need to be idealistic; they also need ethical values. Part of the trend for animal rights is a search for moral substance. The moral vacuum at the heart of Western civilisation has been filled with concern for animals.

On the other hand, there is growing evidence that the tide of opinion, especially among women, has turned against permissiveness. They recognise more and more that, principally, they are the victims. They are certainly now seeing the moral attitudes of the 1960s as outdated.

The growing revulsion against the 1960s came too late to prevent the passage 5 years ago of the Bill on Embryonic Research and Abortion. Following days of debate, in which a mere handful of Members participated, and countless votes took place late at night, which left most Members of Parliament bewildered and scarcely understanding, if at all, certain extraordinary consequences emerged, and are now enshrined in law.

For example, an embryo which is used for experiments must be destroyed at 14 days, but an unborn child can be destroyed - for the same reasons of personal convenience - up to six months, and if it is handicapped, right up to the time of birth. In retrospect, this staggered many Members of Parliament. How did it happen, many still ask each other. They also question increasingly the confusion that currently envelopes the policy on frozen embryos. There is much, much worse to come.

Yet those Members of Parliament have no desire to re-open the related questions of embryos and abortion on the floor of the House, even though the debate goes on outside Parliament. A State Supreme Court in the USA - South Carolina - ruled in July that a pregnant woman who takes drugs can be prosecuted for abuse of her *unborn* baby. More and more the media is now disposed to described the foetus as the unborn child. The unborn child is capable of feeling pain from the 10th week of pregnancy, according to a group of scientists, reported in *The Times*, also in July (18.7.96), thus raising yet again further doubt about the ethics of abortion. Why then, we may ask, does Parliament continue to shy away from the question? One explanation is that MPs are nervous of moral questions, and even more nervous of those of their colleagues who are prepared to grapple with them.

Another, perhaps more profound explanation, is the growing insecurity of MPs. They have to satisfy a variety of people, time and again. Not for them the appeal to an Industrial Tribunal. Somehow they must manage to satisfy their Party in Parliament, their local parties, the voters and single interest groups - all at the same time. Thus MPs are now put to the test, as are few of their fellow men and women. They often fear to speak their minds. For MPs - like governments - prefer to survive.

Where and when electors look to their Member of Parliament to challenge the surviving fashions of the 1960s, they must recognise how difficult and complex is his situation, and take active steps to assist. Whatever the frequency of moral dilemmas in the home lives of ordinary people, we have seen that they keep trying to break through into Parliament. How can ordinary people assist their Member of Parliament, therefore, and encourage him/her to always tread the path of duty? What can electors do to protect their "man for all seasons"? For electors also have responsibilities.

The next time we examine our conscience prior to Holy Communion, we should ask ourselves whether we do our duty as a citizen: not merely in voting, but also in making our voice heard on social and moral issues. Just as important, do we ever consider extending our protective support to those public figures who are prepared to take such a stand? A more rigorous examination of conscience by each one of us is thus essential if we are to see a revival of conscience issues in Parliament.

There can be little prospect, therefore, of a positive move from Government and Parliament, unless the electorate shows more concern, as in the United States. The dissolution of the family will almost certainly have to get worse before public anger compels a reversal of permissive legislation.

How long shall we have to wait for that public anger? How far can we look to ordinary people? There is little doubt that most people believe that Britain is in severe moral decline. Few seem to know what to do about it. A Gallup poll in early July painted a grim portrait of a nation ill at ease with its conscience, worried about issues of religion, sexual morality, honesty and a willingness to make sacrifices for others. Institutions are under attack, respect for them is in decline, individual behaviour in many areas is appalling, the outlook is bleak.

Yet, the current fascination for the soaps on TV - they now extend to Sundays - and the enormous sale of the tabloids, suggest something more than base titillation. It indicates enormous anxiety.

People today are morbidly curious about how other people relate to one another, because with the undermining of the family, personal relationships are all many people have. There are fewer secure groups, such as the family, in which expectations about behaviour are handed down. People now fill the void with a search for emotional experience and an insatiable need to see how others manage it. There is a tremendous hunger among people for family life. With no moral framework, gossip and the soaps are all that many people have to cling to.

According to that Gallup poll in July, three quarters of the population believe that society is less moral than it was 50 years ago. Half think the Church does not provide adequate moral guidance. Previous polls in Britain found that in spite of the rise in divorce and single-parent families, most people support marriage and believe that the Church should do more to emphasise its sanctity. What then of the Church, now that the Archbishop of Canterbury has entered the fray, and called for a form of moral crusade?

The media response to Dr Carey was very critical. A number of commentators dismissively remarked that a debate on morality started by the Church of England - in the words of Clifford Longley (*Daily Telegraph* 28.6.96) "would be all very well if everybody knew what the Church of England stood for. Dr Carey is a good man trying to fulfil his vocation as a moral and spiritual leader and giving it his best shot. But he must not be surprised or disappointed if his campaign raises more questions than it can answer - nor, at the end of the debate, if the ball is then back in the Church of England's own court."

The Archbishop was challenged on two counts in particular: the first, in respect of his call for the involvement of the schools and, second, for what is seen as the failure of the Anglican Church itself to provide leadership.

For my own part, I do not see how morality can be a matter of style or fashion, like 'political correctness', if it is to be regarded also as a beacon of truth.

When relativism rules, one man's adultery becomes another man's flirtation. Moral boundaries are moved at whim, and dust is allowed to settle upon age-old, God-given lines of ethical demarcation. The message that there are certain moral values which never change is one that needs to be heard. What is called for now - I suggest, with respect - is for the wind of a collective moral change to blow all the dust away, and reveal that beacon of truth.

If the Churches do rise to the challenge, they will have to put aside the doubts that have plagued them in the recent past. They will need to rediscover their own sense of confidence and certainty. They will be able to draw upon an increasingly conducive climate. For the Churches will be assisted by new allies.

Among these new allies are powerful critics - from the left as well from the right - of an antisocial male - whom they see as plain feckless and irresponsible.

Other allies include Bryan Appleyard who attacks - in his book *Understanding the Present: Science and the Soul of Modern Man* (Picador) - an era that is shrunken, demeaned and impoverished by a science that tells us nothing about anything that matters! Nothing about where we came from, where we are going, why or how we live.

Yet other allies include such as Anthony Hopkins, Clint Eastwood and Richard Dreyfuss. Appalled by the fashion for gratuitous violence and sexual sadism in the contemporary cinema, they loudly voice their fears in public.

Their revulsion has found a focus in Michael Medved's caustic book *Hollywood V America*, which accuses the film business of waging war on civilised values. These are encouraging signs of an overdue cultural awakening. But is it urgent enough?

So, what of the Church itself and it own inner strengths? First, there is the Church's remarkable historic survival. Through the turbulent experience of 2,000 years, despite lapses and confused purposes, on the eve of the second millennium, Christianity has stood firm against a futile Marxist onslaught and now stands supreme.

Secondly, there are the saintly, from the Apostle Paul to Mother Teresa, all of whom in one way or another have contributed towards reanimating the faith which is the Church's mainstay from generation to generation.

Thirdly, there is the intellectual strength of the Church, as evident in those vast libraries and the glory of its architecture up and down Britain and throughout Europe.

Finally, we also have the encouragement - and surely he is entitled to have the last word - of that outstanding Englishman and intellectual giant, John Henry Newman. I was co-sponsor of an Early Day Motion on his behalf in Parliament 6 years ago. The motion recalled that he spent 45 years of his life as an Anglican, and 45 years as a Catholic, and asked that he be created the first cross-denominational, the first ecumenical saint. For, as we put it, "he remains a kindly light" - indeed, a wonderful, a saintly inspiration - "amid the perplexities of modern life"."

APPENDIX J - Tom Clark Says Thank You (1985)

"Readers with long memories will recall that, during the Miners' Strike in 1984 when I firmly supported the workers from the pits, I wrote frequently about parliamentary exchanges at the time. Many of the speeches were outstanding. Mrs Thatcher was at her most militant, but she met her match when people like Tony Benn and Dennis Skinner said their pieces.

There was one speech then which I thought to be quite spellbinding, and I said so at the time. It was the speech of Geoff Lofthouse, the MP for Pontefract and Castleford, and it was something special. Geoff came from a mining background - and it showed. It came over as sincere, superbly well informed and from the heart as well as the head; and it struck a vital chord for decency and fairness.

I remember Sean Hughes, Harold Wilson's successor and an historian, (who sadly died at a very youthful age shortly afterwards), being completely overawed as people in the Gallery put their heads forward so as not to miss a word from this man who was not a household name and yet who articulated everything we felt.

Geoff later published a book on his life and times, which he named *A Very Miner MP*. I reflected on these events this week when Geoff, now promoted to the post of Deputy Speaker, used all his tact and diplomacy to avoid what could have been a very embarrassing moment for myself.

It happened like this. As the Shadow Minister for Disabled Persons' Rights, I organised an arraignment to present a giant petition from Labour MP's all over Britain in support of a genuine anti-discrimination Bill for disabled people. Although these things look simple, they really demand a lot of behind-the-scenes activity and meetings with Clerks to the House and other Commons officials.

The plans completed, I sat in my seat with the petitions in a large white box, complete with purple ribbon and a seal to give it a 'legal' appearance. The 10 o'clock vote (on the notorious Job Seekers Bill) duly took place and I was present, supported by the whole of the Parliamentary Labour Party, when Geoff looked across to my seat and gave me a wink. As I waited to be called, the agenda suddenly changed: some Members below the gangway called for another vote, which few had expected.

One of my senior Shadow Cabinet colleagues told me it was not an official vote, and so front-benchers like myself were not expected to take part. Fine, I thought, I'll just pop up to the loos above the 'No' Lobby and I'll be back in plenty of time. I returned a little casually and was astonished to find there had been a change of mind, and that nobody was in the Division lobbies - just as I was to be on next!

I broke through a group of MPs who were standing around the doorway and ran for all I was worth, right down the middle of the Commons up to my seat: even the huge Labour cheers around me did not diminish my stunned reaction. Seconds after I sat down beside my big white box, Deputy Speaker Geoff calmly stood up and called my name. I looked across at Sebastian Coe, now a Tory MP, who gave the appearance of a man who had just seen his world record broken and I quickly regained my composure.

Everything afterwards went superbly, and my Labour colleagues were delighted at our demonstration of support for disabled people.

As Members left the chamber, showing thumbs up, slapping me on the shoulder and shaking my hand, I breathed a few sighs of relief. But to my mind the night was not mine: it belonged to Geoff Lofthouse who miraculously had delayed the proceedings and kept within the rules. A minor MP? Certainly not! In my book Geoff will always go down as a parliamentary giant."

APPENDIX K - Speech to the House of Lords on the Wakefield Health Authority (2 December 1998)

"My Lords, I shall confine my speech this evening to matters arising from the gracious speech on health. I quote:

"A Bill will be introduced to replace the NHS internal market which put hospitals, doctors and nurses in competition with each other. In its place will be decentralised arrangements based on partnership, quality and efficiency to put doctors and nurses in the lead in shaping local services."

Your Lordships will have heard my noble friend Lord Winston caution against too much decentralisation. I follow the noble Lord's argument. I shall express the situation as I find it to be in the area in which I live. I do that only because I know that in many parts of the country we will find similar experiences.

I have recently studied the British Medical Association and Royal Colleges consultative document Provision of Acute General Hospital

Services. I understand that that report followed a report from a joint working party of the British Medical Association, the Royal College of Physicians in London and the Royal College of Surgeons of England which states that the effective size of a hospital to provide most acute services for medicine and surgery is one serving a population of 250,000 to 350,000. The report goes on to suggest that the ideal unit for fully comprehensive medicine and surgery is a hospital or integrated group of hospitals serving a population of 450,000 to 500,000.

While I recognise the expertise serving on the joint working party, I wonder whether we are getting too big and moving away from the loyalty and love people have for their own hospitals. I also wonder whether these new units will become so distant the average person will not be able to associate with them. Although I am sure that the public do understand that it may be necessary for there to be alternatives locally to hospital admission and that better outcomes may be achieved by travelling further to receive specialist services, I am sure they feel distance should be minimised as much as possible.

When I think about the situation which is developing as to whether we have larger units, thus obliging people to travel further, I well recall the famous quote from Nye Bevan in 1947. He said: "I would rather be kept alive in the efficient but cold altruism of a large hospital, than expire in a gush of warm sympathy in a small one."

I can well understand that. However, when we consider that hospital services in this country have grown up around traditional populations in towns and cities, it is easy to recognise people's fears that, the longer the distance is from the area that they reside in to an acute unit, the more lives may be put at risk.

Since my younger days, and up to the present time, I have been accustomed to visiting the hospital in Pontefract where I live. I do not make that point to be parochial, because I have already said that many other areas in the country are probably in the same situation. I regret it now, but in fact the services of Pontefract, which have been provided for many years, may have to change and probably move to another part of the area. That will obviously cause people to engage in much more travelling.

I recognise that Pontefract is no different from any other town. I am aware that many other authorities in the country are undertaking to work to close traditional general hospitals and develop services on a single site so as to serve a much larger population. However, there is current concern in the Wakefield district, as I am sure there is in other parts of the country, over the proposals to follow this pattern. People are worried about access to services that they have traditionally found available close to their homes.

I realise that technology has moved on and that the skills of doctors need to be used to the best effect. In many cases this involved sub-specialisation where a doctor is an expert on a particular part of the anatomy rather than on a specialised subject; for example, surgery. But people are worried over the balance between availability of services and the travelling time with which members of the public are increasingly having to cope.

I should like to quote a few statistics to the House and do not apologise for doing so. I shall use them to emphasise the need for acute services in the areas such as Pontefract and Wakefield. This is quite understandable when you consider that Wakefield's aged standardised registration rates are the highest in Yorkshire for breast, lung, stomach and prostate cancer and that Wakefield's standard mortality ratio is 108 for all cancers - 125 for lung cancer and 187 for cervical cancer. Moreover, Wakefield's aged standardised mortality rate is the highest in Yorkshire for lung and stomach cancers, second highest for breast cancer and third highest for prostate cancer. The five-year survival rate for breast cancer in Wakefield is joint worst in the country, at 54 per cent. For cervical cancer, Wakefield women have the second lowest five-year survival rate in the northern and Yorkshire region at 56 per cent.

I am sure that your Lordships will appreciate why the population of the Wakefield district is keen that an ideal unit for fully comprehensive medicine and surgery, equipped with the latest high quality medical and surgical services, should be provided. While people believe that the ideal would be a unit at each end of the district, as is the case at present with a general hospital at each end, it is recognised that the demand for funding of two such units is probably not realistic.

However, there is concern among a substantial number of the population because both the Wakefield Health Authority and the Pinderfields and Pontefract Hospital Trust have made the Strategic Outline Case for capital investment, including a preferred site. As I see it, this is the major problem and this is where the decentralisation comes in. Let us take, for example, a preferred site in an area which consists of about 315,000 people, as is the case in the Wakefield metropolitan district area, with probably 100,000 on the perimeters. If a hospital is to be built at one end of the area, like Pinderfields at Wakefield, it means that there will be no other acute services between Wakefield's Pinderfields site and York, which is something nearing 40 miles. This causes people a great deal of worry, which I am sure noble Lords will appreciate.

If the Wakefield Health Authority is successful with its bid to provide a new modern hospital and everyone hopes that that will be so - there is a strong wish by, I think, the majority of people that it should be a site which is accessible to most of the people. I was very pleased to hear my noble friend Lady Hayman say in her opening remarks today that services should be provided around the people. If in fact areas like my own and others in the country are to be blessed with new facilities, which are very much needed, especially as regards acute services, I hope that they will be placed within the best possible spots, with the best possible travelling distances, for the convenience of all the people and not just a few. Those are the dangers that we face in Wakefield.

I am sure that my noble friend the Minister will agree that the overriding feature must be the availability of care which will improve health. I submit that there must be a middle road which needs to be investigated and identified. Of course, if the recommendations of the consultation documents are given serious consideration, then such consideration must be given to the shortest possible travelling time and access to such facilities to ensure that the NHS is serving the population, with the needs of patients being paramount."

APPENDIX L - Highlights of Speaker Betty Boothroyd's Speeches

Speech to President Yeltsin - "To all in Britain, you, Mr President, will always be associated with a particular photograph. It was one which appeared on our television screens and, indeed, was sent round the World during those critical August days of 1991, it showed you climbing to the top of a T72 Tank and standing there impervious to any threat and symbolising the opposition to the attempted coup. It was a picture of determination and defiance, a picture of genuine heroism.

It is appropriate that you should be with us in a week which marks the third anniversary of the tearing down of the Berlin wall. That event, too, was one of enormous significance. It heralded the end of a regime, just as your defiance meant not only the end of the coup, but the end of Communist rule. Yesterday, you, Mr President, and our own Prime Minister, signed a treaty. It was the first treaty between Russia and Great Britain since 1766. The signatory on your side then was Catherine the Great, a woman, it is true, but hardly one who could be said to have advanced the democratic process."

Speech to President Clinton - "Mr President, Lord Chancellor, fellow Parliamentarians: It is my pleasure, as Speaker of the House of Commons, to thank you most warmly, Mr President, for the speech to which we have just listened with such appreciation. Here, in this Royal Gallery, where heads of government are traditionally received by both Houses of Parliament, I join with the Lord Chancellor in extending to you a particular welcome.

There is often talk of a special relationship between our two countries. It is not for me - a non-political figure, in sharp contrast to the highly political nature of the United States Speakership - to comment on what that relationship entails. What I can say, however, is that I have a special relationship with the United States of America.

Just as you studied British politics as a Rhodes Scholar at the University of Oxford, so I studied American politics as a Congressional assistant on Capital Hill - a rather unusual role for a resolute British subject. It was, therefore, not a coincidence that I chose Washington for my first official visit abroad as Speaker. There I was fascinated once again to observe how our procedures mirror each other in so many ways. This, of course, is not entirely surprising in view of the origins of the Founding Fathers.

I am reminded, Mr President, of those origins daily as I walk through Speaker's House. For there, in the State Apartments, is a wonderful piece of Steuben sculpture which was presented to the House of Commons by the State of Virginia. The sculpture symbolises the three English ships which sailed on their historic voyage in 1607 to establish the first colony in Virginia and its first town, Jamestown. You can almost feel the wind in the sails as you walk past the sculpture. Each time I am reminded of the courage of my fellow countrymen who set out on that great adventure. The names of their ships summed up their hopes - "God Speed", "Discovery" and "Susan Constant".

It was a later Virginian, Thomas Jefferson, one of my political heroes, who used our common language to express in the Declaration of Independence the sentiments and cadences which still send a shiver of excitement down the spine among democrats the world over. The Lord Chancellor has cited Sir Winston Churchill's admiration of that Declaration. So, even though George the Third is staring down at us today from one of the portraits in this Royal Gallery, I feel emboldened to defy the shades of that monarch and quote Jefferson's words once again. When he declares: 'We hold these truths to be self-evident... that all men are created equal' and then lists the inalienable rights with which all men are endowed by their creator... who can fail to find fresh inspiration each time they are heard?

I have only one criticism to address to Jefferson across the centuries. I feel sure that many will join me when I query two words: "All men ..." In one way at least we have progressed beyond the Declaration of Independence. I think I can say with some confidence that it would be impossible now for Thomas Jefferson to leave out one half of the human race.

We have been reminded today of how we share the same language, the same basic legal system, the same belief that no person, however high, is above the law. In two world wars our countries have not only shared the same aims. We have stood shoulder to shoulder. We have shared the same sacrifices. Your visit, Mr President, reinforces the spirit of our alliance. I hope that from these Houses of Parliament you will take back to the United States the feeling that today you have been among friends. For we can take pride in our common past and confront the future confidently as members of the world's two greatest continuous democracies."

APPENDIX M - Highlights of President Nelson Mandela's Speech to the joint Houses of Parliament (11 July 1996)

"My Lords, ladies and gentlemen, it is with a deep sense of humility that we stand here today to address the historic Houses of Parliament of the United Kingdom. The rare honour you have extended to a foreigner speaks to the great age, the extent, and the warmth of the relations between our two peoples. It speaks of the prospect of us further deepening these excellent relations.

Had those forebears had the advantage of education and access to your outstanding cultural heritage, they would have found the words of one of the citizens in Shakespeare's *Coriolanus* most apposite to describe their attitude towards the Great Britain of the day. Let us hear the disenfranchised and dispossessed citizen of that day:

> *We are accounted poor citizens, the patricians good;*
> *What authority surfeits on, would relieve us*
> *The leanness that afflicts us, the object of our misery,*
> *Is as an inventory to particularise their abundance;*
> *Our sufferance is a gain to them.*
> *Let us revenge this with our pikes, ere we become rakes:*
> *For the gods know,*
> *I speak this in hunger for bread,*
> *And not in thirst for revenge.*

We are in the Houses in which Harold Macmillan worked: he who spoke in our own Houses of Parliament in Cape Town in 1960, shortly before the infamous Sharpeville Massacre, and warned a stubborn and race-blinded white oligarchy in our country that "the wind of change is blowing through this continent", he to whom a South African cartoonist paid tribute by having him recite other Shakespearean words,

> *Oh, pardon me thou bleeding piece of earth,*
> *That I am meek and gentle with these butchers!*

Change has come to our country, too, perhaps at last, but bringing with it joy, the promise of a better future and a protracted festival of hope across the globe. Racism is a blight on the human conscience. The idea that any people can be inferior to another to the point where those who consider themselves superior define and treat the rest as subhuman denies the humanity even of those who elevate themselves to the status of gods.

It seems to us that, as the ordinary people of the world came to understand the real nature of the system of apartheid, they decided that they would not permit that their response to that question should be to hang their heads in shame. We take this opportunity once more to pay tribute to the millions of Britons who, through the years and like others everywhere else in the world, stood up to say 'no' to apartheid.

Our emancipation is their reward. We know that the freedom we enjoy is a richly textured gift hand-crafted by ordinary folk who would not allow their own dignity as human beings to be insulted. In the acceptance of that gift is contained an undertaking by our people that we shall never, never again allow our country to play host to racism. Nor shall our voices be stilled if we see that another elsewhere in the world is victim to racial tyranny.

But, above all else, we believe that our charge is to fulfil the wishes of all humanity, including our own people, to ensure that the enormous and sustained universal effort which translated itself into the defeat of the system of apartheid achieves its related purpose of transforming South Africa into a democratic, nonracial, nonsexist, peaceful and prosperous country.

The first founding stone of our new country is national reconciliation and national unity. The fact that it has settled in its mortar needs no advertising. If it were not so, the blood in the streets would trumpet loudly that we had failed to achieve acceptance of the need for all our people, black and white, to live together in peace as equals and as citizens bound together by a common destiny.

Furthermore, recognising the diversity of our society, our new Constitution provides for the establishment of a Commission for the Promotion and Protection of the Rights of Cultural, Religious and Linguistic Communities. This will ensure that our people as whole have an additional instrument in their hands to enable them to avoid the emergence of any situation in which ethnic and other tensions might drive us back to apartheid solutions or to an imitation of the cruel example of Bosnia.

To close the circle, let our peoples, the ones formerly poor citizens and the others good patricians - politicians, business people, educators, health workers, scientists, engineers and technicians, sports people and entertainers, activists for charitable relief, join hands to build on what we have achieved together and help construct a humane African world whose emergence will say a new universal order is born in which we are each our brothers' and our sisters' keeper.

And so let that outcome, as we close the chapter of two centuries and open a millennium, herald the advent of a glorious summer of a partnership for freedom, peace, prosperity and friendship.

I thank you."

APPENDIX N - Speech in the House of Lords - Rugby League (2 December 1998)

"My Lords, I am deeply grateful and indeed privileged to have the opportunity this evening to speak in your Lordships' House and to draw the Minister's attention to the report and recommendations of the Advisory Group on Listed Events, which is chaired by my noble friend Lord Gordon of Strathblane. Any comments I make are no criticism of my noble friend or any members of the advisory group. I am satisfied that they have looked at the overall situation and have come out with recommendations which on the evidence available they believe are the correct ones. Before I present my case, I just want to say to the House that over the weekend a note was sent to my home telling me that my late friend Lord Howell was to support me and speak in the debate tonight. I can do no more than associate myself with the many wonderful tributes which we have seen in the national press this day. He was a personal friend to many other people in this Chamber. We all mourn his loss and we shall miss him greatly.

I shall attempt to speak on two issues in relation to the recommendations of the report made by the advisory group. The first is the principle of listing events. The argument against listing events is that sporting bodies are quite capable of managing their own affairs and have the sense to be able to dispose of their television rights in a manner which is lucrative and which affords them widespread coverage. That is understandable to a point. However, these are times when the numbers of children participating in sport are falling and when youngsters need more than ever to be exposed to the influence of sport for the good of their own health and that of society. The prime marketing tool for any sport is for it to be freely available on television at the press of a button. Children in particular are especially impressionable and acknowledge as their heroes those whom they see on television on a regular basis. There is a fear that, if sport disappears from free to air television, then children will not be captivated by sport and will not be drawn into wanting to emulate their sporting heroes. I certainly share that view. In that respect, the benefits of sporting activities for youngsters, both in terms of their healthy well-being and of the social co-operative virtues which team sports especially convey, are well established. For children to opt out of sport would be for them to miss out on those benefits and so become more and more unhealthy and undisciplined. An extra burden would then be placed on the state, which must pick up the pieces of this decline.

The comparative viewing figures achieved by sport on terrestrial and satellite television speak volumes for what is at stake. As an example, in rugby league the Silk Cut Challenge Cup-ties broadcast live by the BBC regularly attract an audience of between 4 million and 5 million. In contrast, the Super League matches on Sky Sports average between 150,000 and 200,000. Similarly in rugby union, while as many as 7 million watch England internationals on BBC, the matches shown on satellite television have viewing figures similar to those I referred to on the rugby league scene. The marketing effect, then, of terrestrial television making sport freely available is colossal. Its potential impact on youth and the health of the nation is huge. Can we really trust sport to realise the unseen benefits in that regard or are the administrators blinded by the huge sums of cash which are offered by satellite television in exchange for their rights? Do we require instead legislation to save sporting governing bodies from themselves to guarantee that the next generation of British youngsters sees sport for itself and is inspired by its example?

The second point I would like to present to the House is the national spread of rugby league, which means that the Challenge Cup Final is indeed an event of national importance - contrary to the findings of the Advisory Group in Listed Events. I form the opposite view to the review. I do not believe that the group has done enough in-depth research into the case for rugby league. I must emphasise this evening that I am putting the case for only one match a year - the Rugby League Cup Final. There is the international spread of rugby league and the fact that 16 nations now play the game, with 10 recognised as senior test-playing countries, which is more than for cricket. Rugby league in this country has 26 full-time development officers working to spread the game at junior and youth levels in places such as the North East (Gateshead), South Wales (Cardiff), Scotland (Glasgow) and Ireland (Dublin). Each of these target development areas has a thriving amateur league at junior, youth and open-age levels, which gives the lie to the theory that the game is confined to Yorkshire, Lancashire and Cumbria.

Through the Rugby Football League and the British Amateur Rugby League Association, known as BARLA, there has been created a league called the Rugby League Conference, which draws together 16 leading amateur clubs in the Midlands and the South in a competitive environment - which will in time take them to semiprofessional status - including towns such as Birmingham, Oxford, Worcester, Bedford, Ipswich, Cheltenham, Chester and Leicester. That is the spread of rugby league football in our country today.

Rugby league is the fastest growing sport in universities and institutes of higher education, with 68 student teams now playing the game in all parts of England, Scotland, Wales and Ireland, and the first national development officer for the women's game, Jackie Sheldon, was appointed only last year. BARLA itself in a quarter of a century has increased the number of teams playing rugby league from 200 to 1,400 teams. That is success. We wish that success to continue, but we do not believe it will if the youngsters who today are keen on playing rugby league are denied seeing the jewel in the crown, the Rugby League Cup Final. That will be helpful for their advancement.

I say to my noble friend Lord Gordon that each of the factors I have described bears witness to the wrong done by the Advisory Group on Listed Events in denying rugby league a place in the national consciousness. It does and it will continue to grow apace in future years as the professional and amateur arms work in unity together. The Rugby League Challenge Cup is an English institution despite its perceived parochial northern base. As such, the annual final at Wembley goes out to a worldwide audience of millions and is part of the high profile British sporting heritage and should therefore be protected for the benefit of the people. The foundation of the sport is the amateur game under the jurisdiction of the British Amateur Rugby League Association. I have already described its progress. It is estimated that there are nearly 100,000 people playing the amateur game throughout this country. One can imagine the contribution of recreational hours that that gives to many young people who enjoy playing this wonderful game. Many of the players taking part are unemployed due to the industrial decline in the areas where the game has been traditional. Terrestrial TV is the perfect vehicle for promoting this "all-action sport" to the nation. The Rugby League Challenge Cup is probably the most famous rugby competition in the world. The final is staged in the country's national stadium, Wembley, and is watched by a worldwide audience.

I bring my contribution to a close to enable others to have more time to make theirs, but first I must say that, apart from the issue of encouraging youth interest, a major problem has developed especially in the strongholds of rugby league, but also, I believe, throughout the country. In my own area, which I was privileged to represent in another place for many years, most of the rugby league teams received financial help from the mining industry. Many former miners who are now elderly are disabled as a result of chest diseases or have other disabilities. Many are lifelong rugby league supporters who love the game. They cannot get out of their houses because of their disabilities, but they are being denied the right to see the game that they have supported and loved all their lives. Why? Because they cannot afford commercial television. That cannot be right. Of course, I acknowledge that finance comes into most things and that, when somebody like Murdoch comes along and offers millions of pounds, the clubs are under great temptation to accept. In many ways, I think that that is ruining a great game, though I can understand the temptation. However, people are much more important than finance and generations of people, and many old people, are now being denied the right to see sport simply because Murdoch has control.

I was worried when I read the Answer to a Question that had been tabled in another place by Sir Raymond Powell about who had given evidence to the group. I noticed that Mr Maurice Lindsay was among the names. That same Mr Maurice Lindsay was the main negotiator in the Murdoch deal. According to *The Guardian* the other day, a recent poll asked whether such sports should be protected and 73 per cent of the public agreed that they should be. I am being nodded at and it is time for me to sit down. I have gone over my 10 minute limit, but as we all sat in the Chamber waiting for the other debate to finish, we now have an hour and a half instead of one hour for this Unstarred Question, so I do not think that I need apologise."

APPENDIX O - Rugby League: - David Hinchliffe and other speeches in the House of Commons (26 April 1995)

David Hinchliffe MP - "I declare at the outset an interest in this debate. As is declared in the Register of Members' Interests I have 500 shares in Wakefield Trinity Rugby League Football Club. I am not sure what they are worth at present.

The issues are simple and straightforward. Why should a battle between two Australian media magnates result in my constituents losing something very important which we have had for 122 years - Wakefield Trinity Rugby League Football Club? Why should a power struggle on the other side of the world mean that I should lose the team that I have supported through thick and thin since I was a small child? It is very appropriate that you, Mr Deputy Speaker, are in the Chair this morning. You have risen from humble origins in my part of the world to be a highly respected Member of the House. You have achieved a great deal politically but, most importantly to the people who matter, you once played for Featherstone Rovers. I have here your autobiography, *A Very Miner MP*. The front shows a Castleford miner and a Featherstone miner together. There is a gap; perhaps a Wakefield Trinity miner should be included. I refer to the book because it is clear from it that you, Mr Deputy Speaker, more than anyone understand the community in which rugby league is played. You more than anyone understand how the events of the past two and a half weeks have shaken some of us to our roots because your roots, like mine, have been intertwined with rugby league football from the word go.

On Sunday, I attended what may well be the last match that my team, Wakefield Trinity, will ever play. Grown men wept. That grief has turned to anger at the way in which those ruling the game of rugby league in this country - Mr Lindsay, the Chief Executive, Mr Walker, the Chairman, the Club Chairman and others - seem to have allowed us to be used. As you well know, Mr Deputy Speaker, the root of the problem is that rugby league has become a pawn in a power struggle between Kerry Packer and Rupert Murdoch over first, television coverage of rugby league in Australia and secondly, the expansion of satellite television. When Packer won the right to show Australian rugby league on his Channel 9 station, Murdoch's News Corporation retaliated by planning a super league in direct opposition. Murdoch bought up many of Australia's and New Zealand's top rugby league players. When that strategy failed, he turned to Europe and to rugby league in this country. After the £87 million deal between the Rugby Football League in Britain and Murdoch a couple of weeks ago, Packer's representatives came to Britain trying to lure our best players away. The prospect of Murdoch's money being stuffed into players' pockets to outbid Packer is clear; that is the reality of rugby league's present situation. Martin Offiah may become much richer than he is already, but the game of rugby league will be poorer as a direct result.

A couple of dozen suits making a decision on behalf of God knows how many followers of the game is a disgrace. It's a bit like coming home one day and finding that your walls have been knocked through, and from now on you and your neighbour are all sharing one house. What do you say? 'Thanks very much. Another time, perhaps you'd like to ask me first.'"

Ian McCartney MP, Chairman of the All Party Rugby League Group in the House of Commons - "I hoped that today we would be debating the National Heritage Select Committee Report which concluded that after 100 years, the Rugby Football League had been treated disgracefully by organised sports such as Rugby Union and sham amateurism.

In this debate I shall not criticise Maurice Lindsay or Rodney Walker. Maurice Lindsay is a good friend of mine who I have known throughout my public life in the North West. I have been traumatised by what this matter has done to our friendship. My trust in the views of him and other people on the future of rugby league was wiped out in 3 days because of Murdoch's ability to move in and place a gun at their heads.

A small group of players will become instant millionaires while the sport at the grass roots will wither away. Clubs will be left to go bankrupt and communities will see their teams and players made redundant. How can Martin Offiah honestly hold up his hand and say that he did a deal because he wanted to play for his country? The money secured in that contract alone will be sufficient to plough into an investment programme for the clubs left in the first Division."

Kate Hoey MP - "Does my Honourable Friend share my concern that someone - it is difficult not to mention names and personalities - who is involved in this deal, namely Mr Walker, is the Chairman of the Sports Council? Does he feel that people are confident how our sport in this country will be handled when the same person so quickly sells out a major sport?"

Mr McCartney - "My Honourable Friend makes an important point, Rodney Walker is a man of integrity but the deal seriously compromises the whole of the Rugby Football League and the ability of its administrators to be regarded as independent in their role in other non-governmental agencies.

Rodney Walker and others should consider whether before making their hasty decisions they should have thought the issues through more thoroughly. The rugby league family must come together quickly. Some sanity must prevail in Australia and here to attend immediately the cherry picking, bans and prescriptions. Unless that happens immediately, none of the £70 million will be left to invest. It will have gone further."

APPENDIX P - Women in Parliament

In 1992 there were 60 women MPs and in 1997 the number doubled; 120 were elected. It had been an uphill struggle for the campaign, for the admission of women to the House of Commons was preceded by the fight for women's suffrage. The first debate on the subject was initiated by John Stewart Mill, a great advocate for the cause, and held on 20 May 1867. From then on, attempts to pass legislation on the subject were made almost every Parliamentary session, without success, although a few Bills passed the Second Reading stage. It was argued that if women were given the vote, they could not logically be barred from membership of the House of Commons on the grounds that those who must obey the law should be allowed a hand in making it. That done, there could be no argument against universal suffrage; including low paid male workers. From there it followed that if the interests of women were identical with those of men, women's suffrage could not affect the election results or conversely that women's interests were different and so should be directly represented in Parliament. Although the achievements of the campaigners' aims were still many years away at this stage, a small advance was made in 1869 when the franchise for municipal elections was extended to municipal rate payers, including women.

Of the many groups or societies formed to promote the cause of women's suffrage, the best known was the Women's Social and Political Union, founded in 1903 by Emmeline Pankhurst, a Manchester campaigner. In 1905 it was decided that the peaceful method of persuasion which had been employed until that time was achieving nothing, and more militant action was embarked upon. This resulted in repeated arrests and imprisonment.

The outbreak of the First World War brought about a truce in the militancy and propaganda while campaigners devoted themselves to the war. However, the subject came to the fore again in 1916 when it became obvious that the movement of military personnel had rendered the electoral register quite out of date. A conference on electoral reform, chaired by the Speaker, was set up, and in February 1917 this recommended a limited measure of women's suffrage. The recommendations were duly enacted in the Representation of the People Act 1918, this gave the vote to women over 30 years of age.

In October 1918 the Parliament (Qualification of Women) Bill was introduced, to make women eligible as Members of Parliament, and this was passed, almost without opposition, in time to receive Royal Assent just before Parliament was resolved in preparation for the General Election of December 1918. At this election, out of a total of 1,823 candidates, only 17 were women. Most had been active campaigners in the suffragette movement, but the only successful candidate had taken no part in the campaign and was destined never to take her seat. Countess Constance Markievicz of Anglo-Irish background and married to a Polish Count, had contested the election from her cell in Holloway Prison where she had been held under suspicion of conspiring with Germany during the war. She was given early release under an amnesty from a life sentence for her leading part in a 1916 Easter rebellion in Dublin against British rule. In common with other Sinn Fein Members, she did not take her seat in protest against British policy in Ireland. Her action was a forerunner to that taken by modern Sinn Fein MPs, like Gerry Adams and Martin McGuinness, who whilst being elected as MPs have never taken their seat, having refused to take the Oath and Allegiance to the Sovereign, as in their view that would acknowledge British rule in Ireland, which they resist.

Although the women candidates who had stood at the 1918 election were prominent in the suffragette movement or dedicated political activists, it was ironic that the first woman to take her seat in the House of Commons had never campaigned for women's rights. American born Viscountess Astor was elected for the Sutton Division of Plymouth in November 1919 at a by-election caused by her husband's accession to the peerage on the death of his father. In 1923, the Intoxicating Liquor (Sale to Persons under 18) Act, introduced by Lady Astor, became the first Act to result from a Bill introduced by a female MP.

The first woman to hold ministerial office was Margaret Bondfield, who in January 1924, was appointed Parliamentary Under-Secretary at the Ministry of Labour in the first Labour Government convened under Ramsay MacDonald. She lost her seat later that year but was returned again at a by-election in 1926. In 1929 she was appointed Minister of Labour, the first woman Member of the Cabinet and also the first British woman politician to be admitted to the Privy Council. She held this position until her parliamentary career came to an end in 1931 when Labour lost the General Election and she was defeated.

In 1928 the voting age for women was lowered to 21 years, the same as for men, by the Representation of The People (Equal Franchise) Act. This removed the anomaly that had stood since 1918, namely that a woman could be elected an MP up to 9 years before she was allowed to vote in parliamentary elections.

Although women MPs have been active in various committees, it was not until the beginning of the 1946/47 session that Florence Patten became the first woman to be nominated by the Speaker to the Chairman's Panel of Members to act as temporary Chairman of Committees of the whole House and Chairman of Standing Committees. In the former capacity, Mrs Patten in 1948 became the first woman to preside over the whole House during the Supply Day Debate on Scottish Civil Aviation Estimates. She did not, however, sit in the Speaker's chair, but at the table, as is the case when the House is in Committee.

The first woman actually to occupy the Speaker's Chair was Betty Harvie Anderson in July 1970, when she was appointed Deputy Chairman of Ways and Means and took the Chair during the debate on the Queen's speech. She was addressed as "Mr Deputy Speaker". This was changed when the first woman Speaker, Betty Boothroyd, was appointed and in response to a query as to what she should be called said, "Call me Madam." On 27 April 1992, Miss Boothroyd became Speaker. She had served as Second Deputy Chairman of Ways and Means since 1987 in which capacity she had become the second woman to occupy the Speaker's Chair.

Following the Tory victory in the General Election of 1979 Margaret Thatcher became the first woman Prime Minister. Ironically the 1979 election returned the lowest number of women MPs since 1945. It has been a subject of comment on the Thatcher Years that she only ever appointed one other woman to the Cabinet, Baroness Young, Lord

Privy Seal and Leader of the House of Lords in 1982/83. Upon her enforced resignation in 1990, Mrs Thatcher had been Prime Minister for over 11 years, the longest tenure of that office in the twentieth century. The changing attitudes towards women in politics led to the appointment of Ann Taylor as the first female Leader of the House in 1997 and since that time, the first woman Chief Whip in 1998. Ann took over these important posts in the period of influx of women when serious consideration had to be given to the modernising of the procedure of the House.

In an attempt to introduce more women the Labour Party adopted women-only short lists, a practice later disallowed as being illegal under Sex Discrimination legislation. The General Election of 1 May 1997 saw a greater percentage of women candidates. 15 women MPs from the 1992 Parliament either did not stand or lost their seat. Of the 243 new Members elected to Parliament for the first time, 71 were women, (64 Labour, 5 Conservative, 2 Liberal Democrats). There are currently 5 women in the Cabinet, (4 MPs and 1 Peer), with a further 30 women MPs and 4 women Peers in other ministerial positions. Furthermore, two of the Whips in the Commons (in addition to the Chief Whip, who is in the Cabinet) and three in the Lords, are women. Of the current women Members, the Speaker, Betty Boothroyd, has the longest unbroken service among women MPs, having been elected in 1973. Gwyneth Dunwoody was elected earlier, in 1966, but was out of the House between 1970 and 1974.

APPENDIX Q - Maiden Speech to the House of Commons (14 December 1978)

"I am sorry that so many Honourable Members should be leaving the Chamber as I rise to take the opportunity of making my maiden speech and of attempting to bring to the notice of the House what the people of the outside world are thinking and what they want. After my experience over the past three or four weeks in this House I am beginning to wonder how many Honourable Members, especially those on the opposition benches, realise what the people at home want.

I understand that it is customary, when delivering a maiden speech, to refer to one's predecessor. Even if that were not the custom, I would not have been able to make my first speech in this House without referring to the late Joe Harper. I was a personal friend of his. We both had our origins in Featherstone. I felt his loss deeply, and so did everyone in Pontefract, Castleford and Featherstone, because he was their friend too. He was a friend in the true sense. People could always accept what he said, even if he disagreed with them. They knew that he was speaking the truth as he saw it, no matter how unpopular it might be. He never coveted popularity and, for that reason, was extremely popular. No duty was ever too small for him and no burden ever too heavy. He remained always one of the people, outstanding because he had extraordinary common sense and judgement. He wore himself out in the service of the people. We shall certainly miss him.

Although I have been associated with the late Joe Harper for all of my life, and was well aware of his outstanding abilities, it was a little frightening, in my early days in this House, when being introduced to different people, to have almost every one of them, from all parts of the House, bring to my attention the fact that I have a great deal to live up to. I hope that as a result of our close association over the past 30 to 40 years some of Joe's abilities and integrity will have rubbed off on me.

My constituency is a varied one. It has two super Rugby League teams, in Featherstone and Castleford. Like the incomes policy, they have lost a few points recently, but I assure the House that they are on the way back. My constituency has an ancient castle, fine buildings, good libraries and excellent schools. It has a progressive district council, which is trying to uplift and enhance the area. It also has slag heaps galore.

I am delighted when I hear of the concern for the environment which is being shown in connection with the development at Selby. This means that the people there will not suffer what we have suffered. We believe that it is time that some consideration of a financial nature was given to those of us who have lived our lives amid the dereliction of opencast mining. Our parents and our parents' parents have suffered in the same way, and we shall continue to suffer for a long time to come. Cannot the same concern be expressed about us as is expressed about the "pretty places" or is it a case of "they are used to it, it doesn't matter."?

The inner cities have their problems. Quite rightly, money had been forthcoming from Government to assist them. We have similar problems of decay and dereliction. Because they are on a smaller scale, it is easy to dismiss them. If the problems are left to fester, there will be a stronger drift away from the freestanding towns, to the pretty houses being built in Selby, with the result that the public money invested in our schools, housing, water and electricity supplies, will lie idle while more will have to be spent elsewhere. I do not wish to be a prophet of doom and make a gloomy maiden speech, but I point out that it often seems to us that the largest cities get everything to the detriment of the smaller towns.

In my constituency we need a greater diversity of employment, for men and women, but especially for men. We need national assistance to get rid of the eyesores of the coal tips, which are the by-products of the wealth of the country and which have created ugliness for our area. How long must we wait? My constituency is at the centre of Britain and of a rapid communications network involving the M62, the A1 and the M1. If my Right Honourable Friend the Secretary of State for the Environment would like to send money to us now, it could be there in two and a half-hours' time.

I well remember the reports in the press of the maiden speech of my predecessor. One newspaper referred to it as fresh air sweeping through the House of Commons. I do not profess to be able to create fresh air. There has certainly been a lot of air created during the past month when I have been here - from the Opposition Benches. It has not been so fresh. The wishes of the electorate in Pontefract and Castleford are still fresh in my mind. During the election campaign it came over clearly that the majority of the people whom I met, with whom I have lived all of my life, felt that the main priority was to support the Government in their attack upon inflation and in their attempt to control it. That is what they mandated me to do. I am not here for the sake of making party political points to the disadvantage of Britain. If I were so to do, my electorate would never forgive me.

It is only a short while ago that I left heavy industry. Therefore, I can speak on it with some authority. I have some first-class knowledge of the immediate past in industry. Those in heavy industry, and certainly those in the mining industry, of which I am privileged to be a part, do not want wage claims and wage awards that will create inflation. The miners in my area and throughout the country have not forgotten the 1970-71 Wilberforce awards. At that time they enjoyed probably the highest wage increases that were ever awarded to the industry. In a matter of months those wage increases did not mean a thing to them. They represented merely confetti money and their purchasing power was just not there.

The message has come to me - I have been instructed so to inform the House, including my Right Honourable Friend the Prime Minister and the Government - that what is needed is an increase in real wages and that that can be achieved only by the policies of my Right Honourable Friend the Prime Minister and the Government.

I do not want to let the occasion pass without referring to the speech of the Right Honourable and Learned Member for Surrey East (Sir G. Howe), in yesterday's debate. I refer to column 782 of yesterday's *Hansard*. The Right Honourable and Learned Gentleman made reference to the productivity deal in the mining industry. He and others should get the facts right before they briefly refer to

285

percentages. That is tantamount, with assembling all the facts, to misleading the House.

I can speak with some knowledge on the mine workers' incentive scheme as I have only recently ceased administering that scheme. The comparison made by the Right Honourable and Learned Gentleman of the first three months of this fiscal year with the first three months of the preceding year was not representative of the scheme. I admit that the scheme was negotiated area by area and was introduced piecemeal. The scheme started in late December in parts of Nottinghamshire and spread steadily throughout the coalfields until the last coalface agreements were being completed in late March and April. That meant a slow build-up in the early part of the year. Pits had to settle down to operate a unique and novel system that was extremely complicated. The effect was patchy at first and gave a low overall average increase rate.

Results have steadily improved as time has passed and the teething troubles have been overcome. In the first 36 weeks of the current fiscal year productivity at the coalface was 10.8 per cent better than for the same period last year while overall productivity is 3.9 per cent better. All that is against a background of falling productivity in the previous three or four years. To show that this is a progressive trend, the same result for the most recent 13 weeks up to 2 December is an improvement in face productivity of 12.3 per cent and overall of 6.2 per cent. Deep mined output is now more than 500,000 tons up on the same period last year, again showing a complete reversal of the trend of the past three or four years when production as well as productivity declined. Perhaps the most significant fact is that this has been achieved with 7,000 fewer men than at this time last year.

If we assume that those 7,000 men had been available and had been producing, at a conservative estimate, 10 tons a week per man, they would have produced an additional 70,000 tons per week, or a revenue of more than £5.5 million for the fiscal year. Even without those 7,000 men we have increased output by about 500,000 tons. It is not right to suggest, as was suggested yesterday, that the miners' productivity scheme is merely a myth. That is not true. Based on my own experience, I can tell the House that it is working and that it is cutting even. I have made these statements because the House could have been misled by the remarks of the Right Honourable and Learned Gentleman.

As I have said, I come to the House to throw my weight behind the number one priority, namely, that which is most beneficial to Britain - country first, politics second. It has been proved beyond a shadow of a doubt that the Government's policies are working and that the Government should be allowed to remain in office to conclude them."

APPENDIX R - Yvette Cooper's Maiden Speech to the House of Commons (25 June 1997)

"Mr Deputy Speaker, thank you for calling me during this historic debate. I am honoured to be uttering my very first words in the House on behalf of the people of Pontefract and Castleford on Budget day. This is Labour's first Budget for 18 years - and what a Budget. It is hard to know where to begin: resources for education and health, help for the young and for the long-term unemployed, measures to calm growth in consumption, boost for investment or help with child care.

It is also an honour to conclude the debate today, and to hear so many maiden speeches. We have had such speeches from my Honourable Friends the Members for Enfield, North (Ms Ryan), for Redditch (Jacqui Smith), for Eastwood (Mr Murphy) and for Brentford and Isleworth (Mrs Keen), and from the Honourable Members for Witney (Mr Woodward), for Weston-super-Mare (Mr Cotter) and for North Norfolk (Mr Prior). We have had a tour of the country, and we have heard how the Budget will affect people across Britain. It is truly a people's Budget.

Almost 100 years ago, Lloyd George launched his people's Budget for this century. Now we have a new people's Budget to begin the next century. I congratulate my right Honourable Friend the Chancellor on a wise and radical Budget. It faces up to the long-term problems of the British economy. It also takes immediate steps to tackle some of the deep-rooted inequalities faced by my constituents.

I represent a corner of West Yorkshire that is proud of its industrial heritage and its hard-working people; the liquorice fields and factories of Pontefract; the potteries of Castleford; the pits--the heart and belly of the constituency; the power station at Ferrybridge; the glassworks and the chemical works of Knottingley and Castleford; and, near the corner of Normanton that I represent, a Japanese electronics factory.

These past two decades have been hard times in my constituency. Many of the pits are now closed, jobs in traditional industries have gone and, most important, we lack new investment and help to reskill the work force to generate new jobs to replace the old ones that have gone.

I must report to the House that 2,600 people in my constituency are officially unemployed: a third of them have been unemployed for more than a year. The number of people not working either because they have been forced into early retirement or on to sickness benefit is much higher. Too many of my constituents have not had their fair share of opportunities to learn and to obtain the qualifications that they need to prosper in a modern economy. That matters for the future, as one generation follows in the footsteps of another. Evidence shows that the chance of the sons and daughters of miners in my constituency becoming high earners when they grow up is a mere tenth of that of the sons and daughters of well-educated and wealthy professionals. That figure is shocking.

The House must not misunderstand me. It is true that my constituency is plagued by unemployment, but I represent hard-working people who are proud of their strong communities and who have fought hard across generations to defend them. They are proud of their socialist traditions, and have fought for a better future for their children and their grandchildren. In the middle ages, that early egalitarian, the real Robin Hood, lived, so we maintain, in the vale of Wentbridge to the south of Pontefract. It was a great base from which to hassle the travelling fat cats on the Great North road.

Centuries later, Pontefract became home to another true fighter for social justice, Barbara Castle. In her autobiography, she describes her politicisation during the miners' lock-out in 1921. Through the years, my constituency has been home to other Members who have fought hard for the working people whom they represent in nearby constituencies, including the former Member for Hemsworth, Derek Enright, and my Honourable Friend the Member for Normanton (Mr O'Brien), who has helped me so much in these early months.

The people of Pontefract and Castleford owe most to the man who represented them for the past 19 years, and who battled hard for their welfare, Sir Geoffrey Lofthouse, now Lord Lofthouse of Pontefract. I know that Honourable Members will join me in paying tribute to someone who, as a former Deputy Speaker, worked hard for the House, was fair and honourable, and, above all, was a kind man. He governed the House, which can sometimes be rowdy and alarming, with a firm but fair hand.

For some, the traditional tribute to a predecessor is something to be swallowed swiftly, got over as fast as possible. For me, it is an honour and a privilege to be able to pay that tribute on behalf of the House and the people of Pontefract and Castleford to Sir Geoff, as he is known locally.

Sir Geoff was a well-loved constituency Member of Parliament. Like my grandfather, he began his working life in the pits as a teenager. The mischievous among his Pontefract friends describe him as a corner-stint man, but they would never use the same phrase to describe his commitment to his constituents. His proudest achievement was his work for the welfare of the miners with whom he served for so long, getting emphysema recognised as an industrial disease.

I pay a personal tribute to him, too, for Sir Geoff has been extremely supportive during these curious first months here. I hope we can continue to work together for the people of Pontefract and Castleford, a partnership which I hope echoes the strength of this new Government, young and old, energy and experience, women and men, across the country and across the generations working together for common goals. The Budget gives us the chance to achieve those goals.

More important to my constituents than anything else will be the new deal for the unemployed. In Pontefract and Castleford we are raring to go. Already, the Groundwork Trust in Castleford has approached me with a proposal for an environmental task force. We hope to encourage young unemployed people in some of the highest areas of unemployment in our constituency - in Knottingley and on the Airedale estate in Castleford - to join regeneration projects that are already planned. That way, they can take their first steps into the world of work straight from their own doorstep, be part of rebuilding their own troubled estates, learning transferable skills and building their own personal pride in their environment and in their work.

We think that this is such a good idea that we are not even waiting for the windfall tax money to come through. A local partnership is already drawing up a proposal for European money, and I hope that we will provide a successful model for the rest of the country to follow. At the same time, Wakefield council is itching to expand on its successful job subsidy programme, Workline, which it has been operating for the past 11 years. Employers there have a year-long subsidy of up to £40 a week to take on unemployed workers.

I asked one employer involved whether he would have taken someone on anyway. After all, his business was expanding. He told me two interesting things. The first was that the subsidy encouraged him to take on a new employee a year earlier than he would otherwise have done. The second was that, without the subsidy, he would not have considered taking on someone who was unemployed. There, in that one anecdote, was the proof that such a job subsidy can speed up job creation and help people in most danger of being locked outside the work force, trapped on the dole, into jobs.

That is important because it means that the new deal gives us a chance to tackle the long-term roots of inequality - people who are trapped on the dole in my constituency. Moreover, by helping those who find it hardest to get work, the new deal also boosts the capacity of the economy. That means that, as the economy grows, instead of running into the old inflationary buffers, as so often happens, we can have growth that creates jobs and more jobs, because we have boosted the capacity. That is the Budget's greatest strength. At the same time as controlling consumer demand and stopping it expanding too fast, the Budget is boosting the supply side to try to raise Britain's long-term sustainable rate of growth.

I hope that the new deal will receive support from both sides of the House, because it is about our future. In Pontefract and Castleford, I found enthusiasm for these proposals on both sides of the political spectrum.

As recently as Monday morning, a small business man came into my surgery. He admitted to being one of the few people in the area who had voted Conservative for 30 years - until the recent election. However, he said that he was delighted with what he had seen about Labour's plans for young people. He said that he wanted to take on three young unemployed people, asked when they could start, and where should he sign. His enthusiasm was infectious, and I hope that such enthusiasm will encourage more small businesses, both in my constituency and throughout the country, to take up the challenge to provide a new deal for the unemployed. It is something which we all need to work on together.

I am sure that that man will be even more delighted now that he has heard my Right Honourable Friend's Budget. It truly is a people's Budget - a Budget for social justice and for Britain's future. Tough choices have to be made, but they will generate results in the long run.

Keynes said: "In the long run we are all dead" but I say, "So what?" Our children and our grandchildren will still be alive. Therefore, for the people of Pontefract and Castleford and for their children and grandchildren, I welcome the Budget."

APPENDIX S - Maiden Speech in the House of Lords (23 July 1997)

"My Lords, it is a pleasure to have the opportunity of making my maiden speech in this House after many years in the other place and in local government. When I first came to this place I wondered how I should settle down. It tended to worry me a little - until, about a fortnight before I had the privilege of being sworn in, I visited the other place and sat in the Gallery. I received something of a shock. Looking down into the Chamber I did not know anybody. When I arrived in this place it was a great comfort to see many familiar, kind and welcoming faces. It took me back many years to my time in the other place.

I should like, first, to say a big thank you to both the Clerk of the Parliaments and Black Rod, and to all their staff, for the kindness and guidance that they have shown to me and to other noble Lords since we entered this place, and would specially thank the noble Lords, Lord Mason and Lord Gregson, who supported me in my introduction to this Chamber."

After responding to specific points in the previous speech I went on to say, "I welcome the fact that in order to sustain communities and ensure pride for the local population, the Government are also allowing up to 15 per cent of resources to be used for regeneration-linked housing purposes. Again, such an initiative will aid the return to work scenario and could also be used to aid security and crime prevention.

I believe that if there is any aspect which could be enhanced in the current proposals, it is that an indication - say a minimum of 90 per cent - of future years' allocations should be notified to local authorities as soon as possible, ideally at least two years in advance.

The biggest single problem facing local authorities under the current capital control regime is that they only receive the following year's allocation each December. Most capital schemes are by nature large-scale and expensive and the contract period can often exceed 18 to 24 months. Such large schemes require a lead-in time of about 40 to 45 weeks. The most effective way of managing such large-scale projects is to have security and knowledge of the funding arrangements for the period when the actual work and therefore expenditure is incurred. The wealth is very welcome to local authorities with the vast run-down and shortage of housing throughout the country, not least in my own area which is a metropolitan district council, and with the disrepair and lack of new build. To people who criticise and say that the Bill does not go far enough, I say that it is a start, a responsible start, and I wish it a speedy passage through the House and into legislation."

APPENDIX T - All Saints Church Visit to The Palace of Westminster (from the Parish Magazine)

"Our day started at 6.00 am outside the church - and what a miserable time to start out in such miserable weather - the blessing being that it belied the rest of the day! The coach journey was pretty well uneventful. Forty-eight of us had arrived and boarded the coach, we had even started on time - well, all but a minute or two! We had a good time of getting to know one another better, as well as sharing quite a bit of good-natured banter and a variety of London anecdotes and experiences from previous journeys.

We arrived, just about on schedule, at the Houses of Parliament, to be met straight away by our friend, host and organiser of the day, Lord Lofthouse.

He it was who had arranged everything for us to be able to visit the Palace, and had provided three Guides for our party, as well as other things, which will be mentioned later. We all felt that our welcome was sincere and charming from Geoff and the Guides.

The Guides were the staff of Black Rod, who is the Chief of Parliamentary Security in the Palace. They were, as well as being very well versed in the history and tradition of the Houses of Parliament, founts of amusing anecdotes and extra titbits of information on all aspects of the tour. All of us having our interest enlivened by the obvious warmth of the Guides for the subject, about which they were speaking.

We were all very aware that this was the Seat of the Mother of all Parliaments; that there was very little let or hindrance for anyone wanting to view the inside of the Houses and listen to the progress of debate, in the Galleries - although, of course, there had to be a set of rules to abide by, for security as well as for reasons of tradition and smooth running of the Government of the Country; that we were privileged to see not only the splendour of the building's structure but also the outworkings of the everyday business of both Houses of Parliament.

As a whole, the building was much bigger than we had expected, although the Debating Chambers, Lords and Commons, seemed somewhat smaller than we had envisaged, as seen on television.

The technicality of the structure was marvellous, especially given that it was built in an age when there was not the back up of electricity, hydraulic power or any of the high-tech gadgets that we take so much for granted. Of course, there was the overriding feature of that time that cannot be matched today, namely: the people involved realised that "Rome was not built in a day," and so, time was taken to get things right and craftsmanship was not sacrificed on the altar of "Instant Completion". Not only so, but there was a very real sense of artistic taste and grandeur in all aspects of the building and decoration - most of us noting that there was not one piece of bare wood showing and all the stonework was clean and kept beautifully. There was plenty of exercise for our necks: looking at walls, ceilings and floors, which were all sumptuous in their painting, gilding and mosaic tiling - with artfully conceived designs, motifs, and coat of arms integrated into the overall concept of the decoration in that particular area.

The site of the Houses of Parliament was originally the location of the Royal Palace of Westminster, built about 1050 AD. It was the chief residence of the Monarch from the reign of Henry VIII (1509-1547).

Since the 13th Century, most Parliaments had sat there until the fire in 1834, when nearly all of the old palace was destroyed. To a design by Sir Charles Barry, assisted by Augustus Pugin (who oversaw the decorative work until he died in 1852), the building was completed in 1860, after twenty years of working on a site of eight acres with eleven courtyards.

Along with the ancient Westminster Hall, the Palace has royal reception rooms, a Chapel, the Houses of the Lords and the Commons and extensive offices. The Place lies alongside the River Thames, in a line running North to South - with the Clock Tower, popularly known by the name of its chiming bell, "Big Ben," at the Northern end of the edifice.

The party from All Saints were shown round: the Robing Room, where the Queen dons her robes and crown; the Royal Gallery, used for State occasions and for formally welcoming Heads of State, by Members of both Houses; through into the Parliament Chamber, where the House of Lords sits and where the whole of Parliament assembles for the State Opening; into the Central Lobby, where constituents meet with their Members of Parliament; along the 'No' Division Lobby, where Members cast their votes against a Motion or a Bill brought before the House of Commons; thence into the actual House of Commons Chamber, where the Government Party sit to the right of the Speaker's Chair and the Opposition Parties to the left; from there into St Stephen's Hall, which was utilised as the House of Commons from c 1550 until the 1834 fire; to a historical highlight, Westminster Hall, an original, huge, ancient hall, where the Royal Courts of Justice sat, until 1882, witnessing the trials of such people as Thomas Moore and King Charles I, but where more recently monarchs and distinguished statesmen have lain in state before their cortege has escorted them to their final resting place.

Of course, the lack of time and space does not allow for every last detail to be chronicled of what was seen and heard on this memorable day, just to say that there were innumerable paintings, a good number of statues, elegant fixtures, fittings and clocks which would have to be seen to appreciate properly.

All the above inadequately-described treasure and decorations served, for most of us, to evoke a sense of tradition, history and pride along with the privilege of entering in to the very seat of democracy and the epitome of all that a state centre of government should be, only enhanced by the animated commentary of the Guides and occasionally from Geoff himself.

Almost the very last part, and for many, the absolute apex of an excellent tour was our being allowed into the Crypt, the Chapel of St Margaret Undercroft - not on the normal itinerary of a visit to the Houses of Parliament. In a beautifully-decorated, divinely-atmospheric place of worship, we were all able to sit down to listen to Lord Lofthouse, Geoff, speaking to us about the Crypt and the use to which it was still put; about the font where his grandchildren had been christened; and of his evident joy at being able to bring us, his friends and brothers and sisters in the Lord Jesus, into the part of his world of which he is, so justly, proud - having obtained his status by truth and diligence (the latter is our assessment, not his).

It also warmed our hearts to hear Geoff speak so heartily about the Vicar Kevin's ministry and appreciation for the way in which the Kingdom of God was being enhanced and augmented almost daily. Then, his most well-kept and welcome surprise: he introduced our own Bishop of Wakefield, Nigel. The Bishop briefly spoke to encourage and lead us on as Christians; then, as it was time to make our way to the coach, he prayed with us and blessed us on our way - making sure that he was at the door on our way out to shake everyone's hand.

All arrived back on the coach on time, we set off - glancing out to see "our Geoff", in the pouring rain, waving farewell, his face alight with a beaming smile!

The perfect ending to a splendid day!